THE HANDMAIDENS
C⊕NSPIRACY

THE HANDMAIDEN'S C⊕NSPIRACY

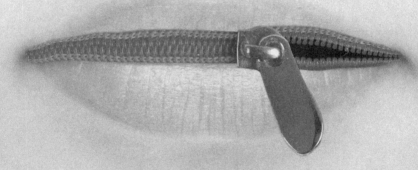

HOW ERRONEOUS BIBLE TRANSLATIONS HIJACKED
THE WOMEN'S EMPOWERMENT MOVEMENT
STARTED BY JESUS CHRIST
AND DISAVOWED THE RIGHTFUL PLACE OF
FEMALE PASTORS, PREACHERS, AND PROPHETS

DONNA HOWELL
FOREWORD BY DEREK P. GILBERT

DEFENDER

CRANE, MO

The Handmaiden's Conspiracy: How Erroneous Bible Translations Hijacked the Women's Empowerment Movement Started by Jesus Christ and Disavowed the Rightful Place of Female Pastors, Preachers, and Prophets

Defender Publishing
Crane, MO 65633
©2018 by Donna Howell
All rights reserved. Published 2018.
Printed in the United States of America.

ISBN: 978-1-948014-00-7

A CIP catalog record of this book is available from the Library of Congress.

Cover illustration and design by Justen Faull.

All Scripture quotations from the King James Version; in cases of academic comparison, those instances are noted.

Contents

Foreword

—By Derek Gilbert, researcher for Defender Publishing; author of *The Great Inception*, *The Day the Earth Stands Still*; chief news anchor and broadcast host of SkyWatch Television; co-host alongside Sharon Gilbert on the weekly *SciFriday*; host and producer of the *PID Radio* and *View from the Bunker* radio shows

Women in ministry walk a tightrope. Many are led to serve, and to do so in amazing, inspiring ways. But there is a line—especially in traditional, conservative churches—that they are never supposed to cross. Paul's first letter to Timothy seems to make it clear: "But I suffer not a woman to teach, nor to usurp authority over the man, but to be in silence" (1 Timothy 2:12, KJV).

Okay, then. We don't let women preach or teach, unless it's to other women. If they try, we smack them back across that line—hard enough so they learn their lesson!

Is that what Paul meant? Did he know about Deborah, who pushed a reluctant Barak (who told her, "If you will not go with me, I will not go") into leading Israel to victory over a large Canaanite army?

What about Huldah, the prophetess consulted by Hilkiah, the high priest during the reign of Josiah? Hilkiah went to her to inquire of the Lord at the command of the king. (See 2 Kings 22 and 2 Chronicles 34.) Think about that. King Josiah had just learned that his kingdom had been ignoring the Law for generations. He wanted to know God's will. So Josiah, the ruler of Israel, sent the high priest, the spiritual leader of Israel, to hear the word of Yahweh...*from a woman!*

Maybe Paul was misinformed?

No. More likely we're not reading the true intent behind Paul's words.

There is *context* we often miss in the Bible because we live nearly two millennia after the last books in it were written. Just as a first-century Jew wouldn't understand some of our idioms—such as "cool," "out of left field," or "selfie"—there are references we miss because of where and how we were raised.

Then there are choices made by translators over the years, and some of the choices in translation are made by pastors and teachers. For example, consider how we handle Deuteronomy 22:5: "The woman shall not wear that which pertaineth unto a man, neither shall a man put on a woman's garment: for all that do so are abomination unto the Lord thy God." Some pastors take that to mean women and girls shouldn't wear jeans, slacks, or pants of any kind. I'm all about women dressing like women and men dressing like men, but as a father with a daughter who had to wait for a school bus in Midwestern winters, the "all skirts, all the time" rule was a non-starter in my house.

The key to correctly applying that verse, and *every* verse in the Bible, is understanding what God *meant* by what He said, not just our interpretation of ancient words on modern paper. And reaching that understanding means first understanding the context in which it was written—cultural and religious.

Donna Howell tackles this issue because she's been pulled out of her comfort zone in recent years. She was happy behind the scenes as researcher and writer for Defender Publishing, but something stirred in her heart. It looks to me as though God is not taking "no" for an answer as He pulls her into a new phase of her life—preaching.

Some people find that disturbing. That was obvious after her recent appearance on *The Jim Bakker Show.* She blew away the Bakkers and the studio audience, who gave her two standing ovations: one during and one after the program. And the reception from those who heard her preach at Morningside Church not long after was just as enthusiastic (again, resulting in a standing ovation). This girl can *bring it.*

And when she preaches, it's from the Word. She points to Christ, and Him crucified.

However, that didn't matter to some. We at SkyWatch Television, proud to know Donna, posted a highlight video to YouTube of some of her most impactful moments with Jim Bakker. The responses, before we shut down comments, were absolutely vile. I mean insulting, inconsiderate, and in some cases, downright profane.

Nice.

Having come to know Donna and her family over the last couple of years, it is a joy to watch her grow into this new role. We know her well enough to say with certainty that she's not after the limelight. Her favorite times are with her husband and their two children (who, by the way, are awesome).

But she feels *compelled.* She can't *not* do this. And yet there are some among us who insist that she *should* not—that by following what feels like the clear leading of the Spirit, she's transgressing, trying to elevate herself above the teachings of the apostles, and should therefore be cast into the outer darkness.

Now then, if the Holy Spirit is genuinely calling her—or you, dear reader—to preach, teach, or even prophesy, then what?

In her book *Radicals,* Donna argued from the book of James that the Church needs a fundamental shift in the way we "do church" to reach a generation that's growing up believing their gods are programmed and saved on silicon chips. Her point was not that we need to throw out biblical doctrine—it's that we need to get *back* to biblical doctrine. We need to strip away two thousand years of *tradition* that has, in places, obscured teachings of the Spirit-led apostles like barnacles on the hull of a very old ship.

This isn't feminism. I know Donna, and she is not about that. This is about loving the Lord our God with all of our hearts, souls, and minds—and doing whatever we have to do to extend that love to the lost. It's about *context*.

If we get the context, we'll get the true meaning of the Word—and we'll find that women have been meant to play a bigger role in the Church than we've been taught.

Introduction

If you or a loved one were to find salvation in Jesus Christ as a result of a female preacher's message, would your salvation be less valid than it if it had come through responding to a man?

I would that you'd ponder that for a moment...

Several years ago, I started experiencing something so supernatural that I knew I, myself, could not have caused it. I would lie awake in bed at night, praying that God would just let me sleep—but in my mind, I was preaching. It didn't start with a few minutes here and there and then gradually increase to occasional all-nighters. This thing hit me as suddenly and powerfully as a silent freight train and wouldn't let up for nearly a year. I admit, it happens now and again even still.

I remember one night, as usual, I was preaching a sermon in my imagination. I looked out to the crowd and there were thousands of people, both men and women. Each time I delivered another point, their response was unanimously positive. I started to quote Scripture passages, and even listed the book, chapter, and verse numbers. I've read the entire Bible several times, and have been well educated in certain theological studies, but for as many verses may sound familiar to me, there are many others that I have not yet memorized well enough to quote, let alone tell you the precise references. Yet there, on my bed, within my imagination, I was preaching to an enormous congregation and listing biblical details I would never be able to recall on the spot during the day.

As soon as I awoke, I rose up, noted the Scripture references, wrote down what I remembered saying in the dream sermon, and then went straight to my KJV Bible. Sure enough, the verses I had delivered in my imagination were an exact match to the words in the Bible.

This happened several times. It's like the Donna of my imagination was twenty years ahead of the Donna who existed on that bed. In the natural, I wasn't nearly as intelligent or articulate as I had been in these intuitions. And my messages weren't limited to verse memory. There were occasions when I would preach on subjects that are profoundly theological, drawing conclusions that are nowhere near what is taught in the sphere of mainstream teaching. When that happened, I would get up in the middle of the night and research the topic, learning afterward that what I had said in the strange vision was a revolutionary truth that leading scholars are only just starting to piece together. In my mind's eye, I spoke of historical and cultural facts that I didn't think I knew—but, again, when I climbed out of bed to look them up, I found that, once again, I had nailed it.

Night after night after night, I was being shown something I couldn't understand. Was God telling me I was going to speak to the multitudes? Was He showing me a picture of my own future? Or was He trying to communicate something else? I had no idea, but I knew, based on the desires of my heart as I could identify them then, that I had not caused these imaginings.

Did I *want* to speak to the multitudes? Did I *want* to be a preacher? No. Not even a little bit. In fact, I had prayed for God to call me into any service *but* that. The very thought of standing in front of even five people to lead a casual Bible lesson during a small church's Sunday school class made me want to hide. With every fiber of my being, I loathed the idea that I would be called into the kind of ministry that persistently popped into my late-night thoughts. These strange occurrences did not originate from my own desires or fantasies, and the bizarrely accurate facts I somehow just "knew" in my mind as I preached were an additional layer of proof that whatever was happening to me on that bed was from Someone higher than myself. I was being called.

The reason behind my resistance is explained in chapter 8, wherein I share the rest of my story. But the purpose of this book was born when I decided to be obedient beyond my own comfort and do what I believe God told me to do.

I opened my mouth.

It was then that the opposition came against me. From everywhere at once, I was under attack—not from the enemy, but from people. Nobody questioned my theology, not a soul said they took issue with what I looked like or how I dressed, and not one person challenged my anointing. The issue, they all stated, was that I was a *woman*.

I was born female, a circumstance I cannot change; therefore, they said I was "limited."

Therein rested my first resolution: If God, Himself, was calling me, a *woman*, to preach in His service, then I would do what He had asked. I couldn't allow myself to be stopped because of critics who wouldn't be bothered long enough to consider what the original Greek and Hebrew texts said about women. I wasn't about to fall under the weight of those who evidently hadn't studied God's heart toward women. I will someday stand before the Lord and be held accountable for the things I have—and haven't—done, so to I didn't believe I owed an answer to those who hadn't looked into what the Bible actually says in its authenticity.

However, it occurred to me early on that an uncountable number of women have experienced the Holy Spirit's call upon them, also—and they stand today with that bitter and invisible tape over their mouths, wanting to obey the Lord yet confused about what that obedience looks like in light of what today's culture allows women to do.

I am not by any stretch of the imagination a feminist, as chapter 1 of this book relates, and this work was not penned to support or begin any kind of "women's liberation movement." Nor was this project motivated by any internal desire to join the raging who's-right, who's-wrong debate that has been going on since the Garden of Eden. But for the women who are caught between the intense, surging sensation of God's call on one side and the muzzle of prohibition on the other, resigned forever otherwise to exist between the duality of these two great forces, a study such as this is in order. My hope is that every woman who feels she is called will be able to look herself in the mirror and repeat the immortal words of T. D. Jakes: "Woman, thou art loosed!"

1

The Cultural Interpretation Debate

At the start, I want to make it very clear that I am not sharing this following story to vent my anger, "get one over on" my aggressors, whine, complain, or be petty. This event in my life taught me a lesson that no college class in the world could have bestowed. I actually couldn't be more grateful for this small outbreak against me, because it lit an all-consuming fire within me to keep going not only in the face of discouragement, but because of the nature of the discouragement. By sharing this with you, I hope to encourage the same fire for Christ in at least one reader. If that happens, I've accomplished my goal. God can and will use *anyone* for His Kingdom work, as long as that person doesn't allow darts (from the enemy or another person) to keep him or her from it.

A couple of months ago at the time of this writing, I went on *The Jim Bakker Show*[1] to talk about my book, *Radicals: Why Tomorrow Belongs to Post Denominational Christians Infused with Supernatural Power*. I spoke on several topics, from the book of James' "faith without works is dead" conundrum, to what "lukewarm" really meant to the Laodiceans in the book of Revelation, to what the Church as a whole needs to do to embrace the current movement of the radical Body that God is raising up all around us—and several other topics. My central message, however, was to embolden members of our current Body to rise up and take ownership of their role in the Great Commission with passion and love for all. This should be done regardless of how uncomfortable it makes people in the Body feel, which is the central message of *Radicals*.

Toward the end of the interview, Brother Jim gave me the opportunity to give a final word to the audience members, who responded with a double standing ovation (one of which occurred off-camera). Several points of discussion led up to and fully explained my final words. However, about a week later, SkyWatch TV emailed me a YouTube video they had made involving only my final—and strongest—thoughts. They asked for my permission to present the video and, of course, I agreed. The video was posted the following day with the title, *Does the Future of the Church Belong to Radicals?*

The short piece opened with the following statements, spoken seriously and passionately as a wrap-up to all that I had said prior about the stagnant and apathetic developments I have witnessed in the Body of Christ:

Listen to me, women. You are not what men have said that you are. And I know I'm not talking to everybody; some of you are like me and you're lucky—you have a man who treats you beautifully. Some of you are not. You have been told that your value only goes so far, and that is not who you are. You are not defined by your outward appearance. You are not defined by what the men in your life say that you are. (Applause.)

Men, you got little boys. You have young men at home, or at church or in your community. They need to be told what a man looks like. Men need to teach the young boys how to separate the boys from the men… So, everybody is called. Look up the Priesthood of the Believer. Everyone is called. There is no such— If you're a Christian, you're "called." There is no such thing as, "Oh, I'm going to go into the ministry; I think that the Holy Spirit is telling me to go into the ministry." If you're a Christian and you have the Holy Spirit living here [I circled my heart], you *are going to be called* into the ministry in your community.

Millennials and teenagers [I pause for the applause to die down]. Millennials and teenagers, I wanna make something very clear to you. You are *so* passionate right now. *Bless you* for your passion. But, you are—some of you are—channeling that passion into pride parades and activism and all kinds of social nuances that are not fulfilling to you. The reason it's not fulfilling to you is because sometimes you're getting things for free that you demanded to have for free and when you get what you wanted, you're not able to appreciate it because you didn't earn it. And the other thing that you need to remember is that as you're going out and you're being all active and you're being all passionate, you're never going to be fulfilled, because there is something else that is needing to be filled here [I circle my heart again], and you're not gonna find it in any other place besides Jesus Christ. But! To those [paused for applause to die down]. To those young people who feel called right now, but who have been told by older people in their life that "You're young, and you're stupid, and you're never going to amount to anything," you have no idea that *you* are tomorrow's leader, but *you are*! And if God decides to raise up a radical, *He only needs one voice for an entire Great Awakening, and it could be yours!*[2]

The crowd was so loud toward the end of these words that I found myself shouting just to be heard above the noise. The funny thing is, my words weren't even that articulate. I wasn't saying anything new, and I *certainly* wasn't saying anything that just about anyone else in the Church couldn't have said with equal zeal. Nothing about my words were particularly powerful or anything most members of the Church aren't already aware of. In fact, the constant applause was a bit surprising to me, which is why I can be seen laughing during the standing ovation. (Well that, *and* the fact that I was joyful to see my words encouraging people out there.) Until this moment, I still have no idea why my words drew such an enormous reaction, but evidently the Church is so starving for encouragement that it only takes one voice to say the simplest thing. There I was, attempting to tell "that other voice out there" to stand up and live his or her ministerial potential to its fullest, and that "voice" in the moment was mine.

It was unreal how that taping went down.

And then I got home…

For the first twenty-four hours or so after the video recap that Sky-Watch TV put up, viewers were allowed to post comments. The comments were coming up so fast that more were appearing even as I read them, and many were replying to posts left by others.

Every single comment was hateful and derogatory.

I was getting slammed with more insults flooding the screen than I could keep up with, and they were *harsh*. But I'm in the media fairly often, and I've written several books, so I wasn't exactly shocked by the Internet trolls, as it was most definitely not their first attack upon me. One must grow tough skin and get used to the idea of being challenged if he or she ever plans to put a message out there, and I accept that. What did shock me, however—to the very core—was *why* they were attacking me. I remember some of these conversations very clearly. One that I copied before it was taken down is as follows (with errors removed):

Person 1: "A woman reverend, eh? Where's the Scripture verse on that one?"

Person 2: "Oh, I totally agree! God is immutable. He never changes, so this Donna Howell character owes the world an explanation for why she believes God is suddenly calling WOMEN to say anything in the Church, including herself."

Person 3: "Agreed. Evidently she hasn't read 1 Corinthians where it is said that women are never to speak in a church."

Person 4: "She really should be ashamed of herself. The best service this apostasy woman [yes, I was really called an "apostasy woman"] could do for the Church is to sit down, shut up, and repent."

Person 1 again: "Glad to see I'm not the only one with a brain in the Body of Christ."

Person 5: "The Bible says that a woman shouldn't speak in a church, yes, but it also says that a woman should not usurp the authority of a man, and she is clearly guilty of this. Who is she to tell men how to raise their sons? She is going against Scripture now in at least two ways!"

Person 6: "Guys, don't be worried about all this. This woman isn't going to stir up anything for the Lord. Nothing will come of it. She'll be thrown out soon enough with all the other garbage ministers and crazies who thought they were gonna start a pretentious women's lib movement in the Church. Rest assured that God will silence her. It's nothing to worry about. ☺"

This final comment immediately reminded me of what Gamaliel said to the Pharisees and Sadducees in Acts 5:35–39 as they stood at the ready to slay Jesus' followers:

Men of Israel, take care what you are about to do with these men. For before these days Theudas rose up, claiming to be somebody, and a number of men, about four hundred, joined him. He was killed, and all who followed him were dispersed and came to nothing. After him Judas the Galilean rose up in the days of the census and drew away some of the people after him. He too perished, and all who followed him were scattered. So in the present case I tell you, keep away from these men and let them alone, for if this plan or this undertaking is of man, it will fail; but if it is of God, you will not be able to overthrow them. You might even be found opposing God!

If I'm a cult leader or some "women's lib movement" leader going against God's will, then, as Gamaliel (the apostle Paul's teacher and one highly esteemed by his Pharisaic companions) said, my words and ministry will eventually fade away. But if I *am* being sent by God to say what I'm saying now, then I should do so boldly and let nothing stand in my way, because I am doing the Lord's work. The issue, then, is whether or not a woman in my place is truly in God's will by being a minister. That is a discussion I will spend the majority of this book unpacking, as it relates to every female under God from Eve to today. (Readers should remember this Gamaliel logic in your own life: God is all powerful. He will not hide from you. If you're off track, He will let you know personally, and He will not allow apostasy to flourish and last amidst His people. But if you're on the right path, you *will* come against aggression and persecution, whether it is a temporary hiccup or a lifelong battle. Pray for wisdom ere you go, as the epistle of James states repeatedly.)

These YouTube comments were a few of many, and *all*—every last one—came against me, *not* because of my message of encouragement, or even because my teaching was in error, but because I'm a woman. I happened to be born female, and therefore (as they say) God cannot use me in this specific platform. I am to "sit down, shut up, and repent." To believe otherwise is to be an "apostasy woman." Even more frustrating than this is that the rest of my message (the earlier portions of the taping that this particular audience hadn't viewed) was important as context to this final stretch. When SkyWatch TV asked if they could only show this last portion, it never occurred to me how "usurping" or "women's lib movement" it may have appeared. So, all this judgment was without full understanding to begin with.

Many more crude things were said about me as the minutes flew by. Some of the names I was called are too profane to even repeat. (Suffice it to say that only by preaching, I have now been compared to a woman who sells her body for money in dark alleyways—this accusation given by so-called Christians.) But I will never forget what I read, not because it hurt me deeply, but because it showed me the level of scriptural ignorance that plagues the Body of Christ…and I am saddened by what people are really garnering from the holy texts of old.

After I read the comments, I called Joe, a coworker, and vented. He, too, was not the least bit shocked that I was coming under attack (as any minister of the Gospel will), but he was equally surprised by *why*. We only talked for about thirty minutes, but it was enough to pull me out of the funk I was in and get my head back on straight. Joe reminded me of one of my own messages:

> If they are *that* bothered by what you're doing, they should find a medium to teach what *they* believe instead of trolling other members of the Body from their PC or smartphones at home.
>
> If the Holy Spirit is behind their work, He will bless it. But online badgering isn't doing anything godly or productive. All it does is the opposite, and your *Radicals* book essentially states that over and over again. You're simply a target of the very kind of attack you're preaching against. What irony! The enemy would love nothing more than for you to "sit down, shut up, and repent" for being obedient to the Lord's radical calling on

your life. What you need to do is the opposite: Stand up, shout, and glorify God.

You know that, don't you? I mean, what did you expect? That the enemy would send you happy thoughts and that the "old suits" in the Church would stand behind you? No way, man! When God says "go," you go. That's in your book, too. What are you waiting for?

I will admit that I have many times been challenged to check, recheck, and check again all the theology I am speaking about right now. Each time someone throws a verse at me, I pray again for wisdom and reassurance. I know that the biblical interpretations included in this book will get me into hot water, and I'm already anticipating the darts. But I also know that true Christianity is frequently uncomfortable. The Bible is packed with proof that the followers of God were recurrently confronted by His own people. Christ, Himself, was heatedly opposed by the Church leaders of His day. I am not Christ, I am not a prophet, and I am no smarter or grander than any other within the Body. My message may not be more intelligently or articulately presented than others'. But this conundrum about women's voices has to be addressed—and from my standpoint, nobody else is taking the reins.

Are we really still—*still*—saying that women aren't allowed to speak in the Church? Is that really, truly, honestly something we're continuing to teach?

The answer is yes.

Ironically, months before I even sat on the panel at the *Jim Bakker Show*, I had already been compiling research on this issue, because I felt that it was long since time that women be seen as the leaders the Bible repeatedly refers to. Voices like those that came against me on YouTube have stifled countless female preachers, teachers, and prophets throughout the ages, and frankly, this must come to an end if we are ever to fulfill the prophecies from the Word that directly declare women to be essential leaders in this—and following—generations. (That's why, when the comments began, I copied several of them. I already had this book underway, and I knew there would be other women out there who could relate to such an incident.)

When I initially heard from the Lord that this book needed to be written, Defender Publishing's release schedule had me booked for research work on several other titles, so the project was shelved until I was once again free to give it my complete focus. Then, earlier this year, SkyWatch TV sent me to a women's conference where the subject of women preachers was dealt with in depth. When I returned home for a debriefing meeting, I sat with CEO Tom Horn and told him that I thought the time was *now* for this message to reach the hundreds, thousands, and perhaps millions of women who *are right at this moment* allowing themselves to remain silent under the misconstrued concepts of a Church that often refuses to balance patriarchal and matriarchal hierarchies. Tom agreed, and the work began immediately. When the comments on YouTube flashed up on my screen, it was merely a confirmation.

But before we discuss what the Bible says, it's important to address the question of culture that so many continue to voice.

Today's Culture Is *Not* the Final Authority

Over and over, I hear versions of the following statement: "Just because our modern culture and society widely accepts something doesn't make it right. The Bible clearly states [fill in the blank], and the Bible is the final authority, regardless of what society today thinks is okay. This day and age continues to blur the lines of what is and is not biblically acceptable, and we have to stand against the idea that today's culture defines what is and is not right in the eyes of the Lord while we pick and choose which Scriptures to accept and which ones to reject."

With that, I emphatically agree. Going against God's Word is sinful—*timelessly* so—and sin remains sin, no matter what the world says or what "enlightenment" season we live in.

Let me say this again in different words, since I anticipate being quoted as saying otherwise: *Today's culture, societal tolerances, ministry trends, and social movements* **have absolutely no bearing on what the Word says is righteous or true.**

If it did, even on the most marginal level, then the Bible's final word on each category of righteous living would fall flat, because the disintegration of one foundational piece will eventually serve to crumble the whole. For example, lying is not considered a big deal today. Sometimes, lying is seen as the "only way out" or a "lesser evil." There are a million reasons to lie, from avoiding hurting someone's feelings to protecting a loved one, and so on.

Case in point: Just the other day, Broken for Good (a Christian music group I'm involved with) was performing at a community event, and during our break, my daughter—who was present at our gig under the watchful eye of a trusted sitter—approached me wanting the same bag of popcorn many of the other kids had. Because I was now with my kids at the break, the sitter was looking to me for an answer. I didn't know where the other children were getting the popcorn, and I couldn't leave the stage for more than a few minutes, so I told her no. (I'm one of "those" moms. I almost never let my kids out of my sight when we're away from home. Even during the performance, I kept my eyes locked on them the entire time.)

Just then, a man who had overheard my conversation hollered for his teenage daughter and, without asking for my input, told her to take my kids down the block for a free bag of popcorn. The girl agreed, told my kids to follow her, and started walking away, at which point my kids looked at me pleadingly. I was in a strange position. Putting a halt to the popcorn entourage could have made that young girl or her father feel awkward, as well as let my own kids down. On the other hand, I would never trust a complete stranger to take my children down the block amidst crowds of other complete strangers, whether my sitter was with them or not, simply because there were droves of people and I had no reason to think they couldn't be snatched when a head was turned. Another acquaintance of mine—a Christian—saw my hesitation and said, "Just tell them your kids are allergic to butter or something!"

That would have been a lie. On the other hand, my kids would be protected. On the other hand… On the other hand…

There are many reasons our society would justify a lie. Telling that man and his teenager that my kids had allergies or that the popcorn was the issue in any way would have been, by the very definition of the word, a falsehood. It simply isn't true. But I didn't want to make anyone feel bad, so I shrugged and said, "Let's all go! But we have to hurry." Had I not been put on the spot, I simply would have kindly explained to the man that I didn't think my kids needed it and the issue would have been dropped, but I had only seconds to react. My choices, as they appeared in my head at the moment, were: 1) lie, which the Bible forbids; 2) tell the man and his daughter I didn't trust them; or 3) go with them all and hope I made it back in time (which I thankfully did).

Even though almost every person I know—Christian or otherwise—would have found the "allergies" lie acceptable (if not completely ridiculous and desperate), it doesn't make it right. Yet, my friend didn't hesitate in defaulting to a lie as the instant and obvious solution, which speaks volumes for how a "white lie" is customary within our culture today, even within the most conservative circles. Today's culture is *not* the final authority on what is or isn't wrong. A lie is still immoral. Modern toleration of dishonesty when it appears to be the "only way out" or the "lesser evil" doesn't bear any weight on the discussion of whether or not it's clearly outlined as a forbidden sin in the Bible. Further, what one generation tolerates in moderation, the next generation tolerates in excess, so if a contemporary "white lie" is satisfactory behavior for our current generation, a "big, fat lie" will be fine tomorrow…and the disintegration of one foundational piece serves to crumble the whole.

So for those who say, "You can't just assume that Scripture no longer applies, because our culture today is different," I agree as heartily as a human possibly can. Let's take today's culture out of the equation permanently, please. Let us forever respect what Paul said when he wrote, "And be not conformed to this world…that ye may prove what is that good, and acceptable, and perfect, will of God" (Romans 12:2).

However—and this is crucial—*the society and culture at the time the Bible was written has **everything** to do with what the Bible commands of believers. Knowing what the Bible **says** is not the same thing as knowing what the Bible **means**!*

If the Bible says women shouldn't speak in the Church, then that's what it says. We as believers cannot pick and choose what we want to believe from Scripture and ignore the rest.

Yes. Agreed.

But it also says—and by the same author, I might add (Paul)—that women shouldn't wear braids in their hair in church, or pearls, or gold, or expensive clothing (1 Timothy 2:9). Yet the Church has no problem writing that one off as a "cultural issue," or correctly interpreting it as the command that women should attend services in reverence, modesty, and humility. (More precise reflection on this verse later.) Many today may rail against women preachers, speakers, teachers, and prophets, but some of these same ministers could care less if their wives come to church with their hair in a pretty braid. Why? Because they will accept the "cultural issue" argument when it suits them and dismiss it when it doesn't. Essentially, they are, as I stated before, "picking and choosing what they want to believe from Scripture and ignoring (or improperly applying) the rest."

In this, they become guilty of the very grievance they're preaching against.

Let me make one thing very clear: I do not believe that all these ministers are intentionally trying to squelch women. I am not a feminist, I don't participate in women's lib movements, and I don't think men are "the enemy." I love my husband and obey him consistently. I submit to him. I am ardently grateful for male ministers and the essential role they have played, still play, and will continue to play in the Church. By no means do I intend to "liberate women from male oppression" or any such nonsense. Some of the ministers preaching this very sermon against women leaders in the Church are doing so out of obedience: kindly, respectfully, and reassuringly. (Others are not so kind in their approach, but in my experience, they are exceptions. More often, the "berating" response comes from men [and sometimes women] who are not in leadership.)

Feminism has, throughout recent decades, caused extreme harm to the concept of equality. What may have begun in its genesis movement as equal rights for women in politics, religion, economics, and social norms has gone beyond anything that benefits the female gender. As it exists today, feminism teaches that in order for a woman to be equal to a man, she must believe men are beneath her and spread the word that men are less intelligent than she is, that she is the superior sex, and that a chief goal among most men is to reduce women to little more than slaves. The only way to achieve true equality, feminism imparts, is for women to act like men and tower above them in the process.

Ironically, this quest for impartiality serves only to forcibly shove men into an inferior position, canceling out equality by default, and disintegrates the feminine and graceful nature that brought balance to the goal of equality in the first place. The answer to what some people view as domination cannot be found in dominating the other.

Though many voices are competing to devalue or eliminate the internal nurturer in every woman, replacing it with an authoritarian aggressor, the result is a degeneration of that which was innately female from the start. The justice that modern feminism fights for results in extreme injustice and subsequent entrapment for those in the fight. In the very moment womanhood is traded for manhood—in the battle to prove we are all one and the same in our abilities, influences, and intrinsic value—the new paradigm becomes, paradoxically, anti-woman. The journey toward "sameness" negates the creation order that God originally designed. Men and women will never be "the same." If they were, then a woman would not be able to offer anything a man could not, and that precious stabilization of the proverbial scales of life would already be hanging evenly, without the contribution of any female.

We should continue perpetuating the goal of equality precisely because of how we are *different*, not in the interest of proving we're the same.

However, the vehicle driving me to address this is not one of retaliation and vengeance, but one of obedience. Scriptures that deal with women leadership in the Body simply should not be interpreted the way they most often are, and many facts prove this.

I will go into more about this in the coming chapters, but for now, I want to explain the Bible study methodologies I have applied in order to explain how I've arrived at the conclusions presented in this book.

Understanding the Voice behind the Text

We should never pull from a biblical text *any* potential meaning until we've taken the proper steps of interpretation. If we don't take these steps, we're guaranteed to arrive at a frequently twisted understanding of Scripture. First, let's look at how easily this can confuse both those who are reading the Bible and their later audience (whether that be a congregation, a friend, or a coworker, and so on).

A cold, black-and-white sentence as read from a page in a book can have many different meanings based on the reader's interpretation. Readers who are willing to interpret the Bible's rules and guidelines for their own selfish agendas and then weigh down the rest of the Body with such miscalculated interpretations will find that the Bible can be a dangerous tool! Such skewed interpretation can—and has—been the road upon which scores of false teachers, preachers, and prophets have led millions of people into misunderstanding. To that, the Church agrees. Every Christian has heard stories of ministers who read Scripture, misinterpreted it (whether intentionally or unintentionally), and then made promises or cast judgments that fell flat when tested. Some of these ministers via televangelism and online media outlets like YouTube have done so to the detriment of listeners all across the nation—and I know I'm not alone in considering that a travesty.

Take the following sentence as an example: "I didn't say he beat his wife." (I am using an example outside the Bible, specifically because it doesn't already have a biased interpretation behind it.) Now we will look at the emphasis as it is placed on each word in turn and observe how this small sentence made up of only seven words can relate *at least* seven different meanings:

- *I* didn't say he beat his wife: "Someone else must have said it, but you didn't hear it from me."
- I *didn't* say he beat his wife: "I didn't say it at all. You're making it up."
- I didn't *say* he beat his wife: "I might have implied it, but I didn't directly declare it as fact."
- I didn't say *he* beat his wife: "I was talking about someone else when I told you that."
- I didn't say he *beat* his wife: "He's just mean to her a lot, but he doesn't actually strike her."
- I didn't say he beat *his* wife: "He beat that other guy's wife."
- I didn't say he beat his *wife*: "He beats the kids and the dog."

To add to this confusion, italics in the King James Bible are only meant as placeholders for when a word was later added to the English translation for flow. This rule first came into practice in 1560, when the Geneva Bible was produced. The Genevan Protestants at the time of John Calvin's influence recognized that a word-for-word translation from Hebrew and Greek left some sentences in English stunted and hard to understand. (Really, no language can be translated word for word without a slight linguistic tweak for flow within the secondary language. Consider the Spanish *tengo hambre*. The word-for-word translation to English would be "have hunger," but in a well-rounded translation to English, it means "I am hungry.") Certain words were added to Bible translations merely to assist English readers in grasping the true meaning behind a sentence when the original Greek or Hebrew phrase, term, or idiom was incomprehensible or ambiguous without it. However, the Geneva Bible was tailored to readers within its locality (as opposed to a widely known form for all English speakers), and it caused errors and confusion. So in 1604, King James authorized fifty-four translators to complete a more accurate rendering. The project was completed in 1611, and the translators followed the model set by the Genevan Protestants. Readers of Scripture today cannot rely on italics to point to emphasis, because they are only present to show a linguistic tweak. Thus, every single word of the Bible must be interpreted without a specific emphasis *until* the proper interpretation methods are tended to.

If there were a sentence in the Bible that said, "I didn't say he beat his wife," and the reader was not willing to practice the most fundamental steps to pulling the true meaning out of what's being said by the original authors, then that one blip of Scripture alone could mean *at least* seven different things, as illustrated above. Then a preacher can merely pick one of the seven interpretations, preach a message focused on that one interpretation, and convince an entire congregation (or nation) into believing the Scripture said what he believes it did—many times without even reading the Scriptures before and after it that likely assist in the overall interpretation (as I will address shortly).

Does this sound sensational? It shouldn't. It happens a lot, actually. As one example: Many prosperity preachers have stood from their platforms and used James' words, "You have not because you ask not"

(James 4:2) as an explanation for why congregants don't have the house, car, money, or other earthly providence they need or want. I've heard more sermons than I can count that use this verse to "prove" people don't get what they want from the Lord because they just aren't asking diligently enough. However, *the very next verse* following "You have not because you ask not" states the reason people don't get what they want: They are asking for something that satisfies an earthly and temporal lust (James 4:3). So this prosperity message referring to earthly gain, when based on James 4:2, meets instant and outright cancellation by the next verse in sequence.

This is a preposterous error that can—and frequently does—pollute the Church's understanding of truth. But sadly, misinterpretation is far more often a side effect of a cultural, societal, or circumstantial issue, and it can have a spiritual (and perhaps eternal) consequence. I'll give another example using three fictional people: Sarah, Jenny, and Amanda (again outside of Scripture, as it will not have any preexisting or biased interpretations associated with it).

1. Sarah is driving home one night when she is hit head-on by a drunk driver. Her injuries are life-changing and painful, and she is lucky to be alive. The accident was clearly the other driver's fault, and she is left wearing the bandages. Her best friend Jenny visits her and tells her: "You poor, dear soul. I'm so sorry for the pain that driver has caused you. This is not your fault. I know you feel lost and lonely right now, and every bone in your body aches, but remember that God is not blaming you for the accident. The Holy Spirit has plans to use you greatly in ministry, and you can rise above this. God works in mysterious ways, and this might be one of them. He can use even this."

2. The following year, Sarah's friend, Amanda, is driving home from a bar after "ten too many" drinks. She has driven drunk many times in the past, and has even run into a few mailboxes,

so she is aware of the dangers of drinking and driving on a personal level. On this particular night, she runs a stoplight and crashes into a smaller car, immediately killing everyone inside. Amanda survives, but her injuries are life-changing and painful, and she, too, is lucky to be alive. The accident was clearly Amanda's fault, and she is left with the guilt of ending several lives as a result of her selfish decision. In a wave of contrition, she vents to Sarah. Sarah says: "I remember when I went through this myself. My friend Jenny had the perfect advice for me. I'll tell you exactly what she said. 'You poor, dear soul. I'm so sorry for the pain that driver has caused you. This is not your fault. I know you feel lost and lonely right now, and every bone in your body aches, but remember that God is not blaming you for the accident. The Holy Spirit has plans to use you greatly in ministry, and you can rise above this. God works in mysterious ways, and this might be one of them. He can use even this.'"

3. Jenny hears that she has been quoted and calls Sarah, irritated about the misuse of her words. In Jenny's opinion, Amanda was irrevocably at fault, and she needs to feel the weight of the consequences over a drunken joyride, or else she might repeat the same mistake later on and potentially take another life. Jenny wouldn't have minded at all if she had been quoted in circumstances that harmonized with the original intent. In fact, she would have blessed that situation, because it would have represented encouragement in despair from one innocent traffic victim to another. But in this specific application, Jenny's advice was circumstantially twisted. Sarah explains that she "didn't misquote anyone." The words she gave to Amanda were *exactly* what Jenny had said, down to the very letter. Therefore, she can't be accused of misquoting. Jenny acknowledges that her words were *said* correctly, but the *application* of them was distorted, and they therefore conveyed an erroneous meaning. She intended

them for Sarah, in Sarah's position. Just before she hangs up, Jenny says, "You haven't used my words faithfully, and therefore you don't have my blessing in the way you've chosen to quote me. I will have nothing to do with this."

Is it possible that Paul's words were meant for the congregations he was writing to, in their position, and in those circumstances? If his words were "normative" and applicable to all women in every city throughout the universe and into perpetuity, then women should not speak in church. Ever. Done deal. If, however, like Jenny and Sarah, Paul's words were meant to apply in specific circumstances, then we need to apply his words only when *those same circumstances* apply today.

A preacher can quote from the Bible down to the very letter. He or she can memorize every Scripture in the entire Word—but if the passages are not properly applied in a way that harmonizes with the original circumstances and intent, they can convey a distortion. This much we can all agree upon. But the central point of this illustration is this: *If a preacher teaches in this way, he or she should not be surprised if or when God says, "You haven't used My words faithfully, and therefore you don't have My [blessing, anointing, approval, consecration, sanction, consent, etc.] upon the way you've chosen to quote me. I will have nothing to do with this message you're giving."*

As a biblical support for this concept, consider 2 Peter 3:16b—which, although written by Peter, again refers to the writings of Paul, who is quoted as saying that women should be silent in church, never attend service with braided hair or pearls, etc.: "As also in all his [Paul's] epistles, speaking in them of these things; in which are some things hard to be understood, which they that are unlearned and unstable wrest, as they do also the other scriptures, unto their own destruction." The ESV renders this: "As he [Paul] does in all his letters when he speaks in them of these matters. There are some things in them that are hard to understand, which the ignorant and unstable twist to their own destruction, as they do the other Scriptures." As for a breakdown of what Peter's words mean here, let's look at the *Barnes' Notes* commentary:

> Speaking in them of these things—The things which Peter had dwelt upon in his two epistles. The great doctrines of the cross; of the depravity of man; of the divine purposes; of the new birth; of the consummation of all things; of the return of the Saviour to judge the world, and to receive his people to himself; the duty of a serious, devout and prayerful life, and of being prepared for the heavenly world. These things are constantly dwelt upon by Paul, and to his authority in these respects Peter might appeal with the utmost confidence.[3]

I can agree that here, Peter is referring to the statements of Paul on these issues listed by *Barnes'*, and not necessarily to Paul's words about women. However, if Peter is placing his "utmost confidence" in Paul's stance on these matters—and, as Scripture proves and strengthens Scripture and all of the Word is "God breathed" (2 Timothy 3:16–17)—we can safely assume that Peter is placing his confidence in Paul's teaching as a whole, and not only within this limited list. *Barnes'* agrees with this interpretation (as follows), then goes on to explain that Peter was not accusing Paul of a poor writing style that nobody could understand, but simply that the truths Paul addressed are so intense that human minds will struggle comprehending them:

> The true construction, so far as the evidence goes, is to refer it not directly to the "epistles," but to the "things" of which Peter says Paul wrote [this would include *all* of Paul's writings]; that is, not to the style and language of Paul, but to the great truths and doctrines which he taught. Those doctrines were indeed contained in his epistles, but still, according to the fair construction of the passage before us, Peter should not be understood

as accusing Paul of obscurity of style. He refers not to the difficulty of understanding what Paul meant, but to the difficulty of comprehending the great truths which he taught [i.e., it's not *how* Paul wrote, but *what* Paul wrote, that is hard to understand]. This is, generally, the greatest difficulty in regard to the statements of Paul. The difficulty is not that the meaning of the writer is not plain, but it is either:

(a) that the mind is overpowered by the grandeur of the thought, and the incomprehensible nature of the theme, or

(b) that the truth is so unpalatable, and *the mind is so prejudiced against it, that we are unwilling to receive it.*[4]

So far, we have *Barnes' Notes* commentary pointing to Peter's open acknowledgment of Paul's authority, followed by the suggestion that 2 Peter 3:16 may very well be referring to people's minds being "so prejudiced against [the proper interpretation of Paul's writings] that we are unwilling to receive it." Yet, what *Barnes'* says next really drives it home:

Many a man knows well enough what Paul means, and would receive his doctrines without hesitation *if the heart was not opposed to it*; and in this state of mind Paul is charged with obscurity, when *the real difficulty lies only in the heart of him who makes the complaint....* An honest heart, *a willingness to receive the truth, is one of the best qualifications for understanding the writings of Paul*; and when this exists, no one will fail to find truth that may be comprehended, and that will be eminently adapted to sanctify and save the soul....

Which they that are unlearned—The evil here adverted to is that which arises in cases where *those without competent knowledge undertake to become expounders of the word of God.* [In other words, "the evil here" is preachers who stand from a pulpit and speak for God without "competent knowledge," which *Barnes'* exposes to be, in part, a lack of understanding the culture at the time the book was written!:] It is not said that it is not proper for them to attempt to become instructed by the aid of the sacred writings; but the danger is, that *without proper views of interpretation, of language, and of ancient customs, they might be in danger of perverting and abusing certain portions of the writings of Paul.* Intelligence among the people is everywhere in the Bible presumed to be proper in understanding the sacred Scriptures; and ignorance may produce the same effects in interpreting the Bible which it will produce in interpreting other writings....

And unstable—... The evil here adverted to is that which arises where those undertake to interpret the Bible who have no established principles...and of course nothing can be regarded as settled in their methods of interpreting the Bible.

Wrest—Pervert—*streblousin*. The word here used occurs nowhere else in the New Testament. It is derived from a word meaning a windlass, winch, instrument of torture [*streble*] and means to roll or wind on a windlass; then to wrench, or turn away, as by the force of a windlass; and then to wrest or pervert. It implies a turning out of the way by the application of force. Here the meaning is, that they apply those portions of the Bible to a purpose for which they were never intended. It is doubtless true that this may occur. Men may abuse and pervert anything that is good....

Unto their own destruction—By embracing false doctrines. Error destroys the soul; and *it is very possible for a man so to read the Bible as only to confirm himself in error.* He may find passages which, by a perverted interpretation, shall seem to *sustain his own views* [in other words, a speaker who twists Scripture to say what he or she wants it to for their own agenda]; and, instead of embracing the truth, may live always under delusion, and perish at last.[5]

Many thanks to *Barnes' Notes* for this thread. It says it all better than I could have. Twisting Scripture can have eternal consequences. And as far as whether God would remove His anointing from a quote given out of context (including the cultural context!), I think that much is clear. In Peter's words, such a practice will deliver a speaker "unto their own destruction." This impression is further emphasized by the next verse in 2 Peter: "Ye therefore, beloved, seeing ye know these things before, beware lest ye also, being led away with the error of the wicked, fall from your own stedfastness." Well before a speaker has been "led away with the error of the wicked," the Holy Spirit's anointing will have been stripped from the speaker's teaching, or else the leading away in wicked error could not have happened had it been sanctioned by Him in the first place.

Thus, we can safely conclude that if a speaker intentionally quotes the words of the Bible, God's Word, out of context—whether that incorrect context is related to a language, cultural, societal, local, or historical issue—the Holy Spirit removes His anointing on that teaching, just as Jenny removed her blessing from Sarah's misuse of her words in my earlier example...and if the speakers willingly continue down this path, they will "fall from [their] own stedfastness."

So what do we do?

Because we are applying words written thousands of years ago to a completely different culture and time, we must take a moment to comprehend the process of getting information out of an ancient culture and making it relevant to our modern lives: understanding the "voice" behind the text. There has been a many-decades-long trend of speaking authoritatively about the stories and advice from Scripture without any thought about the background behind the Scripture, and without studying what the words *really* meant by those who wrote them. People have understandably complained for years that Church leaders take Scripture out of context, and they frequently do, but *why* does this happen?

For one thing, proper exegesis (interpretation) is not taught to the extent it should be. The backdrop of many verses often is not considered before the words are quoted, and the loss of meaning creates confusion. As I once heard from Minister Mark Chironna, "A text out of context is a pretext for a proof-text." In other words, we can find biblical "proof" for anything we say as long as the context is missing. The result of this is nothing less than tragedy, and at times it escalates to heresy and blasphemy.

As it relates to the lost or believers who have been jaded by the Church, the misuse of Scripture only renders a greater disregard for any information of the Word that *is* true. Then, when the facts are later brought up, those burned by the first wave of confusion aren't interested in being misled again, so they ignore the truth entirely, assuming everything is erroneous. They throw the baby out with the bathwater, so to speak. It is then possible that they might hear a more accurate sermon or witness and close their mind to it because of the damage the misinformation of the past has caused.

This tragedy becomes far worse when other preachers and teachers pick up on the trendy form of ministering and repeat the offense. An entire religious and cultural worldview becomes skewed around popular forms and formulas. Young, sincere preachers stand at pulpits and repeat familiar lessons they've learned from their mentors involving verses taken out of context in the first place. As a result, generation after generation becomes so familiar with the newer (but less truthful) concept of the verse that the truth is gradually sapped.

In essence, because of this gradual phenomenon, that old friend by the name of "today's culture" in fact *does* become the final authority on scriptural interpretation, which is deliciously ironic, considering it's the contemporary grievance voiced by those today who say that women ought not to speak in church: They preach against allowing "today's culture" to blur the lines of what's right and wrong, but without studying the culture *at the time of the original writing*, they are only preaching what "today's culture" has warped the Scripture to mean within the limited worldview of Western Christianity. Again: braided hair? No problem. We can throw that verse out. A woman minister? Never, because the Bible says... Paul's words about women are incredibly high up on the charts listing misuse. As a disintegrating foundational piece that is serving to crumble the whole, I can see countries all over the world that have been detrimentally affected by this, and billions of women have likely been silenced as a result (though there appears to be no Pew Research Survey that addresses this specifically).

This type of teaching becomes what the world views as "church," but it means little more to secular minds than an establishment of rituals while the living, breathing Word is cast to the wayside in trade for performance and showmanship. This becomes mounting "evidence" to the lost or jaded that the entire Word—and *all* the claims therein—is based on the product of wild imaginations.

We have to accept the fact that when the injury of misinformation is piled atop a Church that has for so many years accepted unanointed teaching because it's the religious ministry practice to which they're accustomed, we arrive at an equation that spreads distortion like a brushfire. Add to this years and years of the public's cultural familiarity with and acceptance of the skewed ministry concept, and we arrive at a day when any teaching that challenges that norm is marginalized or written off as the ramblings of a nonconformist radical (or an "apostasy woman")—despite how much truth might be presented in the message. It's an age-old social science: When people have largely adopted a way of thinking into their society and slowly built a universal worldview around it, they will not easily receive modifications to that worldview—even when it is based on inaccuracy. They don't want to hear the truth, because that means letting go of all they've known or believed up to that point, so they hold on to what's familiar, what's comfortable, always referring to the others in their support group for confirmation of a path that is biblically incorrect.

In each book of the Bible, the "voice" behind the text is comprised of the original author, certainly, but ultimately the true voice is that of God, the first and last Author of His Word. As such, it isn't just the writer we must know, but the circumstances at the time of the writing, as those details are imperative to understanding the complete message of God.

So, let's take a minute to go over some standardized study points, and then we will dive into precisely how Paul's words were relevant in his time, and how that applies to us today.

Questions that Lead to More Accurate Interpretation

The two most important deductions that any reader of the Bible should be making are these: 1) what God was communicating to His original audience through the human writer at the time it was written, and 2) what normative regulations for daily life that presents for us today. By this process of thinking, we have historically concluded which Scriptures apply only to an audience at a particular point in time (restricted regulations), versus which Scriptures still hold a valuable behavior that must be modeled timelessly, throughout all ages (normative regulations).

I once read a story about an American missionary who went to spread the Gospel in Greece. After his first sermon there, which was well received, he made his way to the door of the church to greet his new congregants as they left for home. As is customary in America, he extended his arm forward, expecting to shake hands. His hand was ignored as he was repeatedly approached by full grown men who leaned in for a holy kiss on the mouth. I can't even imagine the shock the missionary must have felt: the awkwardness of this foreign social situation manifesting right there in front of his wife...

Romans 16:16—as written by Paul—tells believers to "Salute one another with an holy kiss." First Peter 5:14 gives the same regulation:

"Greet ye one another with a kiss of charity." Why? Because in that day and in that culture, that was an appropriate way for a holy man to greet another holy man, and it showed an innocent camaraderie amidst the followers of Christ. Another famously referenced instance of this greeting was from Judas to Jesus on the night of His betrayal (Matthew 26:47–50; Mark 14:43–45; Luke 22:48). The Greek word used here is *kataphileo*, simply referring to a kiss generically, as opposed to *philein*, which refers to an amorous kiss. Some parts of the world still treat such a *kataphileo* greeting as customary, such as the city in Greece the missionary just mentioned traveled to. When this occurs in those specific locations, there is nothing to be viewed out of the ordinary, and it most certainly is not considered a man showing romantic interest in another man. In America, however, especially after the last century's social revolutions involving the homosexual community, there is almost no setting where a man could kiss another man on the mouth (or anywhere else, like the cheek) without it being taken as a romantic gesture (*philein*).

As such, we can easily conclude that almost all Western Christians perceive Paul and Peter's command to "greet with a kiss" as a "restricted" regulation (which is, again, a command or rule pertaining to a specific population of people in a specific time and place) when the verses are analyzed literally. But that conclusion is incorrect. The holy greeting is one that should be seen as "normative" (a command or rule pertaining to all people of every culture and throughout time: a timeless truth), once the intent *behind* the Scripture is deduced. Today's fellow believers should greet each other in whatever "holy" way is appropriate to their culture, so long as that greeting does not go against the intent of Scripture elsewhere. In the States, that is almost always a firm handshake and a hearty smile, and since a male reverend showing a romantic gesture to another man would be forbidden in Scripture, our "holy kiss" becomes a "holy handshake." The intent of the regulation is preserved.

I know that for some, the following review is redundant, but for others, this process is new, so I will say once more: By this illustration, we have quickly satisfied these two items: 1) what God was communicating to His original audience through the human writer at the time it was written (that "fellow believers should greet each other warmly in the way they would have at the time of Paul"); and 2) what normative regulations for daily life that presents for us today (that "fellow believers should still greet each other warmly in the way they do now in their own culture," assuming that greeting does not oppose the *intent* of Scripture elsewhere).

One example of a "restricted" regulation would be the sacrifices of animals upon the altar. This practice, for Christians, was ended when Christ became the ultimate Sacrifice once and for all through the New Covenant (Hebrews 8:13, 9:13–15, 10:8–18). Another example would be when Paul instructed Timothy to drink wine for his stomach problems (1 Timothy 5:23). Obviously, not all digestive problems today should be treated with wine. (My words here should not be taken as an argument for or against the moderate use of alcohol in a Christian's home. That is another debate entirely. I mean only to show that Paul's words to Timothy were not "normative" advice for any believer with a tummy ache throughout all time.)

One major interpretation principle in determining "normative" from "restricted" regulation is called "internal consistency." This can be viewed from two perspectives: 1) what the Bible says elsewhere on a particular subject, and 2) what a specific author (Paul, Peter, etc.) says elsewhere on a particular subject (whether that be the same letter/epistle, or a different book of the Bible, so long as it's written by the same author). In order for the Word of God to have integrity, it must have unity within itself. It has to "agree with itself" from all points to be considered true. It cannot "contradict itself." (Quick note: I know that there has been a raging debate since time immemorial about certain verses contradicting other verses. As a student of the Bible, I have studied many of these so-called contradictions. In every single case, it has boiled down to improper interpretation *or* a translational hiccup when the original

Hebrew, Aramaic, or Greek is forced into the confines of a secondary language, such as English. We studied just now how the Greek has a different word for a casual "greeting kiss" than it does for a "lover's amorous kiss." The Greek language also has many different words for "love," and the English language is once again limited to one word. I do not intend for this book to be a study in every perceived contradiction. I will only state for the record that, once properly understood, the Word does not and cannot contradict itself. When it appears to do so, readers are encouraged to study on their own for answers. For the purposes of this study, the principle of "internal consistency" will be limited to a woman's role in the Church and among men.)

Keep this principle tucked in the back of your mind as we continue throughout the book, because it is crucial to the words of Paul regarding women.

So, within the process of establishing the original culture in order to draw normative regulations for our modern era, we can ask several questions to help us discover timeless truth. Throughout my college studies, I have found that these are the most important questions to ask when reading any of the books of the Bible:

1. What literary genre does the material fall into?

The books of the Bible have been separated into literary genres by many scholars in order to aid study. If we don't know what genre applies to a text, we can't understand what the original text was meant to convey. Most popularly, the canonical list of books within today's Holy Bible fall into eight categories: historical narrative, law, wisdom, poetry, prophecy, apocalyptic, Gospel, and letters (epistles, such as that of Paul).

We wouldn't take in a science-fiction novel involving futuristic medical information the same way we would digest a modern medical textbook at a university. Both books feature heaps of information about medicine, but because they belong to different genres, the material exists for different purposes (one entertains, the other educates). Likewise, we cannot approach apocalyptic Scripture in the same way we would read a historical narrative (one warns, the other informs).

2. Who was the author?

In every conversation—whether between myself and someone else, or between two other people talking on television, at church, or wherever—when I hear someone speak, I consider who the speaker is in order to understand the meaning of his or her words. A person's speech or written works cannot be separated from his or her identity. Two people can be involved in the same cause, but come from completely different angles. Knowing who they are is as important as hearing what they say.

When you listen to a sermon delivered by a pastor you've known for some time, you grasp his words better than you would those of a total stranger. You may have heard this pastor share testimonies, make the congregation laugh by telling silly stories about his home life, and open up his heart passions every Sunday. At times, you may even know what he's going to say before he says it, because you know his personal convictions and you're used to his oratory style. You're familiar with him.

All the writers of the books in the Bible were involved in one central cause: bringing truth to the world. But many came from different angles in their approach to this cause. Paul had a different purpose for writing his letters to the early Church than Moses had when he documented ancient history. Knowing what Paul went through on the road to Damascus is crucial to understanding the passions behind his letters. Knowing what Moses went through during the Exodus helps us understand his anger toward the Israelites when he descended Mt. Sinai. *If you don't know the man behind the text, you won't understand the author's voice and intentions.*

3. Who was the original audience?

Just as with the author, the original audience cannot be separated from the purpose of a written text. New Testament letters address the false teachings, anxiety, persecution, and theological confusion of the early Church that was forming from Jews and Gentiles alike throughout Palestine and the rest of the world when Christ was no longer corporeally present to teach. Who these people were is just as important as understanding the identity of the writer. If we simply take in the text without understanding who originally benefitted from the material, we cannot understand *how* the material was beneficial. As such, we modern readers will find it much more difficult to render that text personally applicable to what we are going through.

4. What were the circumstances that made the writing a necessity?

Knowing what was going on in the world or culture at the time of a writing is crucial to understanding the purpose of the writing. We have to consider what is being addressed, and in what social/cultural setting, in order to properly apply those lessons to our own culture/society. Paul's advice to the churches sprouting up across Palestine after Christ's ascension may at times seem similar in intent or meaning to the words of an Old Testament prophet just before the Babylonian and Assyrian exiles, but they weren't addressing the same events. We cannot apply all of Paul's words to the ancient Israelites, and we cannot apply all of an Old Testament prophet's words to the early Church of Paul's day. In the same trail of logic, responsible readers look for how the circumstances of our current modern world or individuals within it parallel the circumstances at the time of the original writing *before* making assumptions about how verses apply today. (Though this rule is fourth on the list as my college training presents it, for this particular work, it is likely the most important.)

5. What was the cultural language style in use at the time of the writing?

This is one of the most important yet frequently overlooked considerations when studying Scripture. Culture is embedded in language, and language in culture. The two cannot be separated. The way we speak in America is different from how Chinese people speak in China, even when the languages are translated from one to another. For example, I might say, "It's raining cats and dogs outside." To an American, that means the rain outside is heavy. To foreigners, I have just stated that canines and felines are falling out of the sky. If they take my word as gospel, they will apply some kind of meaning to canines and felines being in the sky—whether literally or allegorically—and, to them, that would never relate to heavy rains. This is an example of an idiom: a group of words that sound like one thing, but mean something else, based on cultural use, acceptance, and familiarity.

From Genesis to Revelation, we find many examples of idioms, rhetoric, grammar fluctuation, syntax variations, and semantics that, if considered outside of their cultural setting, do not mean what the author intended. Since no culture today perfectly operates like those at the time of scriptural writings, it can often be difficult to understand what we've read when we dive into the Bible. Therefore, trying to understand the cultural language at the time of the writing seems like a tedious endeavor, but it is well worth the effort when the consequence otherwise is misinterpretation.

6. What does the surrounding text say?

Lastly, once we have, to the best of our ability, figured out the genre, author, audience, circumstances, and cultural language (and consulting commentaries is helpful if we get stuck), we must consider what is being said in context—in the verses before and after any passage, as well as farther out—of the whole book's message.

Take, for example, the popularly quoted Jeremiah 29:11: "'For I know the plans I have for you,' declares the Lord, 'plans to prosper you, and not to harm you, plans to give you hope and a future.'" Many well-meaning Christians take this as a promise that no matter what happens, they will eventually be prosperous. But the surrounding text reveals that this verse was never meant to be dropped in a social setting to inspire a climb up the corporate ladder, to land an audition at a major theater, or have an old car come back to life if we just keep sitting on this verse and hoping the clunker will start. Looking at the broader context, we see that the "you" in this verse refers to a collective people: the ancient Israelites. This was a message given from the Lord, Himself, through the prophet Jeremiah about the future of Israel.

However, that doesn't mean this verse isn't relevant to Christians today. It absolutely is—more today than ever! If we properly consider the genre, author, audience, circumstances, and cultural language behind the verse, and then consider it within the surrounding text, we come up with the following equation: The "you" in this verse—the parallel of that "you" from the ancient writing to today—is the Church, all the people of the Lord. God knows the plans He has *for the collective Body of Christ, the Church*; He has plans to prosper *the Church*. It's corporate, not individualistic.

Exegesis. It changes everything.

One last reflection before we begin our theological study…

I want to be very careful how I say this, because I do believe that the Word is all truth and nothing but the truth, written through the Holy Spirit's guidance, and is therefore the "God-breathed" Word of our Father. Nothing could convince me otherwise. It is this core belief that has driven me to study His Word in great depth every day I'm alive. *However*, I believe that the "God-breathed" and "Holy Spirit-inspired" texts were the original words penned by the original authors. Although this is a risky statement to make, because it might insinuate to some that I don't believe the KJV or some other prized translation (which is *not* the case), I would like to point out how many other Christians also feel this same way, though they may not have put it into these words.

For instance, in November of 2012, a new Bible translation was released, affectionately called the "Queen James Bible." The title was "based upon a theory that King James, the British king who commissioned the famous translation of the Bible, was bisexual."[6] One article opposing the release of this translation reads, "This new translation, the editors say, will 'resolve interpretive ambiguity in the Bible as it pertains to homosexuality.'"[7] The cover is all white with a rainbow-pride cross. I will not go into the translational differences between the KJV and the QJB, as that is not what this book is about, but I will tell you that there are many heavy discrepancies surrounding how this new translation addresses the original Hebrew and Greek languages. Scores of conservative scholars reacted to the QJB release with vehement rejection.

Many Christians would agree with these scholars that the QJB is twisting Scripture, but that doesn't change the fact that it *was* published and now exists for any person wandering a bookstore to find, read, and digest as the QJB translators intended. Does that mean that the QJB is "the Word of God" as He intended it to be when it was written so long ago just because a new translation claims it? No. It means that it's the "word of" and "intention of" the translators from one language into another.

But with so many translations available, how do we know we're reading from the right one? Today, a popular answer is to always to stick to the KJV if we don't understand ancient Greek and Hebrew.

I agree wholeheartedly with this statement, and it's excellent advice.

Yet I still believe "the most accurate translation"—and by extension the most "Holy Spirit-inspired translation"—when deciphering the *intent* of "God's Word" to us humans isn't a "translation" at all. It's the original manuscripts, written by the original authors, in the original languages, as God first delivered it to humanity.

In the following pages, we will address how some words in the ancient Hebrew and Greek were translated into English, and we'll look at the effects those translations have had on our Church's concepts of Scripture today.

Under no circumstances am I saying that the Bible—including the KJV translation—is corrupt, untrue, or questionable as it relates God's intent to mankind.

I only want to stress the importance of taking the original languages into consideration before we hang the entire belief system of Christianity—and all the modern, cultural norms that implies—upon the English (and by default *secondary*) language.

2

Internal Consistency

Some might wonder why I have decided to start the theological portion of this study of women in ministry by focusing on Paul's New Testament words rather than beginning with the first woman, Eve. Whereas it is true that there are a few popular misconceptions about the woman's role in Creation and the Fall that have historically been considered relevant in the Church's resistance regarding women clergy, whenever the subject arises from the pulpit, the strongest argument for the resistance always draws back to Paul's views and writings. As such, I feel this is an appropriate starting place.

In 1 Corinthians 14:34–35, Paul wrote: "Let your women keep silence in the churches: for it is not permitted unto them to speak; but they are commanded to be under obedience as also saith the law. And if they will learn any thing, let them ask their husbands at home: for it is a shame for women to speak in the church." And in 1 Timothy 2:11–12, he said, "Let the woman learn in silence with all subjection. But I suffer not a woman to teach, nor to usurp authority over the man, but to be in silence."

Such powerful and important words require much reflection. But first, let's read these verses *without* proper interpretation, so that we can point out the flagrant application glitches that instantly present themselves.

If we take the words of Paul in 1 Corinthians 14:34–35 and 1 Timothy 2:11–12 and apply them literally and in every scenario, throughout time and into perpetuity—in other words, if we remove the cultural and local circumstances, as well as the nature of the author, from the original text, and apply black words on white paper to every subsequent culture and circumstance—a woman would not be allowed to "speak" within the walls of a church. If this is the correct interpretation, we now have the following issues to address. This list might appear silly, but it *is* necessary because of the "exceptions" arguments such a list presents:

1. If speaking within a church is not allowed for a woman, prophet or otherwise, then, from the moment she enters the doorway, she must close her mouth until her body is once again outside the building. She can't greet visitors, tell another woman she likes her dress, show off her new purse, correct her noisy or fidgeting children, say "amen" during the pastor's sermon, participate in our ever-popular "repeat after me" prayers, or invite Christ into her life at the altar. Our Western world has no problem responding to this list with, "No, that's ridiculous. That's not what Paul meant." Again, without looking at the circumstances under which Paul was originally writing (which we will get to), then what *did* he mean? Is a woman allowed to say hello to her friends before and after the service, but hold her tongue the rest of the time? And what about the "repeat after me" prayers and the altar calls? If a woman can't speak during the prayer, she is disobeying the pastor; if she can't speak at the altar, she's not able to invite Christ into her life, and that goes against everything the Gospel stands for. So, okay, maybe *those two* times are the excep-

tion, but otherwise, she is to remain silent. Then what happens when her kids act up during the sermon? Must she allow them to make noise? If a pastor is greeting his congregation from the pulpit and says, "Glad to have you back home from the hospital, Sarah," is Sarah supposed to only wave in response? One might say, "Donna, you're being petty. These are not the scenarios Paul was talking about." I agree, and that's precisely my point. If a woman is allowed to speak in church, but only at the "appropriate times," *who decides these appropriate times*? Human people? That poses an immediate problem: One church might have more stringent rules than another for women. An inflexible church might apply the "silent while your body is in this building" expectation, which would be clearly oppressive and abusive (not to mention misogynistic if the men are allowed to interact)—while another flexible church allows women to completely disrupt the service, which Paul is clearly against according to his epistles. Where does a church draw the line—from the Word of God? (The answers *are* there, I assure you, but it takes studying more than just what the Word *says*; it requires studying the circumstances to discover why that material was written in the first place.)

2. If a woman isn't allowed to speak, is she allowed to sing? And if so, what if her singing style sounds for a moment like she is speaking, because the fluctuation of her tone is steadier? What if she slips a little "thank you, Lord" in between lines of a song? Is she guilty of "speaking" in the church?

3. And what of the female "prophet" (addressed in the following pages)? If God wants the "female prophet" to share a word with her people, but she is not allowed to speak in church, she would have to step outside the entryway and speak on the church steps in order to share her message with the Body…which means that God isn't able to use her to spread His Word if she is standing

one foot in the other direction. That seems absurd. Is she only permitted to prophesy on street corners and in alleyways then? Why would God gift all His people, sons *and* daughters, with the same giftings like He did in the book of Acts, but only "activate" the gift in women *outside of His own house*?

Many believe that a woman *prophet* is allowed to speak within the church at the appropriate time (based on several Pauline Scriptures, which we will visit in the next two chapters). If she *is* allowed to speak within a church, but only as a prophet and only for a short length of time, we now have the following issues:

1. What if God gives the woman a word of warning that applies to *all* His people, including men? I thought she was supposed to learn from the men, not teach them. And isn't she usurping the authority of men if she utters a warning to them and they don't innately agree with her? A word from God comes from *God*, who is the ruler over *all mankind*, including men, but if God gives a woman a prophecy for men, then who is the true usurper of the male recipients—God or the woman?

2. How long is our Western idea of a sermon? Twenty minutes? Forty? Somewhere in between? If a woman delivers a prophecy that takes this allotment of time, isn't she, by the *Greek* definition of the word "prophet" (*propheteuo*; discussed shortly), teaching and preaching? Therefore, we must have a set time for how long a prophecy can be so that it remains a "prophecy" and doesn't turn into a "sermon." (Again, Western concepts of these terms are not even close to biblical.) What is that time limit? Five minutes? Three minutes? What human authority do we turn to for this rule so we don't inadvertently limit God to our earthly clock?

3. When is a woman allowed to deliver her prophecy from God while she's present within the walls of a church? During the wor-

ship service? During the sermon? During the offering? Any of those times might be perceived as a service disruption, which Paul staunchly opposes throughout 1 Corinthians 14. So, by whose human authority do we rely upon to decide what portion of the service can be interrupted by God's prophecy through a woman, and what is the scriptural justification for why that portion of the service can be disrupted?

4. Since the woman is allowed to be recognized as a prophet, what official permits would our Western world allow her to have on paper? Would she be permitted to carry minister's credentials and say she is "licensed" or "ordained" to use her gift within God's house? Or would that piece of paper with her name on it be taking it too far? Does a certificate drafted by human hands offend God? Or is He simply glad to have an obedient servant, regardless of the papers humans assign? Is the generic "Prophet Mary" perceived as more or less correct in the eyes of God than the official "Reverend Mary" who holds papers within a "liberal" denomination? Western Christianity often says women can prophesy—even within a church, which means "speaking" in a church—but they are not allowed to have a piece of paper in their possession that shows they've studied the Word and have passed a test to show their theological competence as a member of the clergy. By that logic, we might ask: "Why do our churches today want to hear from uneducated women prophets instead of the educated ones?" One might respond, "It's a non-issue. The role of a 'prophet' does not require papers like the role of a 'pastor' or 'preacher.'" But why, and why not? Again, it's a modern and Western concept that "papers" or "official titles" define anyone's purpose.

Some throughout time have claimed to have the answers to all of these issues, but because each of these questions is not addressed specifically within the Word, scores of others have demanded that the "rules" be changed to fit their own theological interpretation. But if what we're talking about truly is a matter of *correct* interpretation, then these questions wouldn't be necessary in the first place, because the circumstances Paul was addressing have nothing to do with these issues.

Do you see how many questions arise when a biblical regulation is applied with modern, Western ideology? In an age when the Gospel message is perhaps more important to a starving world than it has ever been, the entire Church is quickly thrown into petty squabbles and its members are forced to argue amongst themselves about papers and rules and buildings and time limits. The message of James' epistle (just as one example) repeatedly warns against the Church members arguing with one another when people around us are dying every day. But without knowing the rules of appropriate conduct in a worship service, the Church risks being thrown into chaos, as Paul makes clear in *his* epistles. So what's the answer?

We must know the *circumstances* of Paul's words to Corinth and Ephesus before we can correctly apply them today.

In the next couple of chapters, we will look at the cultural backdrop of these verses in order to fully grasp what Paul was speaking about as it pertains to that time and those localities. For now, however, I would like to take a closer look at the glaring evidence that Paul actually *supported* women having roles in Church leadership. By approaching the study in this order, the question later on will not be as much *whether* Paul really wanted women to be "silent," but *when*.

Internal Consistency of Supporting Scriptures

First, let's consider the principle of internal consistency as it applies to the rest of Scripture—that which Paul did not personally write, but what would have been in circulation in his day (or events occurring while he was alive) and what he would have personally accepted as truth. (Other internal support unrelated to Paul, such as women of the Old Testament and Christ's personal involvement, will be discussed in later chapters.)

Acts 1:12–14 says: "Then returned they unto Jerusalem from the mount called Olivet, which is from Jerusalem a sabbath day's journey. And when they were come in, they went up into an upper room, where abode both Peter, and James, and John, and Andrew, Philip, and Thomas, Bartholomew, and Matthew, James the son of Alphaeus, and Simon Zelotes, and Judas the brother of James. These all continued with one accord in prayer and supplication, with the women, and Mary the mother of Jesus, and with his brethren" (emphasis added). We know, first of all, that the women were present in the upper room preparing for the Day of Pentecost, which is documented in Acts 2:1–6: "And when the day of Pentecost was fully come, they were all [the men and women just shown] with one accord in one place. And suddenly there came a sound from heaven as of a rushing mighty wind, and it filled all the house where they were sitting. And there appeared unto them cloven tongues like as of fire, and it sat upon each of them. And they were all filled with the Holy Ghost, and began to speak with other tongues, as the Spirit gave them utterance" (emphasis added).

What we see here is very clear: Men—*and women*—gathered in the upper room on the Day of Pentecost, and then they went out to preach the Gospel in every tongue to every person in their surroundings— *including other men who were present among the recipients.* This portion of Scripture is so powerful and flawless in its representation of women preachers and teachers—who, yes, teach *men*—that if this book ended here, the message would be clear: The Holy Spirit, not mankind, decides who will be chosen for what ministry and in what place on earth, and He communicates that to the individuals He chooses to "go and tell," not to the board members of a religious organization. The Holy Spirit fell on both genders that day, and women went out into the streets to preach the Resurrection to both genders! It couldn't be more obvious…

Sadly, however, this book cannot end here, because although this one portion of Scripture alone proves without any doubt whatsoever that God, Himself, called women to preach, our Western culture believes more proof is necessary. So let's keep trekking.

Acts 2:17–18 says: "And it shall come to pass in the last days, saith God, I will pour out of my Spirit upon all flesh: and your sons and your *daughters* shall *prophesy*, and your young men shall see visions, and your old men shall dream dreams: And on my servants and on my *handmaidens* I will pour out in those days of my Spirit; and they shall *prophesy*" (emphasis added).

The Holy Spirit equips all people for His work, male and female alike. *If the Holy Spirit doesn't place limitations upon women, why does the Church?*

Let us take a closer look at the word "prophesy." Many people in today's society—one that is far removed from the time during which any book of the Bible was written—assume that a prophet is someone who tells what's coming; a kind of fortuneteller for God, if you will. Although the foretelling of events (especially judgment and destruction as a result of Israel's disobedience) was a valid task for many prophets in the Old Testament, the perception of a prophet as *only* a "foreteller" is grossly limited and cheapens the task of those who have gone before us with a prophetic calling as it applies to words of knowledge, etc. The words "prophet" (noun) and "prophesy" (verb) both derive from the Greek *propheteuo*. This word covers a vast array of public exhortation practices, among which is "to teach, refute, reprove, admonish [which means to correct or reprimand!], comfort others."[8] Add these verbs together and place them into a word that today's Western world irrefutably recognizes as the fulfillment of these services, and we arrive at the word "preach." In other words, a "preacher" (or a "pastor" who "preaches") would be one that publicly "teaches, refutes, reproves, admonishes, and comforts others." Whereas the word *propheteuo* certainly meant much more than preaching, scholars of the Greek language unquestionably acknowledge that "prophet" as a noun originally meant the office of a public expounder and "prophesy" as a verb meant the flowing forth of counsel from a person's mouth to his or her recipients (God's nation). The idea that this duty would exclusively be carried out by women "prophets" today (as opposed to "preachers" or "pastors"), especially as that title is allowed in today's American culture, is to place unfounded limitations on the original noun/verb *propheteuo*. That Greek word predated all of the modern Western world's beliefs about what the label "prophet" means, and therefore it is the final authority.

This also raises the question of what label a women prophet would be allowed to have, when she would be allowed to speak, what she would be allowed to say, and for what length of time (the issues of which we just discussed).

This takes me back to a concept I strongly pointed to in the last chapter: No, "today's culture" does not decide what the Bible meant, and we cannot allow "today's culture" to blur the lines of what is or is not acceptable. By that same logic, however, "today's culture" cannot decide what an antiquated word means based on how we wish to interpret it now in our Western understanding. It simply meant what it meant at the time it was written, and the use of *propheteuo* in Acts 2:17–18 does not only mean "a fortuneteller for God," but a vocal instructor for God's holy nation (God's people). Beyond the shadow of any doubt, the original word *did* describe public teachers of the flock, and as the verse implies, those teachers include "daughters" and "handmaidens" (women).

A few weak arguments suggest that Paul simply wasn't fully aware of what was being said by his partners in ministry about women prophesying, or that he wasn't fully aware of what was going on around him at the time, so he wouldn't have had the opportunity to refute them directly. But supposing that were true and Paul *did* utilize his pen to "correct" the false teaching of his peers, the Holy Bible would either include a glaring Paul-versus-them contradiction (and, by extension, that would mean that the Holy Spirit who inspired the Word also contradicted Himself), or those who formed the canon of Scripture would have had to choose which of the intellectual opponents were on the winning side and omit the other's book from the final compilation we have now. Still, by process of elimination, we can rule this theory out by safely assuming that Paul was, as a prized student of the illustrious Gamaliel, aware that this very prophecy exceedingly predated any writings that were in new circulation during Paul's day. The prophecy of Joel 2:28, which Paul would have been aware of if he'd taken his scholarly studies under Gamaliel seriously, says, "And it shall come to pass afterward, that I will pour out my spirit upon all flesh; and your sons and your daughters shall prophesy, your old men shall dream dreams, your young men shall see visions."

In this Old-Testament instance, "prophesy" was the English translation of the Hebrew *naba'*. At the time of its writing, *naba'* was considered a primitive root, meaning that it wasn't derived from a former word. The Hebrews saw the male mouthpieces of God delivering Yahweh's ultimate judgement and warnings upon the people of Israel and assigned a sound to describe it, so the word as it appears in the book of Joel actually originated in the Hebrew language. Here, Joel is without a doubt saying that "daughters" (Hebrew *bath*) will one day be the mouthpieces of God in public exhortation of His people. If we, today's Christians, are God's people, then Joel—God's chosen mouthpiece of that time—predicted a day when women would be preachers/teachers/prophets, once a proper understanding of the Hebrew (and later Greek) word is applied. The Bible says it already happened in Acts, and even Peter "lifted up his voice" to the crowd and identified that the Holy-Spirit outpouring on the Day of Pentecost was "that which was spoken by the prophet Joel" (Acts 2:14–16).

In all of Paul's writings, he never once denies women equal inheritance to the Holy Spirit's gifts, nor does he negate Joel's ancient prophecy. He spoke of the gifts of the Spirit in several passages (1 Corinthians 12–14; Romans 12:3–8; Ephesians 4:4–16) and, therefore, he had ample opportunity to restrict women as recipients, had he considered that appropriate. As a man whose position of apostolic authority in the newborn Church was supremely overriding and final in a time when the Body of Christ needed to be told if women were *not* to be considered equal inheritors of the Holy Spirit's giftings (including preaching and teaching), the fact that he doesn't stipulate women as non-inheritors of these Holy-Spirit-given gifts is telling. (Granted, he does say "men" in some of these passages, but it should be taken as the non-gender-specific "mankind" in order to harmonize with Acts and Joel. More on this in the next chapter.)

The book of Hebrews speaks at length about the model set by Christ, the highest of all priests, and sets the example for all members of the priesthood to follow His lead. Yet, in his first epistle, Peter, the esteemed bishop of Antioch, says: "Ye [Greek *autos*, "himself, herself, themselves; he, she,"[9] referring to all Christians, male and female] also, as lively stones, are built up a spiritual house, an holy *priesthood*, to offer up spiritual sacrifices, acceptable to God by Jesus Christ. But ye are a chosen generation, a royal *priesthood*, an holy nation, a peculiar people; that ye should shew forth the praises of him who hath called you out of darkness into his marvellous light; Which in time past were not a people, but are now the people of God: which had not obtained mercy, but now have obtained mercy" (2:5, 9–10; emphasis added).

The English word "priesthood" is translated from the Greek *hierateuma*: "the office of a priest; the order or body of priests."[10] Today's equivalent of "priest," at least within the confines of Western Christianity, translates "pastor." (Certainly, "priest" is still in use today, but as it pertains to Western religion, a "priest" is a clergyman of the Catholic order or a leader of other religions.) I believe the meaning of this verse is clear, but as a necessary repetition: 1 Peter 2:5 and 9–10 is including women ("Ye," *autos*) among the order or body of priests (preachers/pastors).

Paul doesn't refute that women are among this priesthood. He personally knew Peter and was well aware of his theology, as they had been in communication with each other during the early developments of the Church. That Paul would not exclude women from inheriting a role within the priesthood is, again, telling.

As Scripture proves Scripture, here is another internal reference to this equality, though, by traditional dating methods, it would have been written after the death of Paul: "Blessed is he that readeth, and they that hear the words of this prophecy, and keep those things which are written herein:… And from Jesus Christ, who is the faithful witness, and the first begotten of the dead, and the prince of the kings of the earth. Unto him that loved us, and washed us from our sins in his own blood, And hath made us [Christians, male and female] kings and priests [Greek *hiereus*] unto God and his Father; to him be glory and dominion for ever and ever. Amen" (Revelation 1:3–6). Nearby verses state: "And hast made us unto our God kings and priests: and we shall reign on the earth" (5:10), and "Blessed and holy is he that hath part in the first resurrection: on such the second death hath no power, but they shall be priests of God and of Christ" (20:6).

Some state that because we aren't literally all kings, we wouldn't literally all be priests, either. That's a fair statement, but it limits both offices—*and their purposes in the light of eternity*—to an earthly enterprise. No, all Christians do not have palaces, servants, crowns, etc. like an earthly king. Nor is every Christian believer also filling the role of a public expounder like a priest (or pastor, preacher). Figuratively, allegorically, and spiritually, however, we are all both kings and priests—and we are all equal in the eyes of Christ within the definitions of these two offices as applied in the unseen and spiritual realm. Therefore, if a female feels called to serve Christ (an earthly duty, but a spiritual significance), and we are all one *in* Him, this verse at least speaks of the *divine* equality she would hold among men in ministering to others in this current, earthly life. As far as how that is implemented regarding ordination, time limits, rules of speech, location of ministry (pulpit or no pulpit), and so on, that is sadly now restrained within the narrow confinement of Western interpretation.

Lastly, David's Psalm 28:11: "The Lord gave the word: great was the company of those that published it." The sad reality of the English words chosen for "the company of those that published it" is how ambiguous the KJV translators made it sound. This stems from the Hebrew *saba hambasserowt*, which is used in the feminine form, and the English "published" here is better translated "proclaimed." David was openly acknowledging a group of *women* who were proclaiming the word "the Lord gave." If Paul was the Hebrew scholar we all know him to be, he would have certainly known that David was talking about women who proclaim God's word.[11]

Internal Consistency of Paul's Scriptures

Second, let us consider the principle of internal consistency as it applies to that which Paul *did* personally write. This involves the verses he penned regarding service order, as well as the introductions he made regarding women he knew. (Additional examples of internal consistency from the pen of Paul, himself, will be discussed in the next two chapters in our reflection on Corinth and Ephesus.)

First, we need to revise our concepts of what "church" meant to the New Testament culture. In the first-century, Judeo-Christian religious context, teaching occurred more as a group discussion than a monologue (Christ, Himself, taught in this interactive way). Prior to the third century, before the Roman Empire was "Christianized," Christianity was nowhere near the norm. It took many years and a lot of passionate Gospel work on the ground before believers of the true Messiah began to meet regularly in buildings dedicated to holding Christian services. This is in part due to the expectations that the Jews had regarding what the Messiah was going to be. He was not, as they anticipated, the soldier sent by His Father to crush the Gentile world and bring the Israelite nation to political and theocratic power, and so on. Believers were up against at least two major ancient influences: Jews and Rome. Both of these influences had weighty political power (Jews appealed to Roman political leaders), so many of the early Christians were scattered, out-numbered, and at risk of martyrdom. The resistance Christians faced was such that they had to meet quietly in *homes*, wherein the teaching and preaching of this fresh Gospel message was carried out by the home-owners. (Think back to the Jesus People/Jesus Freak movements of the 1960s–'70s.) Many of the churches that did spring into public arenas for worship, like that of Corinth, began as home gatherings.

It's within these homes that *women* were sometimes known to be the chief teachers. Biblical examples of this were: John Mark's mother Mary in Jerusalem (Acts 12:12); Lydia in Philippi (Acts 16:14–15); Priscilla (alongside her husband Aquila) in Ephesus and Rome (Acts 18:19, 26; 1 Corinthians 16:19; Romans 16:3–5); Phoebe in Cenchrea (Romans 16:1); and Apphia in Colossae (Philemon 2). When Paul and Silas left the Macedonian prison, they went straight to Lydia's home church and personally and directly encouraged the gathering (Acts 16:40). These female home-church leaders were viewed at the time by the early Christians around them as authoritative teachers of the Gospel, and Paul commended them for it in his epistles. This fact refutes the popular interpretation that women can only be church leaders when a man is not present—i.e., only to other women or children, or in a restricted role. It also poses significant questions about whether a woman can be a teacher, leader, or pastor in a church that initially sprouted from within her own home. If women "pastors" begin a church at home that grows to include a congregation too large to meet in that home, are they expected to then step down because their congregations got too large and now have to meet in a larger building? Or do they buy bigger houses so they aren't "caught teaching in a church"? If that's the case, any woman who feels called to preach or pastor can buy a mansion larger than any synagogue in the ancient world and teach congregations large enough to achieve the "megachurch" title, all whilst still being innocent of "teaching in a church." Does a *building* decide who the appropriate minister is? Does the number of listeners decide who is called? If the answer to these questions is, "No, they can still preach/pastor, because they started the church from their home," then we have to decide if other women preachers or pastors are allowed to use their Holy-Spirit-given gifts without first having to spend years opening their homes to the point that they overflow with participants. The issue really should be focused on the qualifications of the *minister*, not on the qualifications of a building. Correct teaching, as well as false teaching, can be carried out anywhere, and it can flow from the mouth of either gender. Many male ministers today are avidly against females being pastors, but they don't see that Paul gives proverbial high fives all around to several female ministers in his epistles, primarily in his greetings to fledgling congregations whom he often told to assist these women.

We shouldn't assume that just because Paul chose not to contest the writings of his fellows, he secretly believed otherwise or was merely oblivious to his cohorts' teaching. He proved as much when he wrote in 1 Corinthians 7 that men and women should share equal authority in their household; chapter 11 (verses 11 and 12) specifically outlines that men and women should be partners. And though many of today's preachers like to say that women should submit to the authority of the man, Paul's letter to the Ephesians, chapter 5 verse 21, states that husbands are to be equally submitting to their wives "in the fear of God."

In the patriarchal society that had so long reigned in Jewish nations, we are befitted to pause for a moment and ask: Why would Paul, the supreme Jew of his time prior to his conversion to Christianity, *ever* suggest that a man submit to his wife? Wouldn't such a concept bleed into the Church hierarchy? Yes, this verse is in regards to mutual submission, and no, it's not about leadership within a church building. However, a student of New Testament culture—one who has read deeply about the importance that honor, patronage, kinship, and purity played in society amidst these people groups and the lesser position that deemed for women[12]—will see certain proof that Paul, by bringing a woman up to par with man in the household first, was essentially *undoing* eons of patriarchal authority within society as a whole as it extended outward from the household. Cultural norms and standards begin with what is taught in the home, because children of tomorrow are raised with that line of thinking and perpetuate it into future generations. Paul saw headship within a home as needing a woman's *equal* guidance, and anyone in his authoritative position would not have pushed that way of life upon his generation if he didn't think it should be adopted as the new norm for the future. So, inasmuch as Paul was redefining societal norms for a woman as a mother and wife, we know he viewed men and women as equals. And that is no surprise to our modern culture, because today's Church has long since accepted that women can teach their children. But in Paul's day, a statement of *mutual* submission would have been a revelatory concept.

Might Paul have been a trailblazer for true equality of women in all spheres of Christianity, not just those relating to the home? I think that's obvious, considering the ministerial partners he chose.

One example is Priscilla. Scholars postulate that she hailed from Roman nobility, which would have meant she was trained in philosophy, rhetoric, and oratory skills, as was the prized training for students of both gender in ancient Roman culture *if* their parents were wealthy enough—i.e., she was a well-educated female. She and her husband, Aquila, were living in the city of Corinth (having fled there after Emperor Claudius exiled the Jews from Rome) when Paul came there to minister, and they allowed Paul to stay with them and build and market tents to fund his missionary endeavors. (Many interpret 1 Corinthians 16:19 to mean that the church at Corinth originated from within Priscilla's home.) Priscilla and Aquila's authority as ministers of "the Way" (the Gospel) is vetted by Acts 18:24–26, which states that they corrected the "eloquent" Jew Apollos' theology. Apollos was documented in this section of Acts as a man "mighty in the scriptures," "instructed in the way of the Lord," and "fervent in the spirit," so this speaks highly of Priscilla's influence: She, alongside her husband, took Apollos aside and "expounded unto him the way of God more perfectly." (Read: "She—a woman—perfected the theology of a man; she *taught* him.")

But maybe Aquila was really the one "expounding" and correcting Apollos' theology while Priscilla stood beside them smiling and nodding, as is a woman's place. Right?

No, not really... Evidence points to the opposite, actually.

It was customary in New Testament times for men to have the first position in nearly everything, as they were the central focus in society. When someone introduced a group with both men and women present, the introduction would begin with the men and end with the women. However, in Romans 16:3, Paul writes to the Gentiles of Rome, "Greet Priscilla [some translations say "Prisca"] and Aquila, my fellow workers in Christ Jesus." *Ellicott's Commentary for English Readers* notes this peculiarity: "It is rather remarkable that the wife should be mentioned first. Perhaps it may be inferred that she was the more active and conspicuous of the two."[13] *Maclaren's Expositions* also notes this oddity: "Did you ever notice that in the majority of the places where these two are named, if we adopt the better readings, Priscilla's name comes first? She seems to have been 'the better man of the two'; and Aquila drops comparatively into the background. Now, such a couple, and a couple in which the wife took the foremost place, was an absolute impossibility in heathenism. They are a specimen of what Christianity did in the primitive age, all over the Empire, and is doing to-day, everywhere—lifting woman to her proper place."[14] *Bengel's Gnomen* commentary, yet again, comes to the same conclusion: "The name of the wife is put here before that of the husband, because she was the more distinguished of the two in the Church."[15] In this case, then, scholars (these mentioned and countless others) agree that Priscilla, in whatever function she held for the Church, was more than an equal partner in the "work of Jesus Christ" (the spreading of the Gospel). And, as we all know, spreading the Gospel requires one to open her mouth and "speak in the church." When Apollos' theology was "expounded…more perfectly," we can't irrefutably prove that Priscilla was the head theologian over her husband, but neither can we prove otherwise. Further, cultural evidence suggests Priscilla was a prominent teacher of the Word, even to such learned *men* as Apollos. At the very least, we know the Bible says that when the act of correcting Apollos' theology occurred, "they," Aquila *and* Priscilla, carried out the act. Priscilla was at least her husband's equal—and likely the leader, in this moment.

The question is then raised of whether Priscilla was an "official" pastor in the early Church or merely a pretty face to compliment what the men were doing—and thus Paul merely meant to honor her with flattery or encouragement in a glittery introduction. Paul's phrase, "fellow worker," is the English translation of the ancient Greek *synergos*: "a companion in work" (derived from: *syn* "together" and *ergon* "work"[16]). From *synergos* we gain the English "synergy": "the interaction of elements that when combined produce a total effect that is greater than the sum of the individual elements, contributions, etc.; synergism."[17] Paul would not have referred to Priscilla as such if she were not considered his equal partner in an effort greater than the sum of the individual contributors. As stated prior, Paul was a student of patriarchal training under Gamaliel, so he wouldn't have risked using such a word to describe a woman if he were opposed to complete gender equality within the Church hierarchy. Paul recognized Priscilla's value as a fellow minister, and introduced her as such.

We can't assume that by "fellow worker," Paul was referring to Priscilla as a pastor, preacher, or teacher, but that is a nonissue since those exact terms hadn't yet originated. The historical etymology of the word "pastor" dates to circa 1325–1375; likewise, the word "preacher" dates to 1175–1225. Both words derive from Latin originally, so he couldn't have referred to her that way even if the duties of Priscilla's work were a precise match to that office. In his day, the word for "pastor" or "preacher" likely would have been "shepherd" (*poimen*) as it related to the cultural understanding of a church leader. But Paul, perhaps because "shepherd" was associated with Christ as the ultimate Shepherd for all, wasn't accustomed to using that terminology either, even when referring to those in his company whom we know *were* serving as pastors in his generation. An example of a similar term is "the Way," as mentioned earlier, which was what "the Gospel" was called (Matthew 22:16; Acts 9:2; 18:25; 19:9; 22:4; 24:14, 22). Back then, we would say something like, "a shepherd of the Way," whereas today, we would say, "a preacher/pastor of the Gospel." So, since the original terminology is so profoundly different from our Western expressions, we have to try to fill in the blanks throughout spans of history and culture. We cannot conclude that Paul saw Priscilla only as a pretty face just because he did not use a modern, Western word to introduce her—especially when the word modern ministers are looking for didn't exist at the time. *Poimen* is used eighteen times throughout the New Testament, and only once is this "shepherd" term translated as a Christian leader in Ephesians 4:11.

"Was it a man or a woman in that case?" one might ask. The answer is *both*. This instance, "And he gave some, apostles; and some, prophets; and some, evangelists; and some, pastors (*poimenas*, "shepherds") and teachers" occurs within the context of the gifts given to the Body of Christ, and it is inclusive of both genders.

This brings me to a side note, and I'll make it brief: For those who say women can preach, teach, and be leaders in certain offices, but they cannot hold the title of "pastor," what argument do they hold for why Paul just used *poimenas*—translated here as "pastors"—as a reference over the *Body of Christ as a whole, including women*? These gifts are irrefutably gender-inclusive. Naysayers have only two options: 1) believe the original Greek, which uses the word "shepherds" for women as well as men in the highest office a church today can hold; 2) believe the English translation, which uses the word "pastors" for women as well as men in the highest office a church today can hold. Either way, women can be pastors. Those who oppose women as pastors might argue that Ephesians 4:11 says this gift is given to "some," and that this "some" would naturally be men. That might be a valid point if it weren't for what Paul said just a few verses earlier in Ephesians 4:8, rendered thus in the KJV: "Wherefore he saith, When he ascended up on high, he led captivity captive, and gave gifts unto *anthropois*." The word *anthropois* is translated in the KJV as "men," which is misleading (and again should be read as "mankind"), because *anthropois* is a gender-inclusive reference that means, generically, "people." The NIV says "gave gifts to his people." If these gifts—including the title of "pastor"—were intended to refer to men only, Paul would have used gender-specific terminology in the authentic Greek, but he didn't. The translators of the KJV made that decision instead.

Women *can be* pastors, friends.

Back to Priscilla… What might "fellow-worker" mean for her?

We *must*: a) begin with Paul's cultural linguistics, b) discover what the original words meant to Paul as a *definition of duties* (the fulfillment of a function), and then c) conclude a rational equivalent of that same definition of duties within today's English language, before we d) boil the issue down to what title belongs to whom.

So, if Paul didn't call the pastoral figures of his time "pastors," he would have referred to them by the description of their function. Was there a *man* in a *pastoral* role whom Paul referred to with the same "function" term as Priscilla (*synergos*)?

As a matter of fact, there was…

We read in Romans 16:21: "Timotheus [Timothy] my workfellow… my kinsmen, salute you." The word "workfellow" here is, again, *synergos*. Timothy was perhaps Paul's most highly praised and revered colleague, and was even referred to as Paul's spiritually adopted son (1 Timothy 1:2). In fact, two of the letters Paul penned to Timothy are widely known today as "Pastoral Epistles." Timothy was the pastor at Ephesus, one of the most important churches of antiquity within Christianity (more on this church later). Yet, Paul did not call Timothy a "pastor" or "preacher" (for reasons just stated; those terms didn't exist yet); he called him *synergos*: the *same word he used to identify Priscilla*. (He also used this word to identify himself, as well as other males such as Barnabas, Luke, Demas, Clement, and Epaphroditus, as ministers of the early Church.)

Thus we know for certain that, by his introduction of Priscilla using the same word in his greeting, she was at least equivalent in ministerial function to one of Paul's most trusted and beloved pastors/preachers/teachers via his own assessment. Additionally, she is acclaimed to this day for "more perfectly" correcting the theology of a respected and learned individual, Apollos (a *man*).

In case you're wondering whether this is a one-time fluke...it's not. Paul also referred to Euodia and Syntyche—female "fellowlabourers," "fellow-workers," or "co-workers" (depending on English translation)— as *synergos* in Philippians 4:2–3: "I beseech Euodias, and beseech Syntyche, that they be of the same mind in the Lord. And I intreat thee also, true yokefellow, help those women which laboured with me in the gospel, with Clement also, and with other my fellowlabourers, whose names are in the book of life." Additionally, the English words "laboured with me" or "contended at my side" (NIV) are from the Greek *synatheleo*, which was a common Pauline descriptor of the ministerial function carried out by men. Here, it is used in reference to women. (Note that there is a KJV spelling discrepancy in the treatment of the name "Euodias." The original text spelled this "Euodia," which was feminine. When the KJV was translated, the name was changed to the masculine "Euodias," and many since have assumed this passage is referring to a man and his wife, instead of two women. If that were the case, then it could be viewed as a man in ministerial leadership who brings his wife along wherever he goes. Therefore, establishing these two names as feminine today is important in the ongoing discussion of women ministers.

And this is not the only time in the KJV that a name was given a slight adjustment to represent a male in Paul's writing. More on Junia in a moment...)

One interesting theory relevant to Priscilla is her association to the anonymously written book of Hebrews. German scholar Adolf von Harnack famously postulated in 1900 that Priscilla—with her close associations to Paul in ministry, as well as her harmonizing theology—makes her a reasonable candidate for authorship. I will not take time here to go over the details of why and how Priscilla might have penned that amazing book, because at best I would only be making a strong case for Priscilla's authorship candidacy. She might have been in the right place at the right time and with the right circulation connections, but the author of Hebrews simply is not identified in the book. Barring some great, new discovery, we simply don't know who wrote Hebrews, and a lengthy discussion of all evidence herein would derail from the central focus of a woman's right to lead in church. This is, of course, only a theory, and it can't be proven true. (Several scholars since Harnack have traced the same lines of evidence and come to the same conclusion, but because a few of them developed reputations as hardcore feminists, their research has been considered biased and has largely been written off since.)

However, the evidence in some points is convincing, and if Priscilla *were* to someday be proven the author of Hebrews, it would certainly show her to be one of the greatest and most authoritative theologians/teachers this world has ever known...and her audience has always included men.

Consider, too, Phoebe, just outside Corinth. (Phoebe is widely accredited as the woman who delivered Paul's letter to the Romans, which later became the canonical book of Romans in the New Testament.) In Romans 16:1, Paul says: "I commend unto you Phebe our sister, which is a servant (*diakonos*) of the church which is at Cenchrea." The interesting issue in this translation from the original text is the English translators' choice treatment of the Greek *diakonos*: literally, "deacon." These same translators, when referring to a man in Scripture in twenty-three instances, spelled out "deacon" or "minister." But in this one instance, when referring to a female, the word "servant" was the choice of translation. At the time of Paul's writing the letter to the Romans, early Church hierarchies (such as deacon, bishop, pastor, etc.) were not formally established, so the "status" of Paul's "deacon" recommendation of Phoebe is ambiguous until we look further into how titles worked in his day.

A deacon or deaconess of modern times is, in most denominations, an *ordained minister*, albeit usually in service to a higher priest or governing pastor. Today, an ordained minister is called a "reverend." If Paul's word meant anything close to what it does in our Western culture, then Phoebe would have been an ordained minister of her time. So how do we get to the bottom of the *intent* of the Scripture?

It is certainly true that this ecclesiastical Greek term had been translated as "servant" in seven other locations of the Bible, but in *twenty locations*, the word was translated as "minister." But regardless of whether *diakonos* appears as "deacon" (and sometimes "deaconess"), "servant," or "minister" in our contemporary renderings, one of the *functions* of this office as outlined by *Strong's Concordance* is the following, under item "G1249-*diakonos*": "a Christian teacher and *pastor* (technically, a deacon or deaconess):—deacon, minister, servant."[18] The other function listed in *Strong's* is "an attendant, i.e. (genitive case) a waiter (at table or in other menial duties)."[19]

So far, we have one of two possibilities as it relates to Paul's reference of Phoebe: a) she was a teacher, pastor, or ordained minister; b) she was a waitress at a "table or in other menial duties." To shed further light on this, consider Paul's lofty words in the following verse, Romans 16:2: "That ye receive her in the Lord, as becometh saints, and that ye assist her in whatsoever business she hath need of you: for she hath been a succourer of many, and of myself also." Paul just said they must assist her in "whatever business" she needed from them. If she were merely a "servant" in the likeness of a table waitress (or equivalent), the notion that her needs would be met by others is a natural opposite. The verse cancels out the intent of the previous verse. Therefore, Paul could only be referring to the former of these two meanings, which is that of a highly esteemed minister. According to the "Outline of Biblical Usage" as listed by *Blue Letter Bible*, the word "deacon" means "(1) one who executes the commands of another, esp. of a master, a servant, attendant, minister; (a) the servant of a king."[20] In other words, yes, a "deacon" is a "servant" as well, but one who answers only to the highest degree of authority, and whose station is above most other servants. This could potentially be a minister who serves the pastor of a church, but considering *Strong's* admission that "deacon" could mean "a Christian teacher and pastor," it could also mean a pastor in charge of an entire church and all its ministers and congregants, but who is ultimately a servant to the King (Christ).

Eddie Hyatt of Charisma News made the following connection: "*Diakonos* does literally mean 'servant,' but [it] became a word for *Christian leaders* as a result of Jesus using it in response to the request by James and John for special seats of power in His kingdom. Jesus replied that whoever wanted to be great must become a *diakonos*, that is, a 'servant.' From that declaration of Jesus [read: out of the mouth of Christ, Himself], *diakonos* became a common designation for Christian ministers, highlighting the servant character of *Christian leadership*."[21] (Interesting note: Christ, Himself, was referred to by the same word by Paul in Romans 15:8!) In other words, before Paul ever referred to Phoebe as a *diakonos*, Christ already inaugurated the word as a reference to a leader of the early Christian Church, so by the time Paul wrote of her, his familiarity with the word would have been accountable to what Jesus deemed it to mean.

At times—such as in the RSV, Jerusalem Bible, and a few other translations—we see Phoebe called the feminine "deaconess" (which would have been the Greek *diakonissa* in the original), but that is not accurate, because Paul specifically wrote the masculine variant *diakonos*, and this was *not* a mistake. It was highly irregular in this day for a woman to be referred to by the masculine version of a term when both masculine and feminine were available, and herein lies perhaps one of the most convincing arguments that Paul was, in fact, referring to a woman in a position of pastoral leadership over a congregation. In ancient Greek, when a masculine noun is used to refer to a woman, "the term is an official or ecclesiastical title."[22] The masculine noun was used over the feminine *intentionally* in cases when the woman was a leader, because women were not usually leaders, and this was a way of distinguishing their societal or religious role as *equal to a male leader in the same position*! It was a stripping away of the subordinate insinuation that the feminine variant of the same noun would have implied. That's simply how it was known amongst the apostles, so Phoebe was a *leader* amidst the apostles' circle, and the translators made her a mere servant, even though they maintained the integrity of the word's true meaning *twenty-three times* when it referred to a man.

Hyatt, in his book *Paul, Women, and the Church*, quoted evangelical theologian E. Earle Ellis, who further describes the function of those who were given this title: "*Diakonos* is used frequently in the Pauline letters for those who exercise ministries of *teaching and preaching*. [!!!] The title is given to Paul and to a number of his associates who are active on a continuing basis as traveling missionaries or as coworkers in local congregations."[23]

Additionally—and this is important—the word "succourer" in Romans 16:2 is drawn from the Greek *prostatis* (sometimes translated in ancient literature as "patroness"). *Prostatis* is derived from the prefix *pro*, "before," and the verb *istemi*, "to stand"—i.e., to stand before others or over others (similar to "overseer") with the authority that a patron would have held at that time. The word was used to identify church leaders.[24] Many believe this word means "helper" or "benefactor," and some Bible translations even use those words instead of "patroness." But in keeping with the truest sense of the word, it is better accepted as a trailblazer who "goes [or stands] before" others in an endeavor. Since this endeavor is closely associated with *diakonos*—and the preaching/teaching function that implies—then Phoebe, as deaconess and succourer, was a trailblazing, preaching patroness. (Again, I cannot recommend highly enough that readers do some deep studying of New Testament culture, for even the word "patron," as they perceived it, was *at that time* a societal leader upon whom all citizens in lower social positions would rely for nearly everything, including financial assistance, as well as guidance and council.) Strong's definition of *prostatis* simply says, "feminine of a derivative of G4291,"[25] the numbered locator for the word *proistemi*, which, *Strong's* says, means "to stand before, i.e. (in rank) to preside, or (by implication) to practise:—maintain, be over, rule."[26] She was, therefore, according to the Greek, a woman who "stood over" or "stood before" others in some aspect within the early Church's Gospel mission. Yet, because of the translation choices made when the secondary language texts appeared, she is now known merely as a servant. Little more than a table waitress…

At this point in the study of Paul's words, we reach a heavy insinuation that could change everything. Paul said, and I quote, "she hath been a succourer [*prostatis*: a "woman who stood before or over"] of many, and *of myself also*" (emphasis added).

She had been a *prostatis* of *Paul also*…

Let that sink in for a moment. Phoebe, this woman leader, is being referred to as a patroness, deaconess, and preacher "of Paul." She had "stood before" Paul in the endeavor of early Church ministry!

Did Paul have a woman as his pastor in the early days of his belief?

The language used here cannot prove this indisputably, but a solid argument can be made that supports this, especially after a reader takes in all the mounting evidence within this book that points to Paul's support of women in ministry as a fact. Consider *how* he instructed the men around her to receive her: "That ye receive her in the Lord, as becometh saints, and that ye assist her in whatsoever business she hath need of you." *They* were to assist *her*, and "in a way that is worthy of the saints" (ESV)! How has Phoebe, over so many centuries, continuously been viewed as a subservient woman?

Without going into the complicated roots of the word "deacon," as it involves an evolutionary process and admittedly varies from culture to culture in Paul's day regarding the authority assigned to the title, I would like to note: It is no secret that a deaconess could be ordained as a minister early on in the development of Christianity in some areas. In fact, according to *The New Advent Catholic Encyclopedia*, "It is certain that a ritual was in use for the ordination of deaconesses by the laying on of hands which was closely modeled on the ritual for the ordination of a deacon."[27] As to their level of a deaconess' public speaking, especially as it relates to being carried out in the company of men, the jury is still out. Scholars haven't yet been able to agree on whether a woman in Phoebe's position would have been given a platform to adjust the theology of, or teach, men. (Maybe we should leave that legacy for Priscilla, that other woman church leader Paul praised who adjusted the theology of, and taught, a man...)

In any case, however, there is yet another layer to add to the "deacon" translation thread. If, let's assume, Paul meant *diakonos* only as "servant" when he referred to Phoebe (which is, in and of itself, not a precise translation, as I just outlined), that still doesn't dismiss the argument that he might very well have been referring to a woman in a position of church leadership. Would anyone—even in today's culture—dare to dispute that Paul, himself, was a leader in the early Church? Certainly not. He was *the* leader, one might say, considering the hefty portion of New Testament Scripture that originated from him, much of which presents itself in the form of a "guidebook" for appropriate church service conduct as well as the correct theology of orthodox Christianity. Yet, Paul referred to *himself* as a "servant," "bondsman," or "slave" (Romans 1:1; Philippians 1:1). The word for this is the Greek *doulos*, which is a well-known synonym for—wait for it—*diakonos*! Paul essentially referred to himself and Timothy, in all their leadership glory, as equals to Phoebe.

The idea that this "women as church leaders" issue has coerced us to dig this deeply into the "deacon"-versus-"servant" and "patroness"-versus-"ruler" debates is actually concerning to me anyway. Aren't *all* ministers, pastors, preachers, Christian teachers, prophets, etc. technically "servants" to the Lord?

Paul evidently thought so.

To those who say, "The Church today needs to follow the example of Paul on this issue," I am inspired to respond, "Yes, please. Can we?"

May we all strive to be as humble as Paul in our subordination to Jesus Christ, regardless of what titles or limitations our Western world wants to place on individual ministers.

Now, on to the issue of Junia. The name "Junia" (Greek literal: *Junian*) is feminine. In Romans 16:7, Paul writes, "Salute Andronicus and Junia, my kinsmen, and my fellow-prisoners, who are of note among the apostles, who also were in Christ before me." This was a man and a woman. The Church Fathers and close-proximity historians—including Origen of Alexandria, Bishop Hatto of Vercelli, Deacon Theophylact of Constantinople, Jerome (translator of the Latin Vulgate Bible), Tertullian, Irenaeus, Ambrose, Augustine, Chrysostom (who served alongside a deaconess), and many others—all recognized Junia to be a female. Yet, in the Latin translations of the New Testament, "Junia" became the masculinized form: "Junias." (Note that there is a discrepancy in Origen's writings. The original work referred to her as a woman, and a late medieval copy of the same work adjusted her gender to a male. Also of interest to our reflection herein: All known instances of "Junia" are recognized as a woman's name, and the alleged masculine "Junias" cannot be found in any Greco-Roman historic records.[28])

The studies available on who originally made this switch and how it remained for so long afterward are so incredibly lengthy and complicated that including the information here would take another hundred pages (at least) to fully clarify. (There are several full-sized books devoted to discussion on this matter.) However, after having reviewed this material myself, I have come to the same conclusion as most others on this subject, and I believe it's accurate to state that the changeover from Junia to Junias found its genesis through Aegidius of Rome (1245–1346), when he masculinized Junia in his commentaries. The concept was solidified within Martin Luther's celebrated Bible translation, which reached multitudes and redefined much of Scripture for hundreds of years, and any hope Junia had of remaining female was lost for centuries. To this day, many are confused about whether Paul's Romans 16:7 reference of Junia was of a man or woman. As to *why* the switch occurred, I will quote from Bernadette Brooten's *Women Priests*: "What reasons have commentators given for this change? The answer is simple: a woman could not have been an apostle. Because a woman could not have been an apostle, the woman who is here called apostle could not have been a woman."[29]

However, as the earliest texts—as well as the men of authority during that era—all point to the name being female (and most translations also dropped the masculine form of the name in the mid-1980s), I will continue via the evidenced conclusion that Junia was a woman. (This evidence occurs both in the testimony of early Church leaders, as well as in modern, exhaustive, and astutely conducted research materials, such as Eldon Jay Epp's, *Junia: The First Woman Apostle* by Fortress Press, 2005.)

An immediate content disagreement arises among scholars regarding Paul's words "who are of note among the apostles." The two possible translations of this string of words are: a) "of note [distinguished] *among*" and b) "well known *to*." The former insinuates that Paul called Junia a "prominent apostle" outright, as she is "among" them (a member of them); the latter insinuates that Junia was a well-known and respected name "to" the apostolic circles, thought she was not, herself, an apostle. It's the difference between whether "of note among" is exclusive or inclusive, grammatically speaking. Some have gone far lengths to prove that every leading Bible scholar (those just mentioned and countless others)—for a thousand years after Paul's words were written—believe that

Paul called Junia an apostle, and their evidence is extremely convincing. Some of the celebrated, historical, and scholarly names who openly wrote of Junia as a woman apostle were: Origen, Jerome, Hatto, Theophylact, Peter Abelard, John Chrysostom, Ambrosiaster, Theodoret of Cyrrhus, John Damascene, Haymo, Oecumenius, Lanfranc of Bec, Bruno the Carthusian, and Peter Lombard (and this is in no way an exhaustive list).[30]

The overwhelming consensus of the Church Fathers and historians—the *men* who are far closer in historical proximity to Paul's writings—is that Junia was a) a woman, and b) an apostle. When a preacher today blares from the pulpit that Junia's identity as a female apostle is a modern "women's lib" or "feminist" alteration of Scripture, they are not paying attention to the *multitudes of men* around or closer to Paul's day who made the conclusion first. The following quote by John Chrysostom surfaces frequently in related research: "O how great is the devotion of this woman that she should be counted worthy of the appellation of apostle!"[31]

A question that arises at this point is: "Why would it be so hard to believe that a woman was an apostle anyway?" The Greek word for apostle, *apostolos*, means "delegate," "messenger," or "one sent with orders."[32] We already know there were more than twelve apostles, as the list also shows the additions of Matthias (Acts 1:26), Barnabas (Acts 14:14), James (Galatians 1:19), and Silas and Timothy (1 Thessalonians 2:6). So the issue is not whether there may have been more than twelve apostles, the challenge is accepting that one was a woman.

A curious pattern begins to develop in these circles as well, and it's a pattern that all the authors of the several books on Junia that I have read are also noticing: Those who believe Junia to be a man interpret "him" to be "among" (a member; one of) the apostles. Those who believe Junia to be a woman say she was "known to" (respected by, but not a part of) the apostles. Those who first agreed that this friend of Paul's was clearly called an apostle quickly change their minds as soon as her gender is revealed as a woman. *Then* she becomes "known to." Why? It's just like Brooten said: "Because a woman could not have been an apostle [a default set by cultural misunderstanding], the woman who is here called apostle could not have been a woman."

Could not a woman be "one sent with orders" or a "messenger"? Why not? But also, this is not to say that the apostolic title is one that Paul would have easily thrown around. Ann Graham Brock, in her book *Mary Magdalene, the First Apostle: The Struggle for Authority*, relates that Paul was protective of the term: "Thus Junia becomes another example of a woman who was called an 'apostle' in early Christian history but whose status has since been mitigated or challenged. Paul's generally sparing use of the term *apostolos* indicates his recognition of the term's significance for claiming authority." Brock goes on to say that Paul's "bestowal of the term upon a woman is in turn strong evidence that the category of 'apostle' in the early church was not only of considerable importance but also *gender inclusive*."[33]

But what of the actual Greek? The English word "among" from Paul's string "who are of note among the apostles" is the Greek *en*: "a primary preposition denoting (fixed) position (in place, time or state)."[34] Thayer's Greek Lexicon states the first meaning of *en* as "I. Locally; 1. of Place proper; a. in the interior of some whole."[35] In other words, a part of some whole, or in the case of a person, a member of a group. The KJV translates *en* as "in" 1,902 times and "among" only 117 times. Additionally, PhD professor of biblical studies Linda Belleville weighed in on the subject from the position of common usage in the New Testament writings, and her academic inference was interesting: In Greek, "primary usage of *en* and the plural dative (personal or otherwise) inside and outside the NT (with rare exceptions) is inclusive 'in'/'among' and not exclusive 'to.'"[36] Her conclusion, based on a rather extensive and meticulous sweeping over Greek nouns, plural nouns, genitive personal modifiers, dative personal adjuncts, and the variations/comparative senses of the language in use during the New Testament times, were that Paul's words "bear the inclusive meaning 'a notable member of the larger group.'"[37]

Eldon Jay Epp, author of *Junia: The First Woman Apostle*, has a fairly impressive résumé, indeed. His Master of Sacred Theology through Harvard University is only one of the many educational triumphs this man can claim. Moreover, he has been a well-respected professor in the field of proper exegesis for decades. He is known for such works as *The Theological Tendency of Codex Bezae Cantebrigiensis in Acts*; *New Testament Textual Criticism: Its Significance for Exegesis*; *Studies in the Theory and Method of New Testament Textual Criticism*; and *Perspectives on New Testament Textual Criticism*. With such a collection under his belt, it's no wonder that he is celebrated for his adherence to true, exegetical, nonbiased studies of the original Greek language. In abundance, Epp has expounded upon the importance of accuracy within biblical interpretation, and his knowledge of the various formations of Greek words throughout history is astounding.

In the conclusion of his book on Junia—after spending well over a hundred pages specifically on the study of the Greek texts, their variations throughout history, the "weigh-in" from numerous scholars, and the cultural implications of it all—Epp states:

Therefore, the conclusion to this investigation is simple and straightforward: there was an apostle Junia. For me, this conclusion is indisputable, though it will not, I fear, be undisputed... Yet, if this perfectly natural reading of [Junia] in Rom 16:7 as feminine, followed by all early church writers who treated the passage, had continued in late medieval to modern times, lengthy and tedious studies like the present one would be unnecessary, as would the manipulations and machinations of countless less male scholars (presumably otherwise enlightened) over the past two centuries. But far more significant and regrettable is the unnecessary alienation of women that has taken place and continues in many quarters of the church....

[I]t remains a fact that there was a woman apostle, explicitly so named, in the earliest generation of Christianity, and contemporary Christians…must (and eventually will) face up to it.[38]

Might I remind the reader at this point—whether he or she is for or against the interpretation that Junia was a woman apostle—that Eldon Jay Epp (to whom the previous quotation is indebted) is a *man*. A theologian and a scholar, yes, but he is also a *man*—and a modern one—who has come to this very learned conclusion through an exceptionally proficient knowledge of the original Greek and exegetical protocol. Folks, *it is not only women* and their "lib movement" or "feminist" mentalities that are bringing a revival to the "women's leadership in the Church" discussion with a lean on full equality.

Another significant detail that argues for Junia's role as an apostle relies on the reader's willingness to acknowledge the profound burdens she carried and the work Paul attributed to her. Once we take a moment to consider the enormous implications of Paul's reference to her as a "fellow-prisoner," we begin to see a boldness that most women of her day wouldn't have been able to conceive, and it no doubt paints her as a leader among men. She didn't allow her gender or social status to stand in her way of spreading the Gospel alongside Paul. She didn't fear persecution or imprisonment, she *embraced* it as a necessary evil in the fight of getting the story into the hearts of as many listeners as possible no matter the consequence. Any other woman in her position might have tightened her apron strings and retreated into the safety of her kitchen, and it would have been a choice that her culture would have supported since women were not expected to don their sandals and march throughout the territory as a minister. But nothing would stop Junia from doing the same work as Paul while she ministered alongside him. It's as if she said, "If you boys think you're alone in this, you're mistaken. I may be a woman, but I believe so passionately in the message of Christ that I will follow the Great Commission if it kills me. If Paul is willing to journey into the wickedest cities and confront thousands of years of pagan culture in the name of Christ, then I'm willing, too. If Paul is committed to throwing his own safety and comforts out the window in trade for seeing souls come to the saving grace of Christ, then I'm committed also. If Paul is beaten, I will be beaten alongside him. If Paul is thrown with his gaping wounds into a freezing prison cell, I will be thrown in as well." She was *with* Paul; she spread the word of Jesus *with* Paul; she suffered as a prisoner *with* Paul. If Paul had written about her actions as immoral or inappropriate because of the fact she was a woman, then her zeal to share the work, as viewed by the apostles, would have likewise been immoral or inappropriate. Yet that's not how he wrote of her. Much to the contrary, her choice to become a "fellow-prisoner" led Paul to instruct others to welcome her as a distinguished servant of Christ "among the apostles."

I believe it's clear that Junia was an apostle, but to those who still interpret her as "known to" the apostles, we are still challenged to admit that she *did the work* of an apostle, and Paul openly acknowledged that as a fact. (Her *function* in the early Church was that of an apostle, just as Priscilla's *function* in the early Church was that of a pastor/preacher.)

In my mind, as well as the judgments of literally incalculable scholars—comprised of men and women alike—Paul clearly showed that women were, have been, are, and will be leaders in the Body of Jesus Christ's Church. In Colossians 1:27–28, we read how Paul describes what he views as the perfect ministry—one that describes his own work, which he expects *all believers in Christ* to follow. In it, he directs that we are all called to a common goal of "teaching every man in all wisdom." Later in the same epistle, Paul lays out the foundation of the Colossian church as one that operates in full mutuality and equality, even among genders: "Let the word of Christ dwell in you richly in all wisdom; teaching and admonishing one another in psalms and hymns and spiritual songs, singing with grace in your hearts to the Lord" (3:16). The

Greek root for "teach" and "teaching" is *didaskein*. Women are called to *didaskein* (teach) within the Body of Christ! (Interestingly, this is the same exact word used in 1 Timothy 2:12, when Paul writes, "I suffer not a woman to teach." This is spoiler-alert intel that Paul's letter to Ephesus had to have been an isolated issue.)

Which brings me to my last verse analysis for this portion of the book. Galatians 3:28 says, "There is neither Jew nor Greek, there is neither bond nor free, there is *neither male nor female*: for *ye are all one* in Christ Jesus" (emphasis added).

Why didn't I begin this whole study with that one, since it appears to put the whole issue at rest? Because the context of this one verse in Galatians is complicated, at least as it applies to this specific study. The Jews believed that when the Messiah arrived, He would be coming only for the nation of Israel. The enormous "Jews and Gentiles" problem that arose within the early Church led Paul to write to several churches throughout the territory, including the believers in Galatia, telling them that as we are all one in Christ, we will all inherit the Kingdom of God together: Jews, Gentiles, slaves, free, men, women, etc. Many pastors are actually correct in stating that Paul's foremost goal in this verse was *not* to talk about women's rights in church clergy, but to lift high the concept of full equality in the inheritance of a glorious afterlife apart from social boundaries.

However, the principle of internal consistency relies on more than just one isolated verse being interpreted correctly—and proper interpretation protocol, as addressed in the previous chapter, only begins after an attempt has been made to digest the whole, which includes the author. *That* is why I held this powerful verse back until now, because it's not just about this verse, it's about unpacking the nature of Paul (getting to know the voice behind the text) so we can understand this verse in relation to all his others. If we don't understand Paul, we can't properly understand his letters.

As a quick recap so far:

- Paul did not attempt to place any kind of spiritual "off switch" upon the giftings of the Holy Spirit in relation to women. He was well aware that the Holy Spirit had equipped both men and women alike for His work on the Day of Pentecost, and that *women* went out to preach the Gospel on that day, even to men. Nowhere in his letters did he specifically say women were not *spiritually equipped by the Holy Spirit* to do the same work as men in the interest of spreading the Gospel. **This shows:** Paul respected the Holy Spirit's anointing upon women to have equality in preaching Christ's message from the Day of Pentecost onward. Equality of all *in Christ.*

- Paul was likewise aware of the prophecy of Joel and the teachings of his contemporaries about women preaching, teaching, and prophesying, and he never set out to "correct" these theological statements. Because of the fact that an entire Church was arising with new questions and new cultural movements around this Messiah in the most important religious shift in world history—and because of Paul's exceedingly apostolic authority being central during this shift—he would have known it was his duty to oppose these prophecies or replace these "false teachings" for the sake of Christ if they were, indeed, false teachings. All eyes were on him, and he knew that. The fact that he didn't oppose, replace, or correct these prophecies displays his acceptance of them. **This shows:** Paul respected the Word of God as it relates to women preaching, teaching, and prophesying. Equality of all *in Christ.*

- In several places throughout his letters, Paul taught of a radical social reformation among the households of believers, cautioning against a patriarchal society where only women submit. He did this despite the implications for future generations. He also spoke diplomatically on the "slaves and masters" issue in his letter to Philemon; he did not attempt to dissolve a master's rightful and legal ownership over a slave, but he spoke of a spiritual equality among all people: "Not now as a servant, but above a servant, a brother beloved, specially to me, but how much more unto thee, both in the flesh, and in the Lord" (16). Over and over again, he taught that there were no "elect" inheritors of Christ, but that we were all one—no longer "Jew versus Gentile," "man versus woman," or "slave versus free." **This shows:** Paul respected the value of every individual—including his or her talents, callings, and gifts—as equal to all others in the light of Christ. Equality of all *in Christ*.

• Paul, in his own choice of introductory terms, presented Priscilla and the great pastor Timothy of Ephesus to be equals (*synergos*). At another time, he presented Phoebe, Timothy, and *himself* as equals in their work (*doulos*, synonym of *diakonos*). Yet elsewhere, he presented Junia (if one chooses to accept the overwhelming evidence of this as fact) as a fellow apostle (*apostolos*)! **This shows:** Paul saw equality in both male and female positions in the Church, and went as far as to introduce them as such. Equality *in Christ*.

Once we "unpack" the Paul of New Testament times, we see that equality was one of his greatest passions. Yes, the verse in Galatians is referring to salvation as it related to believers in Galatia, but the *whole message* of Paul as the author of all his epistles, once pieced together, is one that: a) praises a peaceful camaraderie amongst the saints, for b) the sake of the spreading of the Gospel, so that c) all might be saved no matter the cost (including extreme persecution, which he personally suffered), and that this would be done d) *without the social barriers that existed in his day*!

This verse by Paul is inaugurating a whole new *community*!

A growing number of scholars in the past hundred years have come to this same conclusion, and they, too, are admitting that even though the focus of the verse is upon freedom from ritual, the *whole voice* behind the letter to the Galatians demands liberty from the social restrictions that had for so long dictated whose personal giftings and talents were allowed to be used in the interest of witnessing to others. Professor Gilbert Bilezikian, author of *Beyond Sex Roles: What the Bible Says about a Woman's Place in Church and Family*, puts it this way: "The inaugural texts of the church, one of which was penned by Paul himself, emphatically declare the church to be a community in which distinctions of race, class, rank, and gender become irrelevant (Acts 2:15–21; Gal[atians] 3:28)."[39]

It's what Paul stood for and what he wanted in the short span of his life: to finally observe genuine equality, not just in salvation inheritance, but in the common and universal goal that as many souls as possible would be saved *in Christ*, and he *never* stopped writing about that very goal despite the harsh circumstances of his own literal prison cells—even to the day of his violent death. He saw us all "as one" in the aim of ensuring that the message about Christ was heard and received to the ends of the earth. The whole picture has to be viewed before the whole message can be analyzed.

So the fact that the epistle to the Galatians was written as a response to a salvation issue and not to Church leadership positions is not proof that Galatians 3:28 is irrelevant to that subject. It's another chink in the distracting-competition-within-the-Body-armor. It merely speaks of Paul's innate nature. If anything, it further supports his willingness to see equality in Church leadership, because it's yet another verse that serves to tear the social walls down and embrace a full oneness as a team: the objective being the Great Commission, the tools being Body members who do not squabble against each other about church politics and legalism while thousands around us are dying daily.

Was the verse written to address women as preachers, teachers, and prophets? No, and it would be improper exegetic practice to claim that it was. Does the verse support the *whole* message of Paul throughout the *whole* of the same author's epistles as it stood for widespread and far-reaching equality among believers who are "neither Jew nor Greek, neither bond nor free, neither male nor female" in the work that the Holy Spirit poured out upon everyone equally? Does the verse support the idea that, within the realms of this very endeavor, we are "all one in Christ Jesus"? If a person is willing to see the verse as the heartbeat of the man named Paul, then he or she will "hear" the "voice" of the man who constantly cried out for equality, and he or she will know that this verse in Galatians is yet another extension of the man who saw us all "as one" in Christ's *work*.

John Ortberg said in his book, *Who Is This Man?: The Unpredictable Impact of the Inescapable Jesus*, "Because they share a common humanity, the highest calling of a woman is also the highest calling of a man: The glorious adventure of coming to know and do the will of the God in whose image they are created. Through Jesus, this calling is now available to any woman."[40]

Now onward to the situation in Corinth and Ephesus that led to Paul's words about women being silent in the church and learning in submission.

3

Context of 1 Corinthians

As a reminder: In 1 Corinthians 14:34–35, Paul wrote: "Let your women keep silence in the churches: for it is not permitted unto them to speak; but they are commanded to be under obedience as also saith the law. And if they will learn any thing, let them ask their husbands at home: for it is a shame for women to speak in the church."

After spending so much time in the last chapter reading about the women church leaders Paul kept company with, these words seem out of place now. In order to establish a better understanding of what he could have meant, we have to apply a greater level of interpretational decorum. Let's tackle that first.

Backdrop of Paul's Letter to the Corinthians

Literary Genre

First Corinthians is an epistle. The Greek word *epistole* translates to "letter" or "message." In the New Testament times (prior to phones and email, etc.) communication was limited to messengers and letters. The Bible includes two types of epistles: those to local congregations and those to individuals. This one in particular is a letter from Paul to the newly forming congregation in the ancient city of Corinth.

The purpose of an epistle is didactic (instructional) to one or more recipients in a particular situation that requires advice or correction. Paul's epistles were not originally written to document history, warn about the apocalypse, bestow beautiful poetry, or give another narrative of Christ's life, miracles, trial, and crucifixion. Because we know what this letter is *not*, we must interpret it for what it *is*. The letter was sent from one man to a congregation needing assistance that only he could give for a problem that was occurring at that specific time and place.

This *does not mean* that the instruction from the letter doesn't apply anywhere else or that it has less value than any other book of the Bible. It means:

1. The original circumstances must be determined.
2. Similar (or exact) circumstances of today must be determined.
3. The "relative" instructions apply to today's reader after a fair comparison of the two preceding factors have been determined, and in a way that preserves the spirit of the principles taught.

For instance, Paul's words in Philippians 4:13: "I can do all things through Christ which strengtheneth me." We know that this statement, and the instruction to rely upon Christ that it relays to its readers, is a "normative" one—it applies to every believer throughout history. Nothing about this timeless truth is "restrictive" to one audience, time, or place, and we can be assured of that based on so many other verses (remember the principle of internal consistency) that make the same promise and implied instruction. (Nor does any verse in the Bible refute this one, which satisfies the mandate that the Bible must "agree with itself.") Now the challenge becomes how to make this verse relatable ("relative") to today's readers while preserving its intent. Without following the three steps just outlined, this verse has a potentially unrestrained application. We cannot sprout wings and fly, and no human in history ever has, regardless of whether or not Christ was strengthening their lives. Nor could we, in good conscience, ask for Christ's internal strengthening to help us rob a bank or buy a new home well above our budget without responsible plans for paying it off. But when we follow the steps, the *intent* of the verse is clear, and the "absolute" instruction (relying on Christ's strength in literally every situation, including sprouting wings or robbing banks) becomes a healthy and balanced "relative" (relying on Christ's strength as it applies to similar or exact circumstances that Paul wrote about):

1. The circumstances were: Paul was writing from a dark, dank prison cell. He had been imprisoned for his faith, and much of life seemed hopeless, but his faith remained strong. He knew he had the strength to fight the good fight and keep up Christ's work against all odds, because Christ was empowering him to be strong on the inside, no matter what was going on outside.

2. Similar (or exact) circumstances of today would be: Whether our prison cell is literal or figurative, we can remain strong in our faith and toward good works because we have Christ's internal assistance and empowerment.

3. The "relative" instructions (remaining strong in our faith and dedicated to Christ's work) apply to today's reader after a fair comparison of the two preceding factors have been determined, and in a way that preserves the spirit of the principles taught (we can now rely on the promise that Christ will strengthen us in faith and ministry, even when all odds are stacked against us).

We do not have to be in a literal prison cell for the spirit of the principle to apply, but we have to learn how to separate the "absolute" from the "relative." In cases where one verse appears to contradict another (such as Paul's prohibitions about women in 1 Corinthians and 1 Timothy contrasted to his many accolades of fellow women ministers), there is an added challenge of nailing down what is "normative" (applies to every believer forever, no matter what) from what is "restrictive" (applied first to that audience, and only to modern audiences when the circumstances are the same). This is crucial any time we are dealing with materials that fall into the "epistle" genre, because their nature is to teach us how to live, and we must know those teachings in order to live in a way that is pleasing to God. This obviously includes righteous behavior, but it *also* involves being extremely careful not to place unnecessary (and potentially oppressive) rules upon all believers today when the original instructions were limited to one audience and the circumstances it faced. Choosing to do so anyway, whether out of deliberation or ignorance, can distance us from the Creator and the divine order for humanity He designed.

Author

Saul of Tarsus was a student of Gamaliel, who was a trusted holy man among Pharisee and Sadducee circles. Saul had been trained as a minister of the Jews, and when Christ claimed to be the Messiah, he assisted the Pharisees and Sadducees in persecuting the early Christians. He was present at the stoning of Stephen as a witness who "consented of his death" (Acts 8:1), though he did not personally throw a stone.

Shortly thereafter, "he made havock of the church, entering into every house" and arrested many of the followers of Christ before taking them to prison (v. 3). Despite the increasing conversion number, Saul continued to blast believers with "threatenings and slaughter" (9:1). So dedicated was he to what he perceived to be a holy war against heresy, Saul went to the high priest and received his blessing to take the attack outward to Damascus. His intent was to forcefully arrest the believers in that city and bring them back to Jerusalem for trial.

On the road to Damascus, a heavenly light surrounded Saul, and he personally heard Christ's voice for the first time revealing Himself as the true Messiah He had claimed to be. Saul rose up from the ground to find himself blinded by the encounter, so the men who were with him led him the rest of the way into the city. Saul stayed there for three days without food, water, or sight.

The Lord sent Ananias, a believer in Damascus, to pray for Saul and restore his vision. Afterward, Saul rose, ate, and was immediately baptized. From that moment on, he dedicated his life to the spreading of the Gospel message. Ironically, he became an instant target of the Pharisees, who sought to persecute him in the same way he had persecuted the converts.

As Saul's missionary travels became heavily associated with ministering among the Gentiles, he chose to be called "Paul," which was his Roman name. (The name "Saul," given to him at birth, was his Hebrew name. Dual names were commonplace at that time.) Using his Roman name helped him better relate to the Gentiles, a central focus of his ministry.

Paul's missionary travels are well documented in the book of Acts. He suffered as an apostle of Christ on countless occasions, and was brutally beaten and jailed on several occasions. Even the walls of a prison cell would not silence him, as it was within that setting that many of his greatest works were written.

As a journeyman of ancient cities, Paul launched many churches throughout the land while he built tents to help fund his ministry. Because those churches did not have the authority of the New Testament like we do now, false teachings were corrupting the message of Christ among fledgling believers, so Paul kept in touch with the churches he planted and pastors he trained, writing them letters of correction and encouragement during the earliest phases of Christianity's development. Those letters make up a significant portion of our New Testament today.

Audience

The congregation at Corinth was founded by Paul, who stayed there for eighteen months during one of his many missionary stops. Corinth was a prosperous commercial center for sea trade, and as the capital city of the province of Achaia (the largest territory in Greece), it was the central seat of Roman government. It was well protected by the Acrocorinth, a 1,900-foot-high mountain, which featured a temple dedicated to the worship of Aphrodite, the pagan goddess of love. At the base of the mountain was the temple of Melicertes, the patron goddess of sailors. Biannually, Corinth was the center for the Isthmian Games, a festival of music and athletic competition, and the sea god Poseidon was greatly honored. All around Corinth, pagan worship was experiencing a revival. (Some have hypothesized that this was a manifestation of spiritual warfare: God had just come to the earth in human form, died, rose again, ascended, and the Holy Spirit had poured His power out on the new Christians on the Day of Pentecost. In the spiritual realm, activity was at an all-time high—so, whereas God had His angels and human soldiers at work, the enemy also had his at work, and paganism was rampant.)

Because of the massive number of travelers in and throughout this territory, the population has been reported to be anywhere between one hundred thousand and six hundred thousand residents at any one time. Many religions were being brought to the church at Corinth, and the services of the one thousand cult prostitutes at the temple of Aphrodite were freely given to any tourists with the required coins in his pocket.

These prostitutes, known in ancient Greek as *hetairai*, were higher-class citizens and well educated, frequently maintaining a relationship with the same list of men for some time—which was a contrast from the *pornai* prostitutes (from which we eventually derive the English word "pornography"), who required a more "overnight" expenditure and had little to no education. The *hetairai* heavily populated Corinth as courtesans to the wealthy elite; the *pornai* were available for anyone, anytime,

as long as their "suitors" had money. By far, however, the *hetairai* courtesans were seen as a central part of the "glue" that held society together.
They were richly dressed, articulate, heavily painted, schooled in oratory skills and rhetoric, and every hair was in the right place as they
flitted about society and "owned" every room they entered. They were
not worshiped as gods, themselves—and as women, they were certainly
marginalized in society in comparison to men—but their bodies were
the conduit through which the pagan gods were worshiped and honored. As such, their social standing and cultural status were consistently
respected in a locality where such sexual activity held precedence and
equaled blessings from the gods who demanded orgiastic ritual. Unlike
the Jewish women of surrounding regions that held the patriarchal traditions of society firm, the sophisticated *hetairai* were often welcome to
share their thoughts and opinions regarding spirituality or theology, *especially* in the presence of men who were awed by them. Unlike prostitutes
of our culture today, who are frequently looked upon with scorn, the
hetairai were revered and admired, despite the fact that they were often
considered property. (Corinth dominated the pottery trade, and pottery
still displayed in museums today features artistic depictions of women
ranking above men and animals.)

Pagan idol worship wasn't limited to Aphrodite, Poseidon, and Melicertes. Other gods of antiquity were in revival throughout the region as
well, such as Ashtarte and Baal of the Canaanites, the unseen patron
hosts of the annual fertility and vegetation celebrations of old. Bacchus,
the god of fertility and wine, was also worshipped throughout the land
at that time—as was the mother goddess Cybele—and drunken orgies
in honor of these gods were practiced regularly. With such a large number of voyagers and holidaymakers stopping in Corinth, every day, a
new faith was warping the city Paul had worked so hard to convert,
and the sacred prostitutes made orgiastic worship an unabashedly blatant and delectable indulgence. Before Church leaders eventually ral-
lied together to confront the Gnostic "holy weddings," even "Gnostic

Christians" (true Gnostics at that time who practiced mystery cults but called themselves "Christians") were openly engaging in a public display of intercourse at wedding parties.[41] Corinth was a cesspool of religious prostitution. So known for its sexual perversion and immorality was Corinth that elsewhere, in surrounding regions, any woman known for her loose behavior would be referred to as a "Corinthian girl."[42]

It is no secret that the audience of Paul's letter would have been one of religious syncretism, delivering a great injustice to the purity of the Gospel message. One description documents that the common audience within Corinth was a "mongrel and heterogeneous population of Greek adventurers and Roman bourgeois, with a tainting infusion of Phoenicians; this mass of Jews, ex-soldiers, philosophers, merchants, sailors, freedmen, slaves, trades-people, hucksters and agents of every form of vice...without aristocracy, without traditions and without well-established citizens."[43] As such, the Christians in Corinth were continuously influenced by hordes of incoming religious voices belonging to pagan convictions and mystery cults.

Circumstances Requiring the Epistle

Sometime after Paul established the church at Corinth, word reached him in Ephesus that the saints were squabbling and dividing. Arguments for how a worship service should be conducted were at an all-time high. The Body of Christ was in its infancy, and without a canon of Scripture they could rely on, the notion of a solid and untainted Gospel message seemed hopeless.

Believers were engaging in sexual perversion left and right, at times resulting in incest, and some were actually proud of the high level of tolerance with which the church responded to it (chapter 5). They were taking each other to court and allowing pagans to make legal rulings upon matters that were spiritual in nature (chapter 6). Immoral conduct was warping the sacred communion observances (chapter 11). Doctrinal errors, including the distortion of the Resurrection (chapter 15), were rampant. The believers were tripping over themselves to prove that "their way" was the best way for their church and that "their theology" was correct; this escalated to the point that feuds and disruption during services were commonplace, plummeting each gathering into chaos (chapter 14).

Language / Surrounding Text

In the first chapter's suggested steps to proper interpretation, we ended with the issue of language and the comparison of surrounding texts. However, because the issue of women speaking as leaders in the Body of Christ is the focus of this entire book, and Paul's linguistic style and proximate verses are such a *paramount* piece of that whole puzzle, instead of visiting a few truncated paragraphs of those details here, we will consider the language and the surrounding text as we go, in hopes of doing it better justice.

Message of the Letter

Paul begins his letter by first identifying himself (1:1), and then identifying the recipient, "the church of God which is at Corinth" (1:2). A warm greeting of thanksgiving continues through verse 9.

Verses 10 through 13 are crucial to our reflection, because these are the very first words from Paul from which we can detect the chief concern behind the letter:

> Now I beseech you, brethren, by the name of our Lord Jesus Christ, that ye all speak the same thing [that you are all agreeable in nature and in doctrine], and that there be no divisions among you; but that ye be perfectly joined together in the same mind and in the same judgment. For it hath been declared unto me of

you, my brethren, by them which are of the house of Chloe, that there are contentions among you. Now this I say, that every one of you saith, I am of Paul; and I of Apollos; and I of Cephas; and I of Christ ["I follow Paul"; "I follow Apollos" etc.]. Is Christ divided? was Paul crucified for you? or were ye baptized in the name of Paul?

Remember, the New Testament didn't exist at the time. Believers had no document to turn to when a doctrinal issue came up. Remember, too, that the first-century Judeo-Christian teaching was often a group discussion, not a monologue. The more questions asked about this new Messiah, the more educated witnesses of Him would be, so questions in and of themselves were not prohibited. If someone were to continue asking questions or seeking clarification on a theological issue that was less relevant to everyone present, it would not be edifying to the Body, which is a theme of 1 Corinthians, and the service (read: meeting) would easily become a din of garbled voices.

The church in Corinth was in a constant state of commotion. People were saying the equivalent to, "My theology is more accurate than yours, because I follow Paul." Others were responding, "No, you're wrong. Apollos is a well-educated man of the holy texts, and he said [fill in the blank]." Yet another would weigh in with, "Both of you are wrong! Cephas says…"

Factions and cliques were appearing amidst the brethren, and an extreme division was pulling people apart from the central goal of teaching the Gospel. The foundational purpose of Christ was completely left at the wayside while people engaged in bitter and petty disputes about whose theology was correct. Everyone seemed all too willing to drop names as an added layer of clout in a glorified "I know better than you" exchange. Lost souls in and around one of the largest and most heavily populated cities of the ancient world were heading to their eternal judgment without being gifted with the good news of Christ—all because these men and women could not get through a single gathering without someone starting another round of it.

By asking the believers if Paul, himself, had been crucified for them, or if they had been baptized in his name, he was attempting to remove himself (and other human theologians) from center stage and reestablish Jesus Christ to His proper place among the congregation. Paul continues along this trail of thought (reestablishing the doctrine of Christ and beseeching his audience to revere wisdom by way of the Spirit) through the end of chapter 2. In chapter 3, he's back to addressing division, distraction, and disruption in the church. (Do you see the pattern forming?) In chapter 4, he discusses the ministry of the apostles, but by chapter 5, he's moved on to the issue of sexual immorality and the defiling nature of such sin within the Body:

> It is reported commonly that there is fornication among you, and such fornication as is not so much as named among the Gentiles [read: even the heathen Gentiles aren't engaging in such sexual immorality], that one should have his father's wife [incest]. And ye are puffed up, and have not rather mourned, that he that hath done this deed might be taken away from among you. For I verily, as absent in body, but present in spirit, have judged already, as though I were present, concerning him that hath so done this deed, In the name of our Lord Jesus Christ, when ye are gathered together, and my spirit, with the power of our Lord Jesus Christ, To deliver such an one unto Satan for the destruction of the flesh [yikes, that's serious!], that the spirit may be saved in the day of the Lord Jesus. Your glorying is not good. Know ye not that a little leaven leaveneth the whole lump?... I wrote unto you in an epistle not to company with fornicators. (5:1–6, 9)

Sacred prostitution was influencing the entire city. Men were sleeping with their fathers' wives. Whether this meant their mothers-in-law or their mothers by blood (both have been suggested; neither would be hard to believe in this culture), Paul rightfully saw this perversion as a defilement among the brethren who called themselves followers of Christ. He made no bones about the fact that they were headed straight for Hell through the destruction of the flesh if they allowed this behavior to continue.

Chapter 6 takes a quick break from this subject to talk about disputes *again*—and how the believers were taking issues of a spiritual nature into the pagan courts systems for legal rulings against one another—and then it's straight back to sexual immorality:

> Now the body is not for fornication, but for the Lord; and the Lord for the body. And God hath both raised up the Lord, and will also raise up us by his own power. Know ye not that your bodies are the members of Christ? shall I then take the members of Christ, and make them the members of an harlot [read: *hetairai* courtesans and *pornai*]? God forbid. What? know ye not that he which is joined to an harlot is one body? for two, saith he, shall be one flesh. But he that is joined unto the Lord is one spirit. Flee fornication. Every sin that a man doeth is without the body; but he that committeth fornication sinneth against his own body. What? know ye not that your body is the temple of the Holy Ghost which is in you, which ye have of God, and ye are not your own? For ye are bought with a price: therefore glorify God in your body, and in your spirit, which are God's. (13b–20)

Dissension in the church, then sexual immorality, then dissension in the church, then sexual immorality... These two factors are unquestionably connected. The prostitutes—those who were not only allowed to speak almost anywhere and at any time in the company of males, but who were encouraged to—were controlling Corinth. They were establishing cultural norms that tenaciously opposed both Jewish and Christian values. There certainly were righteous men who didn't agree with what was going on, especially those from Jewish backgrounds, but it was a reality nonetheless. (For those who assume that all churches or synagogues at this time featured separated seating—men on one side, women on the other—I strongly encourage you to look into Bernadette Brooten's studies on the nineteen existent synagogues of the ancient world. Whereas this divided seating was the norm for the Jews for many years, by the time of Christ, the practice was waning. More on this at the end of this study.)

Naturally, within the context of a letter such as this, pure marital relationships had to be addressed. Without taking time to study the backdrop of Corinth, a reader of Corinthians may not understand the significance of the principles-for-marriage subsection in chapter 7. In a city with a thousand prostitutes—most of whom were highly educated and held the best class-seats in society, and whose batting eyelashes drew the Christians out from the house of God and into the house of pagan gods for sacred sexual magic rites—an undefiled husband-and-wife relationship that pleases God had to be firmly attended to.

Some holier-than-thou converts in the church at Corinth had sent word to Paul with the assertion, "It's good for men not to have sexual relations with a woman at all" (7:1)—a concept that Paul gently refuted by admitting that the fleshly temptations in Corinth were so severe that marriage between a man and woman should be allowed (7:2). After admitting that *mutual submission* of man and wife—*one to the other reciprocally*—is healthy both in headship as well as sexual relations (7:3–5), Paul says that there is value in remaining single if one can do so without falling into impulsive desire (7:6–9). In verses 10 through 17, Paul continues to discuss marriage in terminology that speaks of gender equality and the notion of marriage as a joint team. In verses 18 through 31, he praises those who surrender to the call of Christ just as they are (slave, free, circumcised, uncircumcised, etc.); in verses 32 through the end of chapter 7, Paul continues to address the pros and cons of being married versus remaining single. In chapter 8, the apostle speaks of food offered to idols (which again denotes the extent of idol-worship within Corinth), and in the majority of chapter 9, he tells of how those doing Christ's work should find that very work its own sufficient reward.

However, there is a thought-provoking segment of Scripture, 9:19–23, that we should take a closer look at:

> For though I be free from all men, yet have I made myself servant unto all, that I might gain the more. And unto the Jews I became as a Jew, that I might gain the Jews; to them that are under the law, as under the law, that I might gain them that are under the law; To them that are without law, as without law, (being not without law to God, but under the law to Christ,) that I might gain them that are without law. To the weak became I as weak, that I might gain the weak: I am made all things to all men, that I might by all means save some. And this I do for the gospel's sake, that I might be partaker thereof with you.

By no means should this be taken to mean that Paul is inconsistent, that he conforms his convictions to those he is around at any given time, or that by "becoming all things to all men" (a popular alternate translation of 9:22), he flip-flops like a weak, wishy-washy minister between beliefs and principles to flatter the company he keeps.

Heavens no…

A beautiful saying attributed to St. Augustine (but that probably originated from a German Lutheran theologian in the early 1600s) is: "In essentials unity, in nonessentials liberty, and in all things charity." When Christians *must* be united about the essentials—Christ was the Son of God, He died on the cross, He rose again, and His blood has provided redemption for all mankind—then it is our duty to ensure that the essentials are upheld…that no false teachers change, twist, or add to those. However, when we approach a nonessential—"under the law" or "not under the law," etc.—liberty of the individual must be allowed, and squabbles that cause strife in the Body are wicked because they derail the big picture of the Gospel message. But in *all* things, charity and love for others who may or may not agree with what we believe must be sustained if they are ever to be won to Christ. (Even today, voices behind a new Hebrew Roots Movement are demanding that Christians return to the Mosaic Law dietary rules, refuse to celebrate Christmas, etc., and some of these men and women are quite vociferous and demanding. Dissension within the Body over the nonessentials category will continue as long as we are on this side of eternity.)

By showing kindness and understanding to those born and raised in varying cultures and religions, and by *not* choosing to vehemently argue nonessential theology in light of the bigger picture (spreading the Gospel), Paul is a greater fisher of men. His ministry to the lost is increased. More souls are reached through this approach.

Does this show that Paul is compromising? No, because nowhere in his epistles does he ever justify negotiating over of the Gospel essentials. Does this show that he has a natural appreciation for certain cultural and social barriers that believers around him find impossible to let go? Yes. By extension, does it show that he is willing to make exceptions to his Gospel-spreading methodologies (*not the essential doctrines*) based on cultures that receive Christ through different customs, traditions, and techniques as it applies to Paul's time and cultural backdrop? Certainly. If he thought there was a way to lead a Jew living "under the [Mosaic] law" (9:22), then he graciously showed willingness and patience to see past the cultural and societal cultivating that individual had been imprinted with since birth "to gain some" and "save some." If he thought there was a way to lead a heathen, Gentile, or "weak" person to Christ, then he "became as weak" (9:22) in that person's company in order to better relate to him or her and lead that person to salvation—as long as the Gospel essentials were preserved.

Now apply all that we've learned about Paul's support of women ministers to this same pattern of behavior. As clearly outlined in the previous chapter, Paul knew, held company with, and reinforced women ministers. Here in 1 Corinthians 9, he is suggesting—if his example is to be followed—that ministers embrace peaceful witnessing that relates to the company they're in.

What can we learn from this? That Paul, himself, the ultimate apostolic authority, did support witnesses of the Gospel representing themselves agreeably to one audience in one way and another way to a different audience as it pertains to the social and cultural demands/expectations the listener holds if it "gains" or "saves" more of the "some," *so long as he or she is not disobeying Scripture in doing so.* If the 1 Corinthians and 1 Timothy passages are not prohibiting a woman from speaking, teaching, or preaching because they were circumstantial/restricted regulations isolated to the goings-on of Corinth and Ephesus (discussed in this chapter and the next), then they are not "absolute" and "normative" regulations that apply literally in every case, but "relative" regulations that apply in similar or exact circumstances. To an audience whose salvation is not hanging upon a woman's title, she can "become as a reverend," not "under the law" of tradition that states women shouldn't preach, as long as her theology is accurate and edifying. (We will address the "law" referred to in 1 Corinthians 14:34–35 soon.) That same reverend, however, based on Paul's primary teaching here, should not force herself into a church filled with congregants who have been imprinted with the idea that women ministers are immoral. To *that* gathering, she must "become as weak." (I am obviously not referring to "weak" as in a mousey, fragile, or insubstantial female who can't make decisions without a man, and so on. I am referring to her role as a minister. Since this example congregation's view of a woman's role in ministry might only be to teach women and children, then in *that* congregation, she should strongly consider allowing her role or title to be "weakened" to that status, so that the "some" can be increasingly "gained." No minister—male or female—should storm the doors of a church with vigorous proselytizing of his or her own theological convictions and conclusions for the sake of starting or winning a fight or debate. [As to whether there may be occasions when a church's governing force should be challenged, that is addressed briefly in chapter 7 of this book.] When I was invited to speak, teach, and preach at Jim Bakker's Morningside Church as I mentioned earlier, I was in the company of those who *do not* hang their salvation upon a woman's title; I was in the company of those who, like Paul, support women leaders in the Church. So in that place, I "became as a reverend." The papers I hold that certify me as a legal reverend in the sphere of church politics have been assigned by mankind; my spiritual certification came from the same Holy Spirit that sent women to preach on the Day of Pentecost.)

But we haven't yet arrived at the chapter and verse that have caused so much confusion throughout the years, so let's continue.

Chapter 10 deals with idol worship (again), as well as with offering meat to idols, chapter 11 lands at another interesting perplexity: head coverings. For more insight on this, readers must comprehend the Greco-Roman culture's understanding regarding the association between hair and fertility. To a modern reader, the concept of hair and fertility being related in any way is foreign. However, as is heavily documented throughout this era (and especially just following it, as seen in the works of Hippocrates of Kos, the Greek "Father of Medicine"), doctors taught that hair was created by intimate body fluids. From Troy W. Martin's work, the *Journal of Biblical Literature* (2004), we read that the ancients believed "hair is hollow and grows primarily from either male or female reproductive fluid or semen flowing into it and congealing (Hippocrates, *Nat puer* 20). Since hollow body parts create a vacuum and attract fluid, hair attracts semen.... Hair grows most prolifically from the head because the brain is the place where the semen is (78) produced or at least stored (Hippocrates, *Genit.* I)."[44] Of course this "science" seems absurd today, and it is, in light of what we know about hair

ꞮꞮꞶ., but in the interest of remaining exegetically informed, we must understand the world that Paul was immersed in. Paul did not sanction these Hippocratic teachings, but he was responding to a social and cultural issue regarding decency. The world around him believed this medical teaching, and as a result, a woman with an uncovered head was in a sense making the statement in that culture and time that it didn't matter to her if she wandered about displaying her intimacy. Whether Paul and his fellow early Christians accepted Hippocratic leanings is irrelevant. For a woman to go into a place of worship and pray or prophesy with her head uncovered was to blatantly associate herself with the behaviors of temple prostitutes and common pagan practices.

But more importantly than what medicine taught was what Paul taught.

Note that by Paul discussing the proper way a woman should "pray" and "prophesy" while her head is covered *in church* (11:5), he is openly acknowledging that women are allowed to speak in church. Remember, too, that the word "prophesy" comes from *propheteuo*, which, as we discussed in the previous chapter, means "to teach, refute, reprove, admonish [correct or reprimand], comfort others"—not just serve as a "fortuneteller for God" who speaks for a set period of time.

Certain sects of conservative Christianity still follow these "head covering" rules (men cannot pray with their heads covered and women cannot pray without a head covering), especially in foreign countries. However, in the States, most modern preachers—even those who say women cannot teach or speak in a church—have largely rejected this verse as an "absolute." Why? There are many interpretations of this chapter, and we will not take the time to visit each one, but the dominating reason is because a head covering in the ancient Greco-Roman culture showed a woman's modesty, humility, and willingness to submit to her husband. As the principle applies today, a woman should still be modest and humble when she attends church to pray/worship, and she should still submit to her husband. (But remember, as noted earlier, Paul didn't *only* think a woman should submit to a man. He spoke of mutual submission, one to the other, in Ephesians 5:21. It's the principle of reciprocal respect and honor in a marriage.)

Just coming from a reflection on chapter 9, where Paul said he "becomes" what he needs to be for varying audiences, we could also say that if a woman today were to go on a mission trip with her husband to a country where a literal head covering is the decent attire, she should "become a head-coverer" for the sake of the "some," whereas in America, she should respect her husband by dressing modestly. Still, the conflict remains that most ministers today don't think an American woman needs to wear a head covering because of the circumstances (Greco-Roman culture) that initially drove that regulation—i.e., they view Paul's words here as a "relative" and not as an "absolute"—whilst those same ministers will not allow women to teach or preach because they view Paul's words in 1 Corinthians 14:34–35 as an "absolute" regardless of the Greco-Roman and Corinthian culture that drove that regulation. (For those wondering why I haven't tackled the "creation" comments Paul gave here, I plan to do so in our reflection of Eve.)

Carrying on...

Verses 17 through the end of chapter 11 address the "worthy manner" in which the sacrament of communion should be executed (and verse 18 yet again mentions division in the church). Chapter 12 speaks of the spiritual gifts, about which Paul openly acknowledges that "it is the same God which worketh all in all" (12:6): "all" being both male and female. Let's look at his words thoughtfully:

Now there are diversities of gifts, but the same Spirit. And there are differences of administrations, but the same Lord. And there are diversities of operations, but it is the same God which worketh all in all. But the manifestation of the Spirit is given to every man to profit withal. For to one is given by the Spirit the word of wisdom; to another the word of knowledge by the same

Spirit; To another faith by the same Spirit; to another the gifts of healing by the same Spirit; To another the working of miracles; to another prophecy; to another discerning of spirits; to another divers kinds of tongues; to another the interpretation of tongues: But all these worketh that one and the selfsame Spirit, dividing to every man severally as he will. For as the body is one, and hath many members, and all the members of that one body, being many, are one body: so also is Christ. (12:4–12)

We can't take Paul's word "man" in these sections ("the manifestation of the Spirit is given to every man" [12:7]; "one and the selfsame Spirit, dividing to every man severally" [12:11]) to be a reference to the male gender. The Greek word here is *hekastos*: "each or every:—any, both, each (one), every (man, one, woman)."[45] In other words, "every man," "every woman," "everyone," and the universally inclusive "mankind" are all accurate. To suggest that "man" means only males here would be to alleviate women from having to follow all the biblical regulations that apply to both genders whenever *hekastos* is used elsewhere (such as Romans 2:6, 12:3, 14:5; Galatians 6:4–5; Ephesians 4:25; Colossians 4:6; 1 Peter 4:10, etc.). Therefore, we see that women and men alike receive the gifts Paul listed here: the word of wisdom, the word of knowledge, faith, healing, the working of miracles, prophecy, the discerning of spirits, tongues, and the interpretation of tongues. Comparing this section to the rest of the letter to Corinth, which addresses how these gifts are to be used in church, we see repetitious evidence that Paul supported women speaking in church.

Furthermore, in each log of ecclesiastical giftings Paul wrote about in Ephesians 4, Romans 12, and 1 Corinthians 12, no gift is held higher than that of prophecy: "I would that ye all spake with tongues but rather that ye prophesied: for greater is he that prophesieth" (1 Corinthians 14:5). This sentiment is especially prominent in 12:28 when Paul ranks "teachers" (including preachers) even *below* the prophets: "And God hath set some in the church, first apostles, secondarily prophets, thirdly teachers, after that miracles, then gifts of healings, helps, governments, diversities of tongues." Some believe women are *only* allowed to "prophesy" based on the popular interpretations of 1 Corinthians 11:5 and the aforementioned foretelling of Joel 2:28 and Acts 2:17–18. But here in chapter 12 of this epistle, prophets are ranked *above* even the teachers. If we hold steadfast to the "women can only prophesy" idea as an ecclesiastical norm, the implication is that a female prophet outranks a male teacher. On the other hand, if we lean merely on our own understanding (which Proverbs 3:5 commands against), it appears that the Lord's anointing must fall more heavily upon those who perform miracles and healings, because anyone can claim to be a teacher or prophet, but miracles and healings are only proven when an eyewitness observes the almighty manifestation of God's power upon the physical and natural elements. Yet in this list, miracle workers and healers rank number four and five on the list.

This is why it's so important to view the Great Commission as an all-inclusive endeavor! The second that power plays are introduced, it becomes mankind's game!

Through the end of chapter 12 and all of chapter 13 (the infamous "love chapter"), we see Paul's ideal of one Body of Christ working together peacefully—without dissension or division, which is a cyclical key concentration of this epistle. It is made clear that if we do not work together for the sake of the lost, then even the most articulate teachings—words so beautiful they might be heard as the language "of angels"—are nothing more than "sounding brass, or a tinkling cymbal" (13:1). (The ESV renders this "a noisy gong or a clanging cymbal.")

This brings us to chapter 14. *The* chapter 14.

This section of Paul's writing not only has been confused regarding women ministers, it also has launched endless interpretation debates about the use of tongues during the church service. I don't plan to make a theologically "absolute" statement on tongues (as that is not the purpose of this book), but I do wish to point out that Paul, to the church at Corinth, was: a) in favor of tongues (14:5), but b) in opposition to them *under circumstances wherein they disrupt the service* (14:6–25). Consider his words in verse 23: "If therefore the whole church be come together into one place, and all speak with tongues, and there come in those that are unlearned, or unbelievers, will they not say that ye are mad?" The ESV renders this: "If, therefore, the whole church comes together and all speak in tongues, and outsiders or unbelievers enter, will they not say that you are out of your minds?"

Again, the "speaking in tongues while at church" issue is a hot-button debate that would only distract us from our focus on women ministers. But the fact that Paul is—throughout this entire chapter—cautioning against a chaotic service that doesn't "edify" the gathering (14:5, 12, 26) shows without a doubt that the focus is not only upon the use of tongues in church, but also upon the appropriate *circumstances* that must exist before they can be used.

I was raised Pentecostal, and I have seen this precise "out of your minds" event unfold in front of me more times than I can count. I remember inviting a friend (we'll call her Sophie) to church with me when I was in the sixth or seventh grade. It was a hard pitch getting her to come with me at all, since her mother was a self-proclaimed Wiccan priestess (of sorts, though her beliefs were wide-ranging and not limited to any specific theology) who believed in Christ as only a "nice prophet guy who did nice things for people" (her words). I visited Sophie's house a few times, and I vividly recall Sophie's mom—one of the sweetest and most *loving* creatures on the planet. On one occasion, she was in the back room weaving an intricate dreamcatcher while Sophie and I were watching a recorded band concert on television. I was once again inviting Sophie to church, and she was once again turning me down because she was afraid of being judged if people discovered her mother's practice of magic and her oil paintings of "mystic angels." (It is important to know that my mom and dad did not know much about this friend, and a lot of what I told them about her implied that her family was God-fearing. [I stretched the truth about her quite a bit.] They would have *never* allowed me to visit her house had they known more about her mother's hobbies.) I assured Sophie that the church members wouldn't bombard her with demands about her mother, and that she could come with me in confidence that she would have a good time. Sophie's mom overheard our conversation, came into the hallway with strings of beads and crystals strewn about her neck, and encouraged Sophie to be open-minded.

"Sophie," she said, "there is truth in all religions. Jesus was a wonderful man, and it wouldn't hurt you to go with Donna and learn a little more about Him. Would it?"

Sophie came with me the following Sunday, when a guest speaker had been invited to teach about the gifts of the Spirit. The speaker repetitiously followed his louder and stronger statements with a lengthy string of uttered tongues. Increasingly, the rest of the congregation followed suit, and by the time the altar call was given, people all around Sophie were shouting in tongues. Some were dancing, some were moaning, some were conducting a "Jericho march" around the seats, and some were falling to the floor at the altar.

"This is so weird!" Sophie whispered to me. "Are all these people crazy?"

Her question of whether the people were "crazy" is exactly what Paul was referring to when he said, "will they not say that ye are mad?"

I didn't share this memory because I plan to follow it with a study on tongues, dancing, moaning, marching, or falling. I did so as an example of how events like that can be potentially forever stamped upon someone's concept of Christianity. To Sophie, a recipient of teaching that day, the church was a place of complete and total chaos.

Paul outlines in 1 Corinthians 14 how even a blessed gift of the Spirit, when allowed without restraint, produces chaos and disruption in a gathering. The question is not *whether* Paul supported the practice of speaking in tongues, the question is *when*.

The entire focus of 1 Corinthians 14 (and much of the rest of the book) is about order in the church: "For God is not the author of confusion, but of peace, as in all churches of the saints" (14:33). There is to be harmony, peace, and order in the house of God, as in all churches where His children gather!

Verses 34 and 35—the *very next two verses* in sequence—say, "Let your women keep silence in the churches: for it is not permitted unto them to speak; but they are commanded to be under obedience as also saith the law. And if they will learn any thing, let them ask their husbands at home: for it is a shame for women to speak in the church." Coming straight off the statement that our church services should not be confusing but peaceful, Paul says women shouldn't speak in the church. Naturally, this means that the woman speaker in Corinth was viewed as one who caused the confusion he condemned and *challenged* the peace he was decreeing for their church.

However, the Greek word translated "women" here is *gune*, which means "women" as well as "wives," depending on the context, and the close proximity of *gune* in this passage to "husbands" (*andras*) suggests that it was not all women who were instructed to be silent, but *wives*. Tuck this in the back of your thoughts for now…

The word "law" from Paul's words, "as also saith the law," is the Greek *nomos*. It is the same word used in reference to the Mosaic Law, and even *Strong's* acknowledges that. However, to the New Testament culture, apart from the Mosaic Law, it meant "1. anything established, anything received by usage, a custom, a law, a command A. of any law whatsoever."[46] There are only three possibilities for what "law" Paul might have been referring to here: 1) the Mosaic Law; 2) the law of the land; and 3) generically a law amidst the people, such as "anything established" or "a custom." The first of these can be ruled out immediately, because nowhere in the Mosaic Law does it give this regulation. The second can likewise be ruled out immediately because, in Corinth, women were allowed to make all kinds of noises wherever they wanted to. (Not to be crude, but their voices were heard in the temples of the pagan gods in extremely loud and sexual ways, and that was the norm for this society, so the conversation within a newly forming Christian "temple" would have been nothing in comparison. Historical evidence discussed earlier herein also rule out that there had been a "law of the land" for women's silence within this vicinity.) This leaves only the third potential interpretation, and in an age when Judaizers were treating oral tradition (read: "anything established," "custom," "any law whatsoever" [that the legalistic and Pharisaic circles believed]) as "law," such a conclusion is quite plausible. Therefore, this "law" was not one given by God but by mankind, and it was to this authority Paul was appealing (not one that we are held to today). (Note that some Bibles reference 1 Timothy 2:11 in the margins, suggesting that Paul's words in that verse, "Let the woman learn in silence with all subjection," is the "law" that Paul's referring to. But since 1 Timothy was written *after* 1 Corinthians, as historical evidence shows, this reference of "law" could not have anything to do with 1 Timothy.)

The word "confusion" in 14:33 from the string "author of confusion" is the KJV translator's choice English equivalent to the ancient Greek *akatastasia*: "instability, i.e. disorder:—commotion, confusion, tumult."[47] If Paul had never used this word elsewhere, then without another internal comparison, we may think "confusion" might be the best word to pick from amidst "instability," "disorder," "commotion," "confusion," and "tumult." However, he *did* use this same word in 2 Corinthians 12:20, and in that case, the translators chose "tumults": "For I fear, lest, when I come, I shall not find you such as I would, and that I shall be found unto you such as ye would not: lest there be debates, envyings, wraths, strifes, backbitings, whisperings, swellings, *tumults* [*akatastasia*]" (emphasis added). Consider the extreme aggression implied in this list. Now consider the *Merriam-Webster* definition of "tumult": "disorderly agitation or milling about of a crowd usually with uproar and confusion of voices; a turbulent uprising...

violent agitation of mind or feelings; a violent outburst."[48] I cannot say why the translator chose "confusion" in one spot and "tumult" in another when the word *akatastasia* was the same in both places by the hand of Paul, but I can tell you that the nature Paul *intended* for the word based on the other instance of its use was aggressive at least, if not "turbulent" or "violent." This is the same conclusion the award-winning Dr. John Temple Bristow came to in his book, *What Paul Really Said about Women: The Apostle's Liberating Views on Equality in Marriage, Leadership, and Love*: "When Paul faced an unruly mob, he described their noisy confusion and disorder as *akatastasia*, which we translate 'tumult.' It is the same word that Jesus used to describe one of the signs of the coming destruction, in the phrase 'wars and tumults' (Luke 21:9). Now, Paul wrote to the church in Corinth that he did not want *akatastasia* in their public worship."[49] If the church was in such a state of affairs that it took a letter the length of this epistle to the Corinthians to address it, and if so much of the letter concerns service disruption, then Paul wasn't talking about a woman preaching or teaching when she speaks aloud; he was talking about a woman aggressor or agitator—and in the case of Corinth, as Paul's chosen wording implies, it was the *wives* who were aggressive. In such close proximity to the teachings he gave on speaking in tongues, the issue is clear: Wives, stop humiliating your husbands with outbursts, chatter, questions, and speaking in tongues in the middle of service…

I am amazed—so utterly, fully, and wholly *amazed*—that certain members of today's Church still interpret 1 Corinthians 14:34–35 to mean total silence (with tiny exceptions regarding "prophesying," which, ironically, is a form of teaching as well), to the full and literal extent of its meaning, under extreme application, to every audience and reader, throughout all time, in every culture, in every society, in every circumstance, throughout the universe, and into perpetuity. The question is not *whether* Paul was condemning a woman from speaking in a church; the question is *when* such an occasion could be carried out appropriately in order to avoid the chaos he condemns through this entire letter! And, as if we're not already saturated with clarity on this point, Paul sandwiches this note about women speaking between "God is not the author of confusion" and "Let all things be done decently and in order" (14:40).

We know that Paul allowed for women to speak in the church, because he said as much when he: a) acknowledged the gifts of the Spirit—the word of wisdom, the word of knowledge, faith, healing, the working of miracles, prophecy, the discerning of spirits, tongues, and the interpretation of tongues—to be poured out upon men and women alike, just as it was on the Day of Pentecost involving "the women" in the upper room; b) acknowledged these gifts to be carried out *in church* under proper, non-chaotic circumstances; and c) discussed the proper head covering for a woman praying or prophesying in church (11:5). When he did place limitations on who was allowed to say what, and when, he repeatedly included the men in those limitations (as is peppered throughout chapter 14). Everything clearly points to the notion that Paul didn't want wives speaking aloud at inappropriate times.

The thing is, if Paul had written a letter only about women and without the contextual backdrop of the city of Corinth as we know it— with revered *hetairai* skilled in oratory and allowed at all times to dominate in conversation, and influencing other women (married and single) to do the same—we would have no choice but to concede and drop that beloved pop-culture hoorah, "The Bible says it, I believe it, and that settles it." Had he written a letter that only dealt with the subject of women as an isolated issue, we may find ourselves in the same position. However, we *do* have the cultural backdrop of Corinth, we *do* have internal consistency that supports women as leaders in ministry—both from the same author as well as other books of the Bible—and we *do* have a "whole picture" letter from Paul that addresses the subject of disruption and division among male and female as a context.

But perhaps the greatest proof of Paul's intent is in the following fact: Paul had thirty Greek words to choose from in his native language that would refer to the act of speaking. Yes, you read that correctly. He had *thirty* different verbs that all describe differing forms of "speak." Yet the one he chose was telling… Consider how, in the English language, we have "talk," "chat," "state," "say," "express," "address," "chatter," "chitchat," "tell," "converse," "lecture," "preach," "orate," "verbalize," "declare," "babble," "prattle," "rant," "announce," "assert," "proclaim," and so on. *All* of these words (and many others) describe the act of opening the mouth and uttering speech. Imagine that you go to into a church and see a sign hung above the door of the sanctuary. The person who wrote the sign could have chosen a number of ways to phrase what he or she wanted to say, but let's look at these:

- "Please do not proclaim during service."
- "Please do not chitchat during service."
- "Please do not rant during service."

Whereas all of these refer to the act of making sounds come out of the mouth during service, each implies a different act of speech. The first regulation inspires imagery of a person suddenly bursting forth loudly with declaration; the second inspires imagery of people talking casually about the weather in the middle of a sermon; the third inspires imagery of a person being openly disagreeable in a big, tasteless tirade. Whereas "proclaim," "chitchat," and "rant" are not all described by the verb "speak," all three words fall under "speak" as a parent verb that encompasses all varying forms of the action.

When our Western minds see Paul instructing women not to "speak" in church using the parent verb, it falls on our psyche like a binding, solemn commandment of silence—all silence forever over all forms of speech so long as the body is in that building.

In the group, "for it is not permitted unto them to speak," the word for "speak" here is the Greek *laleo*, which simply means "to talk." Paul could have said the women are not permitted to preach, teach, sing, praise, worship, prophesy, address, discourse, expound, advise, lecture, advocate, persuade, and so on and so forth, because—remember—he had *thirty* words to choose from in his native tongue that would have been more specific to the type of activity he was censuring. Instead, however, he chose "talk," which cannot be seen as a binding commandment in all circumstances, because he already said women can pray and prophesy (11:5).

Additionally, from within the lexicology (the study of word usage) and grammar subsections of the textbook, *The Biblical Role of Women*, by New Testament Greek homiletics expert Dr. Deborah M. Gill and theological seminary professor Dr. Barbara L. Cavaness Parks: "The tense of the verb *laleo* is not the most common tense (the aorist) but the less common Greek tense (the present) that emphasizes linear (ongoing) action. Thus, it is better translated 'to *keep* talking.' Paul is saying in verse 34, '[Women] are not allowed to keep on talking,' and in verse 35, 'It is disgraceful for a woman to continually chatter in church.' The kind of verbal action indicates that it is not women's vocal participation but the perpetual disruptive rumble of noise that is disallowed."[50]

Now imagine you're visiting the ancient church at Corinth—or any church, for that matter—and you see a sign above the entryway that says, "Please don't talk in church." Without having to deeply analyze what we're being asked to do and in what language, we all know that "don't talk in church" means "don't be disruptive." By saying women are not permitted to *laleo*, Paul was saying that women are not permitted to keep talking while the service is in session. As to why Paul would have laid this foundation of behavior for only women and not men, it requires understanding the cultural shift taking place at this time.

Christianity was a newborn to Corinth; before Christianity, there was Judaism. In the Jewish custom, women were generally not allowed to express opinions, they weren't usually educated (their rightful place in society was to have kids and obey their husbands), and they certainly weren't allowed to preach, teach, prophesy, or make any kind of noise in the church. In many ancient cultures leading up to the birth of Christianity, Jewish women actually sat in a separate location from the men in the place of worship (though, as stated earlier, Bernadette Brooten's archeological study on the nineteen existent synagogues of the New Testament era likely proves that this was not occurring in Corinth at this time). However, suddenly, a new age was dawning for this new belief system called "Christianity." Thanks to gender-equality spokespersons like Paul, women were finding their voices...and fast. The Holy Spirit had fallen upon women on the Day of Pentecost, and those women ran and preached excitedly. They were allowed to now! And because of this allowance, they were encouraged to educate themselves and form opinions so that they could be successful witnesses of the Risen Christ!

Gone were the days when they couldn't "go and tell," for now they were going and telling...which came along with the expectation that they would *understand* the theology they were meant to communicate to others. So, now that they held a responsibility to understand, they became bolder in their questions. Outside of Corinth, we can safely assume that women were making inquiries, though they—because of the patriarchal culture that dominated for so long—likely remained polite and quiet during the teaching and approached the minister afterward.

Specifically to Corinth, however, thanks to the *hetairai* and *pornai* prostitutes who had already formed an entire cultural acceptance of women who shared "enlightened" opinions and beliefs regarding spirituality and theology, the Christian women in Corinth would have been especially chatty in their newfound freedom. The *hetairai* and *pornai* had "controlled the city" so to speak, and paved the way for women to enter any building under any circumstances and assert themselves with questions, tongues, and other less-than-ideal utterances. Whether the Christians in this church were prostitutes, Jewish converts, Gentile converts, travelers, or simply curious women wandering in from the street (and there is historical evidence to suggest a mixture of these, since

Corinth was such a beehive of commercial trading), they would have walked into a building with confident, well-educated, vocal woman seeking theological answers.

The women in Corinth were talking during service, and in a church where the leaders, themselves, were in constant dispute, they were adding their voices atop the chaos that 1 Corinthians 14 glaringly criticizes. This is why Paul told them not to "keep talking."

In wrapping this up, chapter 15 reminds Paul's readers of the truth of the Resurrection of Christ, followed by the doctrine of the resurrection of the saints to Heaven; chapter 16 is Paul's pledge to return for a visit, words of Paul's beloved fellow-workers, and the warm closing: "My love be with you all in Christ Jesus. Amen" (16:24).

Flaws of Leading Interpretations

Before we tackle the 1 Timothy issue, there remains to be several other popular interpretations of Paul's intent within 1 Corinthians 14, the nature of which are innately flawed. I will address them quickly.

Women Can Teach, but Only in Certain Roles

Some assert that Paul allowed women to prophesy or pray *only* (viewing "prophesy" as a kind of foretelling role, not as the Greek word also defined it as a teacher), and others say that women can teach other women or children, but never men. First, as repeatedly shown herein, Paul never placed gender restrictions upon Holy Spirit gifts, which without a doubt includes public expounding (teaching, preaching, etc.). Second, as mentioned in the previous chapter, internal biblical evidence exists to show women as leaders of the very first fledgling churches that gathered in homes. That list again is: John Mark's mother Mary in Jerusalem (Acts 12:12); Lydia in Philippi (Acts 16:14–15);

Priscilla (alongside her husband Aquila) in Ephesus and Rome (Acts: 18:19, 26; 1 Corinthians 16:19; Romans 16:3–5); Phoebe in Cenchrea (Romans 16:1); and Apphia in Colossae (Philemon 2). Third, Jesus Christ personally inspired women to go and preach the Gospel (see chapters 5 and 6). The limitations and hierarchal segregation that we observe in our culture today—often tied up in arguments of who can have what kind of paper certificate or title—is of mankind's making, not God's.

Paul Was Silencing All Women because of Pagan Outbursts

Greco-Roman state religions sometimes restricted women in leadership roles, but mystery cults did not. Therefore, at the time of the fledgling Christian Church, some women would have just been coming out of mystery cult religions where moaning, wailing, and hysterical shouting (as well as other behaviors unrelated to noise) were the norm. Once converted to Christianity, these same women would have taken their pagan outbursts into the house of the Lord. This interpretation acknowledges that Paul was silencing all women because of the pagan women who didn't know their place in the Church of Jesus Christ. Those who hold to this interpretation at times believe that because women are emotional, the tendency for outbursts will always exist, and therefore Paul's limitation of "all women" because of the "few" is timelessly applicable.

We know that this issue was occurring, and every piece of historical evidence points to the fact that Corinth would have been rife with this kind of activity. However, the application of it for this specific reason is too slim. Had Paul written his regulation as a result of the pagans, this would have: a) suddenly silenced the women Paul had praised, who were teaching from their own homes, and b) unfairly silenced the women present who were not engaging in pagan outbursts (such as some Jewish converts or mild-mannered Gentiles).

Call-and-Response Theory

In the original Greek, there was no punctuation. This Corinthian epistle was written as a response to problems that were reported to him directly (1:11). As such, Paul at times quoted his audience's words back to them to remind them of their initial complaint, and then he followed it with his own response/correction. Today, and in English, quotation marks would be placed around the congregation's original words, followed by Paul's words outside the quotation marks. An example of this would be 7:1–2, within which I have already placed the marks where they would normally be:

> Now concerning the things whereof ye wrote unto me: "It is good for a man not to touch a woman." Nevertheless, to avoid fornication, let every man have his own wife, and let every woman have her own husband.

A popular interpretation theory is that Paul was applying this call-and-response method in 1 Corinthians 14:34–40. If this theory is true, the correct punctuation would be as follows:

> [Paul quotes them first:] As [you say] in all churches of the saints, "Let your women keep silence in the churches: for it is not permitted unto them to speak; but they are commanded to be under obedience as also saith the law. And if they will learn any thing, let them ask their husbands at home: for it is a shame for women to speak in the church."
>
> [Then Paul responds:] What? came the word of God out from you? or came it unto you only? If any man think himself to be a prophet, or spiritual, let him acknowledge that the things that I write unto you are the commandments of the Lord. But if any man be ignorant, let him be ignorant. Wherefore, brethren,

covet to prophesy, and forbid not to speak with tongues. Let all things be done decently and in order.

If this interpretation model is true, then this entire book you hold in your hands is far less relevant, because it shows that Paul wasn't silencing the women at all under any circumstances; he was reproaching the leaders of Corinth for trying to gain Paul's stamp of approval in the silencing of women. In this case, we not only have internal consistency evidence that Paul praised women leaders in the early Church, we also have internal consistency evidence that Paul rebuked any man who would attempt to silence a woman.

Granted, this theory cannot be proven false, since we don't have original-manuscript quotation marks or punctuation. However, it also can't be proven true. Probably the strongest argument for why it's *false* is not because the quotation marks are missing, but because the grammatical consistency is lacking. Unlike our 7:1–2 example when Paul wrote, "Now concerning the things whereof ye wrote unto me"—which is grammatical evidence that he is about to quote them—in 14:34–40, Paul doesn't indicate that he is about to quote one of their delivered complaints. Additionally, our generation would have to add the words "you say" (or equivalent) in the string: "As [you say] in all churches of the saints." The only evidence we have that he is *responding* is the sudden, "What?" in verse 36. Lastly, the historical record of Corinth strongly points to the notion that women were interrupting the service, and a man in Paul's position wouldn't have advocated for such a disruption, especially in a letter largely dedicated to the rebuke of disruption.

If this interpretation were to be proven accurate, then 1 Corinthians 14:34–35 would *not* serve to silence women; it *would* silence the resistance of women leaders in the Church. Alas, we cannot be sure on this one, but it doesn't seem likely in light of all else we've discussed herein.

Subsequent Scribal Additions

The authors of many recent scholarly works have begun to question whether or not Paul's words in 1 Corinthians 14:34–35 were even the apostle's to begin with, and have raised the possibility that these verses were a textual interpolation. Because Pauline literature does not base its authority upon "law" (Mosaic or otherwise), and Paul was against legalism, then these words must have been inserted later by a Judaizer. They simply "don't sound like Paul," these theorists say.

The evidence that supports this theory is not limited to the following list, but these are central: 1) Verses 34–35 complete a grammatical unit in and of themselves, and they are a little sudden, so they seem to "stick out" within what would have otherwise been a perfectly complete thought; 2) the surrounding verses flow more smoothly without them; and 3) ancient manuscript copies mysteriously place these verses, as a complete grammatical unit, in a different location (some place it after verse 33, some after verse 40, some after both verses 30 and 40, and still others insert it as a note in the margins)—and since the very first letter from Paul to Corinth is nonexistent (early manuscripts relied on copying since the papyrus crumbled over time), we can't refer to Paul's original letter for examination.

Late manuscripts settled the matter by placing these words where they are today.

Yet, this theory presents two major issues: 1) For purposes already stated, Paul had many reasons to address women disrupting the church services in Corinth, so if we believe they weren't Paul's, we have to ask why he wouldn't have addressed the problem at all; 2) doing away with these verses completely avoids facing the context of Scripture as we have it now, which leads to questioning the authority of Scripture elsewhere: if we say, "*These* words weren't Paul's," then what stops us from saying, "These aren't either, and neither are those, and neither are those…" This would be a very dangerous game, indeed.

Conclusion

Our best bet for interpretation is to see what is on the page, look into the backdrop, understand all contributing factors and circumstances, and *then* apply the regulations to similar or exact circumstances today.

After digesting all of this in detail, I believe we can make the informed conclusion: Paul never said in 1 Corinthians 14 that women are not permitted to be preachers or teachers of the Word. Paul was silencing the disruption, and if we are to apply his regulation to similar circumstances today, we should *all*—men and women—imagine that there are "Please don't talk in church" signs above the doorways of our sanctuaries.

Respect for all speakers, regardless of gender, so that "all things [can] be done decently and in order" (14:40).

Now onto Ephesus and 1 Timothy.

4

Context of 1 Timothy

As a reminder: In 1 Timothy 2:11–15, Paul wrote: "Let the woman learn in silence with all subjection. But I suffer not a woman to teach, nor to usurp authority over the man, but to be in silence. For Adam was first formed, then Eve. And Adam was not deceived, but the woman being deceived was in the transgression. Notwithstanding she shall be saved in childbearing, if they continue in faith and charity and holiness with sobriety."

In the previous chapter, we established that Paul's words in 1 Corinthians 14 were not meant to be an "absolute" or "normative" regulation against women being leaders of the Church. However, the apostle's words above appear to be quite clear. But if Paul elsewhere attributed the Fall to *Adam*, and *not to Eve* (Romans 5:14; 1 Corinthians 15:21–22)—and if he was so quick to say that women were created because men *needed* women, and that men are even born from women (1 Corinthians 11:8–9; 11–12)—then how do we explain this sudden switch? If Paul so consistently referred to salvation as a result of faith, alone (1 Corinthians 1:21; Ephesians 2:8; Romans 10:9), then why does he here refer to a woman's salvation through childbearing? Why does he say, "I suffer not a woman to teach [*didaskein*]" to Ephesus, if he directed the whole Body of believers in Colossians (3:16), men *and* women, to follow his example and share responsibility in "teaching (still *didaskein*) and admonishing one another" about the message of Christ? And why is it that we know women can be prophets (1 Corinthians 11:5; Joel 2:28; Acts 2:17–18), and we know that prophets are listed even before teachers (1 Corinthians 12:28: "And God hath set some in the church, first apostles, secondarily prophets, thirdly teachers"), but here women must be silent and subjected under the male?

What were the circumstances behind this 1 Timothy 2:11–12 restriction?

Backdrop of Paul's First Pastoral Letter to Timothy

Because the literary genre and author are the same for this reflection as they were in the last, we will not go over them again. Likewise, since the surrounding text and the linguistic style are paramount to our study, we will attend to those matters as we go. That leaves the audience and the circumstances.

Audience

On an immediate level, the audience of this letter is only one man: Timothy, a young and passionate pastor whom Paul referred to as "my own son in the faith" (1:2). Timothy was the pastor of the church in Ephesus that Paul had launched during his second missionary journey; Timothy had traveled with Paul on this journey (Acts 16:1) and was in Paul's presence near the end of his first Roman imprisonment (Philippians 2:19–24). Timothy's initial exposure to faith in God came from his mother and grandmother—Eunice and Lois (two women)—according to 2 Timothy 1:5.

By extension of where this advice would be taken and how it would be implemented, however, the audience could be seen as the church members in Ephesus.

The great ancient city of Ephesus, by the time of Paul's influence, was one of the wealthiest cities in the Mediterranean world. Documents reflect that after the sun went down, the streets were brightly and luxuriously lit with rich oil lamps, an extravagance most cities of this time could have never afforded. Ephesus' greatest pull (based on historic documents as well as art) was likely its education, but it also doubled as one of the most important trade ports and dealt heavily in the industry of idol-making. Heraclitus, the infamously well-known pre-Socratic Greek philosopher known for his treatise *On Nature*, was an enormous inspiration behind the increasing establishment of education in Ephesus. This single papyrus scroll—addressing politics, ethics, theology, and the universe—was dedicated by Heraclitus to Ephesus' prized Artemisium, one of the Seven Wonders of the Ancient World.

The Artemisium in Ephesus (destroyed in 356 BC; rebuilt by the New Testament era) was the temple of Artemis/Diana (daughter of Zeus/Jupiter, twin sister of Apollo), who was the goddess of fertility, considered the Great Mother of Asia.[51] Through her, the Anatolians (from Anatolia, the area surrounding Ephesus) believed, all life began[52] (as opposed to the Christian belief that all life began through the Creator, God the Father). Early Gnostic teachings associated with Artemis/Diana and documented near this time state that Adam was created through Eve's rib—not the other way around—and that salvation came through *gnosis* (enlightenment) of these pagan entities.[53] Artemis/Diana was also the goddess of the hunt (through archery), wilderness, forests, hills, animals, childbearing, virginity, and the moon. It was believed that she could both bring and relieve disease in women; she could control animals with her blessing; she was able to create all life without the need for a male's involvement (a kind of "virginal birth" idea); and she served to protect little girls.

Alongside Minerva and Vesta, Artemis/Diana was considered one of the three "main" goddesses of mythology. However, although she was worshiped throughout the Greek world, the existence of her temple in Ephesus created a proximate superiority claim amongst its residents. Anyone was allowed to worship her, but the Ephesians believed they understood her and her transcendent aims better than any people anywhere else on the planet at that time. She was *their* goddess, and they were extremely protective of her. Idols of her were in many households throughout the city and region, and as far as the Ephesians were concerned, there were no other gods above her. The hundreds of temple prostitutes/priestesses (sometimes called "bees" in literature) that served her in Ephesus were, like in Corinth, considered to be a force of authority, primarily in religious settings. The annual Artemisia Festival held in her honor drew multitudes from surrounding territories to Ephesus, as it was a foundation stone of Greek cultural identity. Anyone living in or around Ephesus at this time would have been exposed to an idolatrous culture, at the forefront of which was a goddess (a *woman*) and the hundreds of temple prostitutes/priestesses who worshiped her.

Alongside the Artemisium was the Celsus Library and the revered School of Philosophy. Ephesus was a concentrated assembly-point city for learning throughout the ancient world, plagued by intellectual arrogance and pretentiousness, and women were equal to men in social rights and privileges from many angles (including religious settings). Records show that women were revered as professors, sculptors, painters, musicians, and philosophers, among many other illustrious offices. (After Christianity took hold of Ephesus, Emperor Theodosius had the schools closed, and women were reduced to second-class citizenship, but at the time of Paul, women were equals in almost every way except voting rights.) Prior to the shaming of the seven sons of Sceva, residents of Ephesus (including the Jews, according to archeological evidence) were deeply entrenched in magical practices and mystery cults (. 30). Within these mystery cults and magic rites, just like in Corinth, were strange sexual practices. Although the population wasn't as swayed by prostitution as was Corinth, Ephesus was afflicted with unrestrained sexual worship, and the influence of that certainly bled into daily cultural and societal norms.

The presence of the occult in Ephesian civilization was *overwhelming*, and the infiltration of these influences in the church was prodigious.

Timothy, the one-man addressee of Paul's pastoral epistle, had a lot on his plate with this audience.

Circumstances Requiring the Epistle

When the Gospel was first being spread in Ephesus, Demetrius—a wealthy silversmith who made silver idols of Artemis/Diana—instigated a near riot when he perceived his idol-making trade was vulnerable under the increase of Christianity. Acts 19:23–29, 20:1 documents a tumultuous few hours when the entire city was thrown into chaos and many voices in one accord decreed, "Great is Diana of the Ephesians!" A gracious town clerk brought the matter to an end, but not without a lasting impression that this "Christianity" was a powerful force to be reckoned with. The incident concerned Paul, who thereafter headed to Macedonia. But those who remained in Ephesus had already heard that a new religion was forming, and it was one that centered around a Savior who required nothing more from His followers than faith and love.

This new "Christ religion" *also* centered on a Savior who was brought to the world without the involvement of a human male...which was a concept that would have been familiar to the women in a city that worshipped a goddess who created life without a male's participation. We can already see a connection forming here. These pagan women, as well as recent converts to Christianity, would have already viewed themselves as the "experts" of such theology. Keep that in mind.

What followed for the next few years was a turbulent and agitated relationship between theologians/ministers of pagan, Jewish, and Christian conviction. The area was rampant with not only well-learned men and women of the pagan religions, but with professional graduates of philosophy who fervently applied their esteemed intellect to exceptionally persuasive doctrines that had been culturally adapted into every crevice of Greco-Roman identity for *eons* before Paul ever visited Ephesus. Whereas today, most people follow the ideologies, doctrines, and tenets of a specific religion that suits them, in Paul's day, it wasn't at all abnormal for a person to cherry pick what he or she liked to hear from several religions and mesh them together, simply as a result of so many years of pagan eclecticism in the ancient world.

Priests and religious leaders at that time could be gurus of several different cults at once. By the time religious personalities were rising to the call for Christ's Gospel, many of them would have viewed such syncretistic practice as routine. For instance, there might have been a priest whose central doctrine was of the Messiah, Christ, while his creation doctrine was that of Artemis/Diana as the Great Mother, preaching that all must bow to the authority of the Roman imperial cult, demanding all males to be circumcised (Judaism), and cautioning all his followers' behaviors to reflect those within oriental religion. (Any devout and learned Christian or Jew would know better, but these kinds of leaders still existed aplenty.) That's five religions in one, and although we might consider that to be a sellout today, at the time it was a blending of strong suits. Such a motley collection of beliefs understandably presents believers with several holy deities to follow, and the roads to salvation were not through Christ alone, as Paul strictly taught, but through several various gods.

Again, without the New Testament as a reliable training tool for the early Church (because it had not yet been written), Christianity was subjected to false teaching to the maximum extent. Women were equal to men behind nearly any secular platform in Ephesus, so female converts to Christianity were becoming deceived by all the diverse religions and presenting a syncretized version of the Gospel with a pagan slant to their listeners (2 Timothy 3:6). (Men were as well, and Paul mentioned several of them by name: Hymenaeus, Alexander, and Philetus [1 Timothy 1:20; 2 Timothy 2:17; 4:14–15]. This same behavior was happening around the same time in the city of Crete when Paul wrote to Titus [1:10–11, 14–15; 2:11–15; 3:9–11].) From every angle and all at once, Paul was beginning to feel bombarded by false teachers, and the problem was *still* occurring in Ephesus by the time Paul wrote his second epistle to Timothy (2 Timothy 2:14, 18, 23; 3:1–9, 13; 4:3–4).

In the meantime, there was an interesting development specific to the Artemis/Diana priestesses in Ephesus. In the last chapter, we discussed how a woman's body was seen as the pathway to blessings from the gods. In Ephesus (and in Sardis), the thinking was similar, but with a more spiritual application. The priestesses of Artemis/Diana saw themselves as the divine mediators between gods and men, and they were revered as such by the males in and around the city. (There are many records of this same "woman as mediator" type of religious practices around the time of, and predating, the priestesses of the New Testament age in Ephesus. Consider the oracles at Delphi, Didyma, and Dodona. Only these women could intermediate between Zeus or Apollo and men.) Documented accounts of these divination/oracle-type incidents describe the women going into a trance-like state, whereupon they would moan or convulse and even go into hysterics. Because of so much emphasis on virginity, fertility, and orgiastic worship throughout this part of the world during this time, even when sex wasn't directly involved, the episodes were often known to be of an erotically charged nature, as documents show: "Female priests (such as the Pythia at the oracle of Delphi) played a more trance-like, inspired role. The unintelligible prophecies of these women had to be interpreted and delivered by men. The worship of the mystery cults was enthusiastic, and all those present—including women—took part. Hysterical shouting and wailing of women was a valued part of the meetings. Ancient texts record even the sounds and syllables they uttered."[54]

By the Gnostic enlightenment age, which was in early stages of development at the time this epistle was written, women were frequently prized mediators who were observed to be the principle mouthpieces of the gods. When Christianity was introduced to Ephesus, these same women embraced the Messiah's story as truth, but they also made a smooth transition into positions of spiritual authority, as the mediators of the Savior, Jesus Christ, as only one god to fellow believers, while they maintained belief in the final authority of Artemis/Diana.[55]

Imagine you are a new male convert to Christianity in the city of Ephesus in the first century. You have heard of this man, Paul, who knows all there is to know about Jesus Christ, as he not only had a personal experience with Him on the road to Damascus, but he was also in the company of Christ's very disciples and learned His doctrines first-hand from those who walked with the Messiah daily. Paul is not present to speak to in person, and there is no idol of Jesus Christ nearby, but you wish to further sharpen your understanding of the Messiah. You've heard that there is a church within city limits that Paul, himself, established with the help of a woman, Priscilla. You assume, as would anyone else within your culture, that Priscilla was the mediator between Jesus and men. Men could not gain truth from the Son of the Living God without going through some kind of female oracle, you believe, so you head over to the meeting place to seek assistance from the priestess. When you arrive, you are told that Priscilla is not available, but there are many women among the congregation who also serve as priestesses of this new and "true" religion. One of them offers to help, and she takes you to her home that afternoon, lights candles, and tells you about Christ. You're as happy as ever to hear of this "way" to salvation through the blood of the Messiah, and you're even more thrilled when you learn that it's free to all who believe. You're a little confused when she tells you that all life began through the Great Mother of Asia, Diana, without her ever having to

124

engage in sexual relations with a male god...but if Jesus Christ was born of a virgin, then maybe the goddess of virginity and fertility could have been the true creator of Adam as well. And if Diana was the creator of all life, and this priestess is a mediator of the goddess and Jesus Christ, then she is undoubtedly the right person to teach you the truth of this new, popular religion sanctified by Paul. The priestess begins to chant, moan, sway, and "communicate with the spirit of Christ" on your behalf. It's not surprising to you, because you've been taught to believe that this is normal behavior for a mediator—and after all, this woman is a graduate of the School of Philosophy in Ephesus, so she can't be just another crackpot minister, because the reputation of the school stands behind training only the greatest minds. She elucidates Christ's message to you with impressive articulation and intellect. After a few minutes, she escalates her vocalizations to the ultimate, spiritual, euphoric ecstasy (use your imagination), and then finally releases a hefty sigh and returns to a peaceful countenance. You believe that you've been given the greatest gift of all: salvation through Christ and Diana. As you turn to leave this strange and erotic affair, the priestess gives you one last thought: "Thank the gods Paul came to Ephesus when he did, or else you may never have been reached with this gospel. Doesn't it feel so good to be cleansed?"

Do you have this picture of insane pagan-Christianity syncretism in your mind? Then you may now have a better understanding of what historical and cultural circumstances were in play when Paul wrote the epistle that theologian Dr. Gilbert Bilezikian said held an "exceptional character" of "emergency measures."[56]

Paul was reacting to an emergency.

Message of 1 Timothy

Paul begins again by identifying himself (1:1) and then his recipient, "Timothy, my true child in the faith" (1:2). The apostle wastes no time in diving straight into the central crisis—false teaching—in verses 3 through 11. He spends a brief moment telling his personal testimony in verses 12 through 17 in order to pack a more powerful punch behind his charge to Timothy, who, like Paul, will have to remain vigilant in these trying times of unbridled false teachers: "This charge I commit unto thee, son Timothy, according to the prophecies which went before on thee, that thou by them mightest war a good warfare; Holding faith, and a good conscience; which some having put away concerning faith have made shipwreck: Of whom is Hymenaeus and Alexander [false teachers]; whom I have delivered unto Satan, that they may learn not to blaspheme" (1:18–20).

Chapter 2, verses 1 through 8, include Paul's instructions for how to pray and what to pray for, so that Christ will be ever at the center of the church's focus. The transition between verse 8 and 9 is telling: "I will therefore that men pray every where, lifting up holy hands, without wrath and doubting. In like manner also, that women adorn themselves in modest apparel..." Notice that he does *not* say, "I will therefore that men pray... Now onto the issue of women's apparel." He specifically writes "I will therefore that men pray... In *like* manner also, that women..." First, he describes the humble way he wants *men* to pray in the church, and then he writes *hosautos*: "in the same way:—even so, likewise, *after the same (in like) manner* [as the men he just instructed],"[57] referring to how he wants the women to pray *in the church*; he wants them to do *kai* ("also"; "and"; "likewise,"[58]) with modest apparel. Both genders are receiving instructions on how to pray (which involves speaking) in the corporate setting of service. So, later remarks about silence cannot be seen as Paul describing a "silent woman" in the church.

Focusing more completely on verses 9 and 10, we hit a strange snag: "In like manner also, that women adorn themselves in modest apparel, with shamefacedness [Greek *aidos*: "modesty"[59]] and sobriety; not with braided hair, or gold, or pearls, or costly array; But (which becometh women professing godliness) with good works."

126

As pointed out earlier, almost every minister of the Gospel today dismisses these verses as a "cultural issue." The exception might be in conservative churches that follow the Word to the literal extreme, but by and large, there is a common shoulder shrug that modern readers apply to the prohibition of braided hair, gold, pearls, and expensive clothing. Barring extremists, *nobody* in the Body of Christ today has an issue with a woman coming to church with her hair in braids or pearls around her neck. If a Western minister today were to stand up and proclaim a necessary return to these prohibitions with literal application, his message would be met with the exasperated sigh of a million theologians. Why? Because we all know Paul's concerns were not with braids, pearls, gold, or expensive clothes. His concern was with a woman attending church in modesty and humility, and in making sure that her appearance in a place of worship would be for the right reasons (to worship, not to attract the attention of surrounding men).

In ancient cultures, women didn't wear miniskirts or low-cut blouses. They didn't wear six-inch heels, fishnet stockings, or skin-tight, celebrity-designer clothes. If a woman wanted to dress in a manner that alerted all the men around her that she was ready to have a good time, she wore eye-catching accessories and expensive and colorful robes— and she would braid her uncovered hair intricately, weaving flashy pieces of precious metals or gems into it. In fact, the literal, word-for-word translation from Paul's Greek was not "braided hair, *or* gold" (*plegmasin e chrysio*), it was "braided hair *and* gold" (*plegmasin kai chrysio*).[60] (Note that in order to see this translation, the interlinear must be done from Greek to English first. The interlinear cannot be like some of those tool-Bibles online that start with the KJV and simply show the Greek equivalent above or below. That is essentially translating from our known English *back to* ancient Greek, and in this case, because the KJV has "or," the Greek will show *e* as the equivalent. A true Greek-to-English interlinear comparison will show that *kai* ["also"; "and"] was the word Paul wrote originally.) Paul was aware that women were weaving gold *into* their braids, which was a common practice for prostitutes who wanted to wear an ongoing advertisement in public that they were "available for hire." These women knew that the culture around them considered their hair to be an extension of the body's most intimate fluids, so they drew even more attention to it with gold, fine metals, and gemstones.

The *hetairai* spoken of in the last chapter were women of the professional courtesan or prostitution vocation. Well before their bodies were ever offered to their first clients, older or retired prostitutes had trained them in the fine art of cosmetics and fashion so their beauty and ornamentation would secure the interest of potential patrons. Throughout the ancient world at this time, as in Corinth, there was a certain kind of attire that "loose" women (especially prostitutes) would wear in order to gain the attention of men and let them know what kind of work they were in. (In Ephesus, it may have been the aforementioned "bees" [priestesses/prostitutes] of Artemis/Diana setting this trend.) As time went by and the *hetairai* had influenced the other matrons and single women who belonged to the soul of upper-crust society (i.e., educated women with well-paying jobs who hobnobbed with the elites and could afford gold, pearls, and fancy clothes), women began to imitate this form of adornment simply because it looked feminine and pretty. So not *all* of the women who wore braids, gold, pearls, and costly array were prostitutes, but since the fashion trend principally began in those circles, even an innocent maid would be seen as indecently dressed if she went out in public wearing her hair and clothing in a similar, flashy way. They "looked the part," so to speak.

According to the celebrated book by Richard and Catherine Kroeger, *I Suffer Not a Woman: Rethinking 1 Timothy 2:11–15 in Light of Ancient Evidence*—whose work has been cited numerous times (including within university textbooks, although their treatment of the Greek *authenteo* [addressed shortly] has drawn much scrutiny)—Paul may have even been responding to a report that women were either lifting their skirts to their waistlines as a symbol of fertility or taking their clothes off during service. Erotic art from the surrounding regions shows women participating in mystery-cult celebrations (the book mentions Dionysus) while nude.[61] This sounds extreme, and we cannot guarantee that this specific lewd behavior was taking place in the church at Ephesus, but we *can* be sure it was happening in the area—and, as stated before, Paul appears from every angle to be responding to an emergency.

Food for thought...

Whereas many modern ministers may not be aware of the *plegmasin e chrysio* versus *plegmasin kai chrysio* comparison—or of who began the trend (prostitutes/*hetairai*)—they are aware that the verse in 1 Timothy demands modesty and humility. They preach that women today *can* wear braids, gold, pearls, or expensive clothing, as long as they don't dress in a provocative way that "advertises" that their presence in church is for the wrong reasons. Why? Because it's a "cultural issue."

By this, they are successfully completing the steps we outlined before:

1. The original circumstances must be determined. (Women were attending church in attire that *their* culture perceived as immodest.)
2. Similar (or exact) circumstances of today must be determined. (Women sometimes attend church today in attire that *our* culture perceives as immodest.)
3. The "relative" instructions apply to today's reader after a fair comparison of the two preceding factors have been determined, and in a way that preserves the spirit of the principles taught. (Women today should not attend church wearing immodest clothing or accessories.)

See? Easy peasy. Obvious and clear-cut. The regulation is understood and then applied as it relates to the original *intent*.

Now to the most glaring (and frustrating) fact in all of this: The *very next verse in sequence*—you know, that one *right after* the one about braids and gold—is not given this same allowance. Many, *many* preachers today who interpret 1 Timothy 2:9–10 as a "cultural and relative regulation" state that 1 Timothy 2:11–12 ("I suffer not a woman to teach, nor to usurp authority over the man") is an "absolute [normative] regulation for all times." These ministers may not personally be hypocrites, but their willingness to go from "relative" to "absolute" one verse over—without even a shred of evidence that *this* verse was intended to be an absolute regulation (especially when there is so much evidence to the opposite from Paul, the same author: that women were praised as *prolific* leaders and theologians of the early Church)—is hypocritical. These men may not aim to be hypocritical, and I understand that many are simply teaching what their mentors/pastors taught them in the first place, but a willingness to look at ancient culture in one verse and not the next is—at the very least—duplicitous, if not intentionally neglectful of the proper hermeneutical responsibility they hold as teachers of the Word.

In light of all our studies throughout this book, it's noteworthy to mention that before Timothy was the pastor in Ephesus, Priscilla and her husband, Aquila, were equal partners in establishing, growing, and maintaining the church there. And, as we stated earlier, historical evidence makes it clear that Priscilla was an astute early theologian of the doctrine of Christ, likely ahead of even her husband. As such, the reader needs to remember that Priscilla (a woman) perfected the theology of Apollos (a celebrated holy man), which was met with accolades from the apostle Paul in Ephesus, the very recipient city of this pastoral letter. The original readers of Paul's letter to Timothy (meaning Timothy, himself, as well as all those affected by Paul's instruction through Timothy) knew Priscilla personally. She was their archetypal "pastor" before Timothy was. Therefore, the Ephesians would have immediate insight into the nature and regulations that 1 Timothy addressed. If Paul had gone out of his way to verify Priscilla as a significant leader of the Christians in Ephesus (2 Timothy 4:19); if she was honored and recognized by "all the churches of the Gentiles" (Romans 16:3–4); and if the residents of Ephesus knew her as their previous teacher who perfected even Apollos' theology (Acts 18:24–26)—then the readers of 1 Timothy would have known that Paul was, himself, in support of women like Priscilla leading a congregation. (And that is only to list close-proximity proof. Chapter 2 of this book thoroughly examines a trainload of other evidence that proves Paul's acceptance of women as church leaders, and we haven't even arrived at what Christ thought of them yet…which presents a whole other gamut within the "internal consistency" proofs.)

Therefore, we have only two avenues by which to travel down Logic Road here: 1) Paul supported women in ministry, until he suddenly and inexplicably began to contradict himself; or 2) there were isolated, cultural circumstances that applied at the time, and it was those very circumstances Paul had to address. If we agree to the principle of internal consistency—and we must, if there is any truth to the Bible at all—then we must also agree that Paul wouldn't suddenly contradict himself and still be included within the canon of Holy Scripture, which leaves only the latter of these two possibilities.

The prohibition against women teachers was a "cultural issue" also! It had to have been, or else Paul could not have commissioned women leaders in the early Church, as we well know by now that he did!

If "braids and gold, or pearls, or costly array" are allowed to be a "relative," then the very next verse should be allowed that same interpretational accommodation if there is enough evidence to justify it—and there is…in spades.

Speaking of our trip down Logic Road: Why didn't Paul, in his letter, say that he supported women leaders of the church, and then give a full explanation as to what circumstances might require otherwise? Simply because he didn't feel he had to. Timothy, as well as the other leaders of the church in Ephesus, already *knew* how Paul felt on the issue. Priscilla—a *woman*—had been their pastoral figure in the beginning! Their familiarity to her gave them insight into what Paul was forbidding in his letter that we modern readers have to look harder to find than the original readers did. They knew what their problems were, they knew how Paul felt about women, they knew that Paul's response was related to a specific and unique issue, and Paul wrote to them via the conclusion that Timothy (and others) would have an immediate and clear understanding of precisely what cultural issue he was referring to. Just because *we* do not have that explanation in this very spot of Scripture does not mean that it doesn't exist in the historical record. Simply put by the authors of the textbook, *The Biblical Role of Women*: "They knew that the apostle Paul, who had left Priscilla to pastor this very congregation, was not prohibiting, once and for all, women as spiritual leaders. Historical context (especially these details surrounding the founding of the church) disallows such an interpretation."[62]

So what were the problems that led Paul to such an extreme prohibition of the women *in Ephesus*? As mentioned in the "Audience" heading in our "Backdrop" section prior: Sex magic, mystery cults, pagan idolatry, prostitution, and women as mediators and oracles between God and men were infiltrating the teaching of the church Paul had launched. However, at the center of all of this was the worship of Artemis/Diana.

Several internal consistency clues support the idea that Paul was responding to the Artemis/Diana/Christianity syncretism in Ephesus, and that this false teaching was a threat to the church's big-picture operation. If this is the correct interpretation, the proof of which we will consider momentarily, then Paul's prohibition of women in ministry would be a matter of correct theological adherence to the Gospel as he would have taught it, not a matter of permanently silencing all women from teaching. First, the "surrounding text" step of proper interpretation is crucial. All the guidelines listed from 2:1 through 3:13 are related to the same thing: establishing order within the church. Within that box as the dominant category, we can draw the following chart of internal subcategories:

I. Order within the Church; 2:1–3:13
    a. *Prayer for Peace 2:1–8;*
    b. *Issues regarding women 2:9–15;*
        1. They must dress and act humbly and modestly; 2:9–10
        2. They must be taught properly; 2:11
        3. They must be silent and cannot teach; 2:12
        4. They were formed after Adam; 2:13
        5. They were deceived; 2:14
        6. They will be saved in childbearing; 2:15
    c. *Bishops' conduct as husbands and heads of household; 3:1–7*
    d. *Deacons' conduct as husbands and heads of household; 3:8–13*

To avoid isolating one verse out of context, we need to establish borders around the text that forms a group. In the context of 1 Timothy, a natural group forms around verses 2:1 through 3:13, all pointing to a call for Timothy to establish order within the church. Today, we may find ourselves picking from the middle to distinguish what is "absolute" from what is "relative," but the whole picture as the original author intended was to address the concern at hand: false teaching and the reparative phases of correcting it. Paul—whom we already showed in the last chapter as prizing a peaceful and systematic service gathering to prepare the saints to carry the message to the rest of the world—is here showing that the theological hiccups of false teachers were disturbing the orderly ministry of the Ephesians. So the "relatives" and "absolutes" can't be identified until we link them to the "group" of correlating Scripture to form a whole. In other words, 1 Timothy 2:9–15 (from braided hair to childbearing) might seem like a garbled knot of information about women, but to the original readers of Paul's epistle, they were unified as a *whole* teaching about women—which I have labeled "Issues about Women"—and they were further clarified by Paul's intent to bring amenable worship parameters within the dominant category of "Order within the Church."

As such, verses 9–15 must be considered together. What do child-bearing and the Creation order and the Fall and braids all have to do with a woman teaching in the Ephesian church?

Let's look at this verse by verse.

In like manner also, that women adorn themselves in modest apparel, with [modesty] and sobriety; not with braided hair [and] gold, or pearls, or costly array.

We have already discussed this verse, and the meaning is clear: Paul wanted women to attend church with a humble and modest appearance. He didn't want their hair or clothing to resemble the *hetairai* and *pornai* of that day who were beginning to set trends for women even outside their profession.

But (which becometh women professing godliness) with good works.

If a woman is "professing godliness," then she should dress in a way that matches her claim.

Let the woman learn in silence with all subjection.

Here we arrive at an interesting plot twist that is repeatedly and tragically skimmed over. So much focus is placed on the "silencing" aspect of Paul's words here that many don't even realize the radical and countercultural gender-equality leap that Paul is introducing in his day. For only a moment, let's consider only the beginning of this verse and allow the profound historical and cultural implications of these words sink in: "Let the women learn." Today, because our culture and Christianity allow women to go to Bible colleges or seminaries, attend conferences, ask pastors questions, browse YouTube's countless theological vlogs, buy study Bibles catered to women's issues, etc., we gloss right over the first half of this verse. We can't appreciate the veracity of Paul introducing a whole new freedom for women. Our eyes land on "silence" and "subjection," and we let out a collective sigh over that moment we perceive to be Paul's misogynistic lapse in judgment. Yet, nothing could be farther from the truth! Both men and women need to stop, pull the cloud of regulation out of this moment, and be still long enough to deeply perceive what Paul just did with those four short words.

Women of the synagogue were not allowed to learn nearly *anything* in the days before Christ. Their place was in the home. The Mishnah (the first major compilation of Jewish oral traditions, also known as the "Oral Torah") highlights this profoundly. Gamaliel II (the grandson of Paul's immediate teacher) was an associate with Rabbi Eliezer, who was quoted more in the Mishnah than most other rabbis in the final redaction. In Mishnah Sotah 3:4, he sheds some light on a bygone era when he says, "If any man gives his daughter a knowledge of the Law, it is as though he taught her lechery."[63] According to the *Merriam-Webster* dictionary, "lechery" means "inordinate (see inordinate 2) indulgence in sexual activity"[64]; I followed the suggested redirect of "inordinate 2" and it read: "exceeding reasonable limits."[65] That is to say that a leading rabbi just a handful of years after Christianity's birth suggested that merely by teaching his daughter the Law (oral tradition or Mosaic), a Jewish father was committing an offense so heinous as to be compared to teaching her to exceedingly defile her body. Although Rabbi Eliezer's conclusion was an extreme one that may not have been shared by all rabbis throughout time, this "women don't need to learn" mentality was the Jewish way of life for hundreds of years before Paul, who was, himself, a devout Jew trained under the very same traditions.

Outside of Jewish culture, women sometimes had equal rights to men when it came to being educated—as was the case in Corinth and Ephesus—but now Paul was setting a new precedent for *all* women from every background within the Church of the Messiah to learn! Such a concept would have been radical! Today's reader stops at "silence" and "subjection," but readers of Paul's day would have stopped aghast at the words, "Let the women learn," as a direct command from a man who had dedicated his entire life to Jewish tradition before Christ drastically changed him. *That* would have been their focus. In order to fully comprehend the innate tone of gender equality in Paul's intent, we have to take a mind-journey back to the era in which he wrote and conceive the immensely countercultural scale of his words. He wasn't just "letting them" learn as a casual acceptance of a norm within pagan culture, as Paul frequently condemned pagan culture. In an era and setting when and where many women weren't expected to be taught, by saying "let them," he was commanding that the practice of teaching women would be carried out. He *wanted* the women to be taught. This is the opposite of misogyny! Hold onto that concept for a moment...

Now consider how we, *today*, perceive the words "silence" and "subjection." Because our culture places such distasteful associations with these words, we picture in our collective mind's eye some woman sitting up straight in a pew or behind a desk with a head covering, enduring a chauvinistic lecture by a domineering male who is just reveling in his hierarchal power. But a more sincere and respectful picture can be painted when we look at the words in their original form. Paul said that a woman should learn in "silence," which is translated from the Greek noun *hesychia*: "stillness, i.e., desistance from bustle or language."[66] It is used its adjectival form in 1 Thessalonians 4:11 to describe a peaceful life: "And that ye study to be quiet [*hesychios*], and to do your own business, and to work with your own hands, as we commanded you." It's also used in 1 Peter 3:4 in this way: "But let it be the hidden man of the heart, in that which is not corruptible, even the ornament of a meek and quiet [*hesychios*] spirit, which is in the sight of God of great price." Nowhere is it meant to suggest an aggressive mandate of overbearing silence upon a person; contrarily, it suggests an enthusiastic and cooperative spirit from a person who is willing to learn more in an area of life in order to please God. In fact, there is an instance of its use in extremely close proximity to 1 Timothy 2:9–15. In the same epistle and the same chapter, we find in the prayer of peace: "For kings, and for all that are in authority; that we may lead a quiet [*hesychios*] and peaceable life in all godliness and honesty" (2:2). If we were to apply this word in this sentence the same way our modern culture wants to apply it to women, it might read: "For kings, and for all that are in authority; that we may lead a mandatorily and continuously silent and oppressed but peaceable life in all godliness and honesty." See how quickly an assumptive interpretation can dramatically change the meaning of the Holy Word? *Hesychia* is a harmonious kind of silence, not an oppressive kind. Paul is saying that a woman's nature during the learning process should be peaceful, not argumentative.

The second word, "subjection," is the Greek *hypotage*: literally "subjection," which is further described as "the act of subjecting; obedience."[67] In a military application, the word describes one showing respect to the ranks above them. As Dr. John Bristow notes, "The word for subjection is the noun form of *hypotassomai*, which...is the voluntary willingness to be responsive to the needs of others (in this case, to the needs of others to listen, of themselves to hear, and of the teachers to communicate without noisy competition)."[68] More simply, it describes a woman willing to sit through a teaching without giving into the temptation to *laleo* ("keep talking")—which Paul addressed in 1 Corinthians—and that they should "subject themselves" (obey) under that teaching while they are actively involved in learning. They must become "quiet learners" who obey what they're taught before they can even think about becoming teachers of a material they don't understand. Indeed, as other scholars have pointed out, Paul, himself, learned in quiet submission under his tutor, Gamaliel, before he became a rabbinic scholar among the Jews.[69]

And why might Paul want a woman to learn? Because he knew that—despite what any human thought or wanted—the Holy Spirit on the Day of Pentecost had already equipped the women in the upper room to preach the Gospel to both genders, Jesus Christ personally inspired them to do the same (we're getting there...), and it was *imperative* that these women do so *with knowledge*!

How should a woman sit in on a lesson today—a lesson of any kind, not just those limited to religious settings? If she has been taught any respect whatsoever, she will sit still and be quiet while the class is in session. She will learn "in silence" by not disrupting the class with retorts or chatter, and in "subjection" by submitting herself to that lesson. Think back to what we learned about 1 Corinthians 14 and Paul's unwavering standards of respect between a teacher and a student. Paul held high the ideals of a professor or preacher being allowed to share knowledge (even interactively, if it's done so with respect) without having to bang a gavel. In 1 Timothy 2:11, Paul wasn't saying that all women throughout all times and under all circumstances have to take a man's word as the final one and have no opinions for themselves. Why does our modern culture make so much more of Paul's words here than what is actually said? As this rule of respect is golden for every age, why *wouldn't* we want *all* students to respect a teacher while in the learning process?

The important thing to remember is that this sentence of Paul's not only carries an order of how the teaching should be received while the recipient is a student; it also commands that women should be allowed to be students. If they are never students, then they can never be teachers of correct theology. The issue of whether they can eventually become teachers by Paul's following words, however, is the next natural question in sequence, since it appears to starkly contradict internal consistency.

But I suffer not a woman to teach, nor to usurp authority over the man, but to be in silence.

First of all, since the gifts of the Body members Paul wrote of in several places were gender-inclusive, we already know that a woman teaching the Gospel cannot be prohibited. Also, if women are here forbidden to teach or hold authority over the men, and that is an "absolute" regulation for all times and places, then we have to figure out why Paul: a) allows women to be prophets in the church (1 Corinthians 11:5), and b) lists prophets as the greatest authoritative ministry in the Body of Christ, just under the apostles but *above* the teachers/preachers/pastors in 1 Corinthians 12:28. If we apply all of this brand of logic to a military-rank comparison, as Gilbert Bilezikian did in *Beyond Sex Roles,* this is like telling a woman she has to lower herself to a "captain" whilst simultaneously being promoted to a "colonel."[70]

The words "I suffer not" here are from the Greek *ouk* ("not") and *epitrepo* ("do I permit"). The verb *epitrepo*, the exact grammatical variant of the word as Paul wrote it in this sentence, is first person, singular; it is being used in the *present* tense. So, a more accurate rendering into English would be, "I am not currently permitting," as opposed to the inaccurate, "I will never permit." After a serious dig into the uses of this word in the Septuagint (the Greek Old Testament; Genesis 39:6; Esther 9:14; Job 32:14; also: Wisdom of Solomon 19:2; 1 Maccabees 15:6; 4 Maccabees 4.17–18), Professor John Toews notes that the word is used to address isolated, *present-tense* circumstances (i.e., affairs occurring at the time it was written), not universal situations throughout all time.[71]

But the really tough meat to chew in this verse is the relationship between "teach" (*didaskein*) and "to usurp authority" (*authentein*). The word "teach" here has been isolated by some scholars as its own "absolute" regulation, but the majority of available research points to the conclusion that *authentein* is a copulative word to *didaskein*. Put more simply, the *kind* of teaching prohibited here is defined by whatever *authentein* means within this context, because *authentein* serves to qualify *didaskein*. Logical support for this, based purely on common sense within the overall "internal consistency" picture, is that: a) Paul commissioned women to teach; b) Jesus Christ commissioned women to teach (next two chapters); c) the Holy Spirit commissioned women to teach, so therefore; d) if teaching is anywhere prohibited within Scripture, it *must* be qualified (limited) to a certain *kind* of teaching, and therefore it is a "relative" and not an "absolute." Thus, the qualifier here, *authentein*, is a key element to our study, as it explains what kind of teaching the prohibition addresses. But before we visit the exasperating complications raised around the translation of *authentein*, it's crucial to point out that Paul normally used a completely different word with a much more common understanding in the Hellenistic period.

When Paul wrote 1 Corinthians 6:12, the words "be brought under the power" were translated from the Greek *exousiazo*: "to control:—exercise authority upon, bring under the (have) power of."[72] The feminine noun variant of this word is *exousia*: "(in the sense of ability); privilege, i.e. (subjectively) force, capacity, competency, freedom, or (objectively) mastery (concretely, magistrate, superhuman, potentate, *token of control*), *delegated influence:—authority*, jurisdiction, liberty, *power*, *right*, strength."[73] And this is in no way the only time Paul used *exousia* or its variants; he used it in plenty of other verses when describing "authority over" (1 Corinthians 7:4, 9:4–6, 9:12, 11:10; 2 Corinthians 2:8, 10:8, 13:10; Colossians 1:13; 2 Thessalonians 3:12; Romans 6:15, 9:21). In the *Strong's* database, this word is translated sixty-nine times in the KJV as "power," and twenty-nine times as "authority."[74] Twice elsewhere, when Paul was referring to "having dominion over," he used the word *kyrieusei* (Romans 6:14; 2 Corinthians 1:24). One would think that if Paul was prohibiting a woman from "bringing a man under her power" or "having authority/dominion over," he would have used *the same words he had already used in other writings* that were: a) clearly known at the time, and b) familiar to his reading audience by default of repetition. Yet here, in this one specific instance, Paul uses a very uncommon verb, *authentein*, which the translators of the KJV chose to mean "to usurp authority."

The first peculiarity is that *authentein* does not occur anywhere else in the Bible—Old or New Testament. Because we cannot rely on Paul's use of this word elsewhere for an internal comparison of how *he* would have used it in a sentence, the only places we can look are in extrabiblical documents in ancient Greek. Understand that some words—even in English—can have more than one common meaning, even when the word is spelled the same in all variables. This is called a homonym. For instance: "Row" as a verb is the action that propels a boat forward, but as a noun, it refers to a line of regularly-spaced objects. *Authentein*, as it appears in ancient Greek documents, is similar. It means different things to different writers as it is used in a sentence. However, despite all available instances, it remains a very rare word with definitions in such contrast that it's harder to pin down what Paul would have meant.

From the list provided by Henry George Liddell and Robert Scott in the *Greek-English Lexicon*, we retrieve the following instances of *authentein* in its noun form, *authentes*: "murderer" (Herodotus 1.117; Euripides, *Rhesus* 873; Thucydides 3.58; Euripides, *Hercules Furens* 1359; Apollonius Rhodius, *Argonautica* 2.754); "suicide" (Antipho 3.3.4; Dio Cassius 37.13); "one from a murderer's family" (Euripides, *Andromache* 172.2); "perpetrator," "author" (Polybius 22.14.2; Diodorus Siculus 16.61); generally "doer" (Alexander Rhetor 2S); "master" (Euripides, *The Suppliants* 442; *Leidon Magical Papyrus W* 6.46); "condemned" (Phyrnichus Arabius 96.3); "murder by one in the same family" (Aeschylus, *Eumenides* 212; *Agamemnon* 1572).[75]

Thesaurus Linguae Graeca, an online computer database, uncovered only 306 uses of *authentein* between 200 BC and AD 200 (four hundred years total, at the center of which was Christ). Although 306 sounds like a very small number, in light of how often it is discovered in ancient texts, this was actually a thrilling find. Among the uses listed, these were the most common: "doer of a massacre," "author of crimes," "perpetrators of sacrilege," "supporter of violent actions," "murderer of oneself," "sole power," "perpetrator of slaughter," "murderer," "slayer," "slayer of oneself," "authority," "perpetrator of evil," and "one who murders by his own hand."[76]

New Testament scholar Scott Bartchy lends the following insight: "The verb *authentein* clearly bears the nuance of using such absolute power in a destructive manner, describing the activity of a person who acts for his or her own advantage apart from any consideration of the needs or interests of anyone else."[77] Based on Bartchy's conclusion, the following verses in 1 Timothy regarding the creation order are perfectly aligned, because women are not supposed to dominate men. Women and men are to rule alongside each other in mutual unity.

Egalitarian Walter Liefeld writes in his article, "Women and the

Nature of Ministry," from the *Journal of the Evangelical Society*: "A perplexing issue for all is the meaning of *authentein*. Over the course of its history this verb and its associated noun have had a wide semantic range, including some bizarre meanings, such as committing suicide, murdering one's parents, and being sexually aggressive. Some studies have been marred by a selective and improper use of the evidence."[78]

One of these "marred" translations Liefeld referred to (and I am tempted to agree) might have been the one given by Richard and Catherine Kroeger. Their calculations, based on a substantial cultural investigation into the word, was that *authentein* should be translated "to engage in fertility practices" (1979 conclusion) or "to represent herself as originator of man" (1992 alternative conclusion; although this one holds some merit, as we will see shortly).[79] Cultural support for this interpretation would be: a) we know that one meaning of the word *authentein* is "author" (i.e., "originator"); and b) native religions of Anatolia (surrounding Ephesus) taught that Artemis/Diana was the divine source through whom all life began. Who would teach such a thing? False teachers. What does 1 Timothy centrally condemn? False teachers. Surrounding text support would be that the very next verses in the epistle reestablish the creation order, essentially putting such a woman teacher in her place.

However, many scholars have refuted the theological and lexicological breakdown of the Kroegers' conclusion, and for many (lengthy and complicated) reasons related to even the tiniest syntax and accent relationships. I, too, believe that swallowing their conclusion to the extent that they implemented it takes a lot of imagination and stretching. Yet, for all the scrutiny they gained in their interpretation of one word (that was already widely recognized to be one of the most mysterious in ancient Greek), they *did* put together the following list of cultural and linguistic factors, a list that has been extensively acknowledged among scholars for hundreds of years, and one their book exhaustively and credibly cited: 1) Ephesus, as well as the surrounding regions, was simply *crawling* with people who practiced erotic pagan religions that placed women equal to, and often above, men in aggressive and sexual positions of authority;[80] 2) historical evidence shows instances in Ephesus and nearby regions that women had collectively usurped the authority of men in religious settings (especially those related to the temple of Artemis/Diana in Ephesus);[81] 3) the words *authentein* and its noun form *authentes* are repeatedly associated with some form of extremely aggressive behavior;[82] and perhaps most importantly, 4) there exists a substantial argument based on historical evidence that *authentein* and *authentes* were *not employed to mean* "having power or authority" until *"the second century after Christ"*![83]

Wow...now *there's* a thought.

Professor of Religion Albert Wolters came to the same determination about the final item on this list in the *Journal of Greco-Roman Christianity and Judaism* (note that I have removed Greek characters and replaced them with English characters for flow):

> With respect to the meaning of *authentein* in 1 Tim. 2.12, my investigation leads to two further conclusions. First, the verb *authentein* should not be interpreted in the light of "murderer," or the muddled definitions of it given in the Atticistic lexica. Instead, it should be understood, like all the other Hellenistic derivatives of *authentein*, in the light of the meaning which that word had in the living Greek of the day, namely "master." Secondly, there seems to be **no basis for the claim that *authentein* in 1 Tim. 2.12 has a pejorative connotation**, as in "usurp authority" or "domineer." Although it is possible to identify isolated cases of a pejorative use for both *authentein* and *authentia*, **these are not found before the fourth century AD 135.**[84]

At the time 1 Timothy was written, the common language in the Hellenistic era was Koine Greek. Insight for what the verb *authentein* might have become by this time can be credited to Dr. Cynthia Long Westfall, exegesis professor at the McMaster Divinity College: "In the Greek corpus, the verb *authenteo* refers to a range of actions that are not restricted to murder or violence. However, the people who are targets of these actions are harmed, forced against their will (compelled), or at least their self-interest is being overridden, because the actions involve an imposition of the subject's will, ranging from dishonour to lethal force."[85]

Don't miss that... "An imposition of the subject's will." Someone's "self-interest is being overridden." Such circumstances do not have to be murderous or violent for them to also be inappropriate, and in the moment that a subject's will is imposed by another to the point that he or she is entirely overridden, a usurpation has most definitely occurred.

The KJV's "usurp authority" was not translated until 1611 (and prior to that, Tyndale used "have authority over"). By then, the "usurpation" connotation was a common one. But at the time Paul wrote 1 Timothy (circa AD 58–65), *authentein* was not used in that way. This might be why the Latin Vulgate and the New English Bible translate the word as "domineer." The most frequent appearance of *authentein* within Hellenistic literature as it relates to Paul's usage would be "master." Therefore, his words should probably be translated, "I do not permit a woman to teach, nor to master over the man." Whereas some would think "usurp authority over" and "master over" are synonymous, we still have to acknowledge that *authentein* has a history of associating with hostile and antagonistic activity, and that "mastering over" suggests a more aggressive takeover than, say, a diplomatic disagreement between a man and a woman over theology (or some equivalent). Yes, there certainly is a chance that the translation of "usurp authority" is correct, and many scholars (even egalitarians) accept this as a fact based on exhaustive lexicological exegesis (even despite the fact that historical evidence likely proves this word was not used in this way during Paul's life). But that does not explain away the fact that, in relationship to the word's etymological/historical roots, the "usurpation" referred to would be an antagonistic or hostile concept—"an imposition of the subject's will" while someone's "self-interest is being overridden"—*not simply a peaceful woman preacher/teacher who is preaching the Gospel for the eternal sake of the lost.*

Moreover: If Paul was accustomed to using the more conventional *exousiazo* or *exousia*, then why does he suddenly switch to a word that is so widely associated with aggression in this instance? Perhaps because he *was* referring to an aggressive or antagonistic takeover…and in this case, it's not far-fetched to say that it would be a priestess/prostitute of Artemis/ Diana whose pagan theology was misleading the believers in Ephesus.

But let's consider, logically please, what we're arguing about here. A woman standing behind a pulpit to draw the lost to Christ through her theological knowledge and the words of her mouth is not "usurping" anybody anyway. To "usurp authority" means to steal authority from someone else and harness it as one's own. The *Merriam Webster* dictionary defines "usurp" first and foremost: "to seize and hold (office, place, functions, powers, etc.) in possession by force."[86] To assume that any woman preacher who uses her pulpit and her mouth to reach the lost is "stealing" the authority from a man and harnessing it as her own just because there may be another male in the congregation is a *huge* stretch! Who is stealing anything from anyone in this instance? If a woman were to stomp up on the stage, grab the microphone from her pastor, and present an uninvited preaching session, then yes, she would be usurping. Let's face it: The evidence is stacked against the idea that Paul was automatically associating any female preacher/teacher to a usurper.

The bottom line on this whole *authentein* debate, in my opinion (as well as in the opinions of several other scholars who have weighed in on the issue), is that the word is rare and mysterious, and even if we were to pin down *exactly* what it meant in Paul's day, we still have scores of preachers, teachers, linguists, and scholars who may all end up at a different contemporary *application* of it based on their own imprinting and cultural/individual approaches to study. For instance, let's say that we were finally able to conclude that *authentein* meant "to hold power over." Now we have a billion voices weighing in on what it really means to "hold power over the man." Additionally, since so many ministers today preach only what *today's culture* determines instead of looking at the circumstances at the time of the original writing—and because we are so far removed historically from the original culture and all that implies for a comparison of contemporary circumstances—many of these voices wouldn't be correct, anyway. They would be basing their interpretation of what "holding power over" means within the limited concepts of a world radically unlike our own. This is already happening in regard to Scripture that is imminently clearer to present-day readers, so the "corporately conclusive" determination of such a rare and mysterious word as *authentein*—along with a "corporately conclusive" application to the calling upon women's lives today—is likely never to happen on this side of eternity. Sometimes there is great wisdom in agreeing to disagree when it comes to the nonessentials.

Case in point: Aggression and domination aside (as those are the most obvious topics within the debate of *authentein*), does a woman "hold power over the man" simply by preaching the Gospel so that more lost souls will inherit the Kingdom of God? The Holy Spirit, Paul, and Jesus Christ evidently didn't think so, or else *all three* of them contradicted themselves. If we rule that one out, it only leads to other questions: Does a woman "hold power over the man" by contradicting or correcting his theology like Priscilla was praised for doing? Perhaps, but then what happens when a female teacher recognizes a male heretic spreading false doctrine, and *oh so many* verses point to intervening? Should she disobey the verses that tell her to step in because she may otherwise be guilty of "holding power over" the heretic just because he was born male? (And don't get me started on the gender/sex identification that would explode overnight in our modern day if Paul's words were "conclusively" applied this way. We currently have churches popping up all over the country with ministers who feel they were created by God to "be" the gender opposite of their sexual identification at birth. If the day comes when this is the final word on the whole issue, a simple sex-change operation and legal-identification swap would be the only thing standing between a woman minister "becoming" a male minister. I'm not saying that this argument would hold any ground in conservative circles, but I *am* saying that there are people out there who—like some readers of the Queen James Bible, perhaps?—will make this connection.)

Suffice it to say that we must allow Scripture to interpret Scripture, and with as much proof that Scripture holds in support of women being allowed to teach, we have no choice but to conclude that whatever *authentein* meant to Paul, 1 Timothy 2:12 couldn't have been an "absolute" or "normative" prohibition of all women teachers throughout all time—the evidence that Paul was addressing an isolated, cultural/local issue and "relative" regulation pertaining to the church at Ephesus is overwhelming. Again, this does not mean we shouldn't apply 1 Timothy 2:12 to our lives today; it means we should apply it "after a fair comparison of the [cultural] factors have been determined, and in a way that preserves the spirit of the principles taught." A comparison of the original circumstances must be similar (or exact) to our circumstances today when dealing with a "relative" and "restrictive" regulation such as this one, given by a man who elsewhere manifestly supports women teachers.

Now we come upon a set of verses (13–15) that, in light of all we've studied, appears to be rather confusing and unrelated.

For Adam was first formed, then Eve. And Adam was not deceived, but the woman being deceived was in the transgression. Notwithstanding she shall be saved in childbearing, if they continue in faith and charity and holiness with sobriety.

Several questions arise immediately: If the creation order assigned the authority to who or what was created first, then wouldn't Adam be under the authority of all the animals? Paul already said that Adam, not Eve, was to blame for the Fall (Romans 5:14; 1 Corinthians 15:21–22), so is he now saying that the guilty party—the one "in the transgression"—was Eve? And if a woman will be saved in child-bearing, what about a woman who never has, or can't have, children? (More on the Fall in the next chapter.)

Countless ministers have connected the dots in this portion of the letter to say that because Adam was formed first, but the woman was deceived, then the man is supposed to be the head of a ministry or church and a woman cannot become a leading teacher or preacher because she might (and some say "will") become deceived, like Eve was by the serpent. I don't need to point out again how many times Paul commissioned women as church leaders, as I have done so already, but that fact dismisses this interpretation. Likewise, many speculators (of both genders) have pointed out, just as Paul did, that Eve was deceived, but Adam *chose* to do wrong. By this logic, male ministers are just as vulnerable to concocting false teaching, because their flesh tells them to twist Scripture to make it read how they want for their own agenda. So if interpreters want to use these verses about Eve to justify prohib-iting female ministers who might be deceived, they should also allow Adam to be the justification for prohibiting male ministers on account that they might willfully teach falsely—and the fact that ministers are twisting Scripture all over the country at lightning speed for their own gain is not a secret. We all know it happens all the time. The argument here is not the fact that men would be considered more or less guilty of this "transgression" than a woman just because Paul said Adam was the guilty party. This is by no means a "gotcha" sentiment against men or a statement that women would be "better leaders" or any such nonsense. The argument here is that *both genders* are equally vulnerable to false teaching, *both genders* will be tempted via deception (Eve), *both genders* will make bad choices willfully (Adam), and these verses on the Creation order don't say anything about church hierarchal order.

Conclusion? It doesn't have anything to do with who's allowed to preach, teach, or pastor a church.

That still doesn't really answer the question of why these verses are placed here, so let me connect some dots of my own, based on the research compiled herein (and upon the conclusions of respected scholars):

1. It's clear by this point that women believed Artemis/Diana was the creator of all life (including the first man). So Paul, by pointing out that Adam was formed first, then Eve, would be reminding false teachers in Ephesus that even if Artemis/Diana existed in the minds of her believers, she couldn't have been formed first—and these false-teacher women would be wise to accept that they, like Eve, were not given an authority advantage in the Creation order just because their goddess religion told them so.

2. These false-teaching women, like Eve, would have been guilty of "transgression" if they had been deceived by this pagan idea and followed through with teaching others to partake of this theology, just as Eve followed through with coaxing Adam to partake of the forbidden fruit.

3. Notwithstanding "she"—Eve!—shall be saved in childbearing (Genesis 3:15–16; 20) through the birth of the eventual Savior, which relied on Eve's willingness to have children of her own to populate the earth as the first mother of the human race. Paul was referring to the promises made in Genesis that the Savior would arrive through the foretold childbearing of Mary, and that this Messiah would then be the Savior for *all*. This would also involve the male seed of Adam to produce the eventual Mary (mother of Christ), unlike the theology taught by the priestesses of Artemis/Diana that the Savior Jesus Christ might have been created by the goddess entirely without a male's participation. These false-teaching women, like Eve, can be saved as well through the coming of the Savior "if they continue in faith and charity and holiness with sobriety." This also serves as a logical explanation as to why the "she" becomes "they" in such close proximity.

However, one insight has yet to be shared…

The very first thing the reader should note within the "trouble passages" (verses 9–15) is Paul's seemingly unexplainable grammatical switch in number. He refers to women (plural) in verses 9–10, then, in verse 11, he shifts to the singular, "Let the *woman* learn," Greek *gune* (nominative case): "a woman; specially, a wife:—wife, woman."[87] He remains focused on one woman through the first half of verse 15, and in the second half of that verse, he reverts to plural.

Within my personal library, several university-level study materials point to this as proof that Paul was silencing only one woman who was guilty of false teaching.[88] This interpretation suggests:

1) Paul received word that one woman was misleading one man, "the man" in verse 11 (likely her husband, since *gune* often referred to a wife). Between Timothy and himself, both knew exactly who these people were, so a lengthy explanation from Paul regarding what this woman was teaching wasn't necessary within the letter.

2) Paul sent word back to Timothy telling him how to resolve the issue of "the woman."

This is a fair and logical interpretation, in part because it answers all the questions that arise from this group of verses:

1. It wouldn't make grammatical sense to go from plural to singular and back to plural the way Paul does. Paul was a gifted writer, and if the Bible is inerrant and infallible, as Christians believe (and as the Word, itself, claims), then the switch from "women" to "the woman" and back again is not a mistake. It should be taken seriously.

2. Despite all the evidence that ancient Ephesus was populated with domineering women who would have seen themselves as mediators between men and a deity (Artemis/Diana, Christ, etc.), many continue to reject the notion that this city was as full-scale pagan as the evidence suggests. Whether their resistance to

all the evidence is rational or not, this interpretation allows the issue to drop, permanently. One does not have to accept the idea that Ephesus was wholly entrenched in a state of constant and chaotic paganism in order to accept that one woman could have been a completely sold-out heretic with much influence in her own marriage.

3. Throughout 1 Timothy, Paul uses gender-inclusive pronouns when he addresses the problem of false teachers (1:3, 6; 4:1; 6:21). Therefore, we have proof that women and men—both genders—were teaching falsely. Here, however, he switches to "the woman," suggesting a solitary female was at the center of at least some of the false teaching that Paul's whole letter addressed. Based on historical and archeological evidence of religious activity at the time, we can reasonably conclude that women—and within this interpretation, *the* woman—had bungled the Creation order to include Artemis/Diana, the Great Mother of Asia from whom all life originates, in the mix.

4. Understandably, the Creation order section of text poses many interpretational problems. However, if the concern in the trouble passages is a solitary woman and her false teaching about the Creation order, then Paul's reestablishment of the Creation order was needed to correct one woman's false teaching. We can never know what the woman's exact teachings were, but based on evidence, we can glean what the correction was: 1) The man was created before the woman, and therefore, a woman did not create man—i.e., Artemis/Diana (or any other venerated pagan goddess) could not have created mankind; 2) Paul recognized that the "woman" false teacher in Ephesus was deceived, like Eve was deceived; Paul's letter to Timothy does not negate that Paul said elsewhere that the sin was Adam's, it only serves to enjoin Eve in the "transgression" through the error of allowing herself to be deceived by the "false teaching" of the serpent; 3) while

151

Paul is discussing the Genesis account here, he points to child-bearing (with Adam's involvement) as the way that Christ eventually came to save us all, including the "woman" false teacher, through Mary's giving birth (Genesis 3:15).

If this interpretation is correct, all the questions of how the Creation order relates to Paul's message to Timothy fit flawlessly into context of one female false teacher.

For those who may be wondering why Paul referred to this false teacher as "woman" instead of calling her by name, he was also known to do this with men, such as the contentious person in Crete (cf. Titus 1:5, 11; 3:10) and the man guilty of incest in Corinth (1 Corinthians 5:1, 5).

From this point, Paul deals with the qualifications of overseers, pastors, preachers, bishops, deacons, and the subject of godliness in chapter 3. Verses 3:6–7 list a telling instruction for the overseer: He must "Not [be] a novice… Moreover he must have a good report." He must have built up a good report, i.e., he can't be a recent convert. Paul is holding the men accountable to being quiet learners before being leaders, in the same way that he is holding women accountable to learning before teaching. No male or female should teach until he or she has learned.

But it is also within this section of the epistle that we observe what might be *the biggest argument within this entire investigation* that the modern-day Church is abusing 1 Timothy!

Please, if you haven't digested anything else I've written so far in this chapter, digest this…

Here, in chapter 3 verses 2–13, Paul tells the church in Ephesus that *male leaders cannot be*: single; married without children or married with only one child; married with children who aren't in complete subjection to his authority "with all gravity;" married to wives who gossip; or married to wives who default in their faithfulness. Further, a male leader must not be abusive to his wife, a recent convert without "good report," lacking in self-control, unteachable, or without a stable reputation even to those outside the church. If 1 Timothy 2:11–12 applies as an "absolute" that women cannot be leaders in the Church just because "the Bible says so," then 1 Timothy 3:2–12 applies as an "absolute" for the men because "the Bible says so." No male is allowed to be in leadership if he hasn't yet taken a wife and had at least two kids who are old enough to prove themselves obedient in "all gravity" and at all times. No male is allowed to be in leadership if his wife gossips or shirks her "faithfulness" responsibilities. No male is allowed to be in leadership if other people—even those outside the church (3:7)—have slandered his public reputation. And what of the "self-control" issue? Does that regard temperament? Or does that extend to other subjects of behavioral restraint, such as diet? (I know a great number of obese pastors whose eating habits are "out of control.")

The list goes on and on. Yet, how many single pastors do we see today? How many are still waiting for the Lord to bless them with a child? How many have children who misbehave? How many are married with well-behaved children, but whose wives always have a big, juicy story to tell? How many are married with well-behaved children and submissive wives—and whose ministry and teaching are dead-on correct according to Scripture—but who aren't accepted in their town?

None of these men is qualified to lead. Not one of them. Nope.

Sorry to break that to you.

That is…*unless* we are able to acknowledge that 1 Timothy 3:2–13 is a "relative" regulation for men. Have we done that in our modern culture today? Irrevocably so, yes. Have we done the same for women? Absolutely not, because our culture embraces the double standard when it suits a particular agenda, such as power. Women who stand up and preach despite the resistance are told to "sit down, shut up, and repent," lest they be an "apostasy woman."

The condition of the church in Ephesus was so bad that Paul had no choice but to implement what Professor Gilbert Bilezikian called in *Beyond Sex Roles* "a sort of congregational martial law."[89] The rules had to be as strict as ever…and *fast*. Weeding out the false teaching was Paul's number-one priority, and at least one female was (and perhaps many were) at the forefront of the pollution. We should still apply all these rules if we find ourselves in the same position as Ephesus, but if not, then we shouldn't find ourselves under the same rules. Period.

In chapter 4, Paul once again acknowledges the harsh realities of those who "depart from the faith by devoting themselves to deceitful spirits and [false] teachings of demons" (4:1–5), followed by godliness again, and in chapter 5 he gives instructions on how to live as a family unit in the church. Chapter 6 returns for one last sweep through warnings regarding false teachers, and it ends with the exhortation to fight the good fight of faith. The apostle's farewell is, as usual, warm: "O Timothy, keep that which is committed to thy trust, avoiding profane and vain babblings, and oppositions of science falsely so called [false teachings]: Which some professing have erred concerning the faith. Grace be with thee. Amen" (6:21–22).

In conclusion: Paul and Timothy, as a team, had a lot of damage to repair in the city of Ephesus. I believe Bilezikian nailed it when he summarized 1 Timothy, concluding that a comprehensive understanding of the cultural, historical, linguistic, and circumstantial study on the epistle shows, and I quote:

- that the apostle Paul wrote this epistle to a church in a state of terminal crisis;
- that he drastically curtailed the ministries of *both* women and men to save the church from self-destruction;
- that the restrictions Paul laid down in this epistle were temporary measures of exception designed to save this particular church from disintegration;
- that the remedial crisis-management provisions mandated in this passage remain valid for all times since they are relevant to churches that fall into similar states of dysfunction.[90]

Without skipping to the very end of this reflection just yet, one last string of verses in 1 Timothy need to be shown herein. The ESV renders this beautifully: "If anyone teaches a different doctrine and does not agree with the sound words of our Lord Jesus Christ and the teaching that accords with godliness, he is puffed up with conceit and understands nothing. He has an unhealthy craving for controversy and for quarrels about words, which produce envy, dissension, slander, evil suspicions, and constant friction among people who are depraved in mind and deprived of the truth" (6:3–5; emphasis added).

Let that "absolute" from Paul sink in for a moment…

If any person does not agree with the words of Jesus Christ, he or she only craves—with an "unhealthy craving"—to bicker over words…

Sounds pretty clear to me.

But if Jesus Christ inspired women to preach—with the words of *His mouth*—then wouldn't those who disagree with Him be guilty of this—guilty of craving this very kind of petty-semantics rivalry and "quarrels about words"?

I could not have asked for a better segue into this next chapter.

5

The Women Jesus *Knew*

Paul's words have been the central cause behind why women have been forbidden to hold leadership positions within the Body. It seemed fitting that the first deep studies would begin there, in order to replace our contemporary interpretations of an ancient text with the proper *intent* of the ancient text. This was a crucial step in our journey toward seeing the true and biblical role of women, because what we're about to delve into is the highest authority of all Scripture: *what Jesus Christ thought about women*!

However, before we delve into those whom He *sent*, we should first consider those whom He *knew* in order to understand how He came to view women as a whole. This includes the women He interacted with personally, as well as some of the names He would have studied from Old Testament Scripture (New Testament wasn't written yet), as those women would have been the natural basis of His theology at the time.

Jesus Knew of Eve

Many today have an inadequate perception of what took place in the Garden of Eden. In spite of what Scripture says, we still tend to rely on the "cartoon" depiction of the Fall: Adam is off somewhere else taking a nap; Eve is surprised when a green snake coils up the trunk of the forbidden fruit tree; after the snake convinces her to eat the fruit, Eve goes looking for Adam and deceives him into believing that eating it would be a good idea (in some versions, Adam doesn't even know it's the forbidden fruit he's taking a bite of); later, when the voiceover actor for God calls out to the couple, Eve acts guilty and Adam acts surprised. The book *Paradise Lost* by poet John Milton in the seventeenth century played a key role in establishing these, and other, inaccurate portrayals.

Likewise, some members of the Church cling to the misconception that God made *only Adam* in His image, whereas Eve was simply "plucked" from the man's chest—a kind of warped, Eve-made-in-the-image-of-Adam theology.

For generations, these ideas have been the "truth" taught to children of the Church, and it concerns me, because it's one step lower than the at-times contextually dismissive "the Bible tells me so" interpretation method; it becomes that terribly misleading "the cartoon tells me so" reality. Then, when teachers of the Word come along with a deeper understanding, they are written off either as extremists or scatterbrained fruitcakes by the legions of now-grown men and women who skim over the true facts; if those teachers are *women*… Oh boy. I see the patriarchal cynics waving their "feminist" and "women's lib" warning flags even now.

Nevertheless, Jesus Christ was present during, and actively involved in, the formation of the world (John 1:1–4). He would have known who was made in whose image, and He would have known what went down on the day of the Fall. Since the Fall account is paramount to how women are viewed today—and since Christ's treatment of women would have been in part due to His understanding of that event—it's crucial that we dig a little deeper.

Is it possible that the "Eve" we know is not the Eve Christ perceived?

First things first: Throughout this area, I will be referring to the serpent in the garden by the English word "serpent," but it must be stated here and now that the Hebrew *nachash* (what spoke to Eve the day of the Fall) does not appropriately translate as the kind of snake we see today when we go on a tour through the jungle. I don't have the space or time in this book to do full justice to the study here, but a plethora of exegetically and hermeneutically rich studies have been brought to the table in the last two hundred years focusing on what this *nachash* really was. (Spoiler alert: It wasn't a green snake telling Eve, "Ssssssssssssurely you will not die.") The word used as a noun can be translated "serpent" or "snake." The verb use, however, means "deceiver," "diviner with divine knowledge," or "to practice divination," and the adjective use translates "shining one." Angels and divine beings are often described as shining or luminescent in the Bible, and the name "Lucifer" (Hebrew *Helel ben-Shachar*) literally translates "Shining One, son of the Dawn." Many of the studies I have read therefore consider this entity to be a shining, serpentine deceiver associated with the Divine Council mentioned in the Old Testament that God pronounces judgment upon (Psalm 82:1; 1 Kings 22:19; all of Job).

Genesis 3:14 ("upon thy belly shalt thou [now] go") has many times been the choice proof-text among the Body for why all snakes today don't have arms and legs, and the assumption is that all the animals in the Garden of Eden prior to the Fall were able to speak, and Satan simply possessed one of them or appeared to Eve as one of them. (The cartoons almost all show the snake, with no arms and legs, slithering up a tree, which, interestingly, opposes this mainstream idea, because if this traditional view were true, then the snake in the cartoons would have walked straight up to Eve and its limbs would have been zapped off after the curse. And whereas this might seem like an irrelevant observation to this study, it's actually quite important: Our Church doesn't even know what we believe about ancient Scripture, and even when we think we do, we produce teaching materials that don't reflect that same belief. This is a symptom of a major theology dysfunction sickness inflicted upon the Church today.) Nowhere does Scripture suggest that talking animals were the norm in the Garden of Eden, or anywhere else, before or after the Fall. (Balaam's donkey is, of course, an isolated instance that cannot be taken to represent a "normative" or "absolute" scriptural reality.) And if the curse upon the serpent was merely to render all snakes armless and legless, this punishment doesn't appear to have accomplished anything, since these creatures still thrive in that form—and yes, they can still climb trees. Also, if the curse in Genesis 3:15 says that there will be "enmity... between thy seed [the serpent's offspring] and her seed [human beings]," why isn't there enmity between snakes and humans today? Sure, snakes are territorial, but so is an enormous chunk of the animal kingdom. For the most part, unless they feel provoked or threatened, snakes usually mind their own business—and not every human hates or fears snakes. This doesn't sound like "enmity." Likewise, we all know that snakes don't survive on eating dirt, even though the curse said, "and dust shalt thou eat all the days of thy life."

From Derek Gilbert's *The Great Inception* articles, we read:

Was it a talking snake?

In a word, no.

So who or what was the serpent? Most of us assume it was Satan, but maybe not. The serpent isn't named in the book of Genesis. In fact, Satan wasn't even a personal name in the Old Testament.

Satan means "accuser," written *ha-shaitan* in the OT. It's a title, *the* satan, so it really means "the accuser." Think of it as a job title, like prosecuting attorney.

The adversary in the Garden is the *nachash*, which is the

word translated into English as "serpent." It's based on an adjective that means bright or brazen, like shiny brass. The noun *nachash* can mean snake, but it also means "one who practices divination."

In Hebrew, it's not uncommon for an adjective to be converted into a noun—the term is "substantivized." If that's the case here, *nachash* could mean "shining one." And that's consistent with other descriptions of the satan figure in the Old Testament....

The bottom line is this: What Adam and Eve saw in the Garden wasn't a talking snake, but a *nachash*—a radiant, divine entity, very likely of serpentine appearance....

For centuries, well-meaning Christians have pointed to Genesis 3:14 as the moment in history when snakes lost their legs. That misses the mark entirely by desupernaturalizing the story. God didn't amputate the legs of snakes; He was describing the punishment the *nachash* would suffer in figurative language. Even casual observers of the animal kingdom know that snakes don't eat dust....

The main takeaway of this article is this: Eden was a lush, well-watered garden "on the holy mountain of God," which was where Yahweh presided over His divine council. The council included the first humans. They walked and talked with the supernatural "sons of God" who, based on clues scattered throughout the Bible, were beautiful, radiant beings. At least some of them were serpentine in appearance."[91]

The discussion of this topic is so lengthy that the last book I added to my personal library on it was nearly six hundred pages long. Suffice it to say that this entity most likely was *not* a walking or talking snake, but a bright (perhaps luminescent), intelligent master of deception with arms and legs intact. I will not set out to prove that it was or was not

Lucifer possessing the body of a snake, as that's not my theological area of expertise, and it's not crucial to the purpose of this book. However, as we take a closer look at *the Eve whom Christ would have known as the rabbi He was*, we need to see past this idea that she was just wandering around talking to animals all day and instantly believed the first one that lied to her. This creature was a being of extreme power and persuasion, most likely a "professional" accuser within the Divine Council, and he had a major agenda: to reverse the beauty of what God had created—the subject to which we will now return.

To begin, Genesis 1:26 is clear in its stipulation that men and women are to rule together: "And God said, 'Let us make man in our image, after our likeness: and let *them* have dominion over the fish of the sea, and over the fowl of the air, and over the cattle, and over all the earth, and over every creeping thing that creepeth upon the earth'" (emphasis added). Let *them* rule, it says…together, one alongside the other, in full equality as one working unit. Two verses later, the stipulation is repeated: "And God blessed *them*, and God said unto *them*, 'Be fruitful, and multiply, and replenish the earth, and subdue it: and have dominion over the fish of the sea, and over the fowl of the air, and over every living thing that moveth upon the earth'" (emphasis added).

Sure, Genesis 1:26–27 does state that God "created *man* in his own image," but within the very same verse, it says, "male and female created he *them*" (emphasis added). The "man" in the first half of the verse is in reference to mankind, not as a male person. After a lengthy dive into scholarly translations, interpretations, and commentaries, the most popular consensus among scholars (but lost in lay teaching) is that God: a) created both men and women *equally* in His image; and b) that because God is spirit and not flesh, the "image" we have in common with God is in reference to the spirit of humanity—such as superior dominion, creativity, consciousness, and the draw toward interactive companionship of *Homo sapiens* as a species—*not* as it relates to the physical anatomy of a man over a woman.

And what did God—including all three members of the Trinity who were present—think of this arrangement? He saw that "it was very good" (1:31). Christ—*Himself*—saw that this creation composition was "very good." Christ—*Himself*—saw that this was how the ruling order of men and women was supposed to be. Note that in the back of your mind as we continue.

In Genesis 2:18 we read, "And the Lord God said, 'It is not good that the man should be alone; I will make him an help meet for him.'" Most modern translations choose instead the words "a helper suitable [or "fit"] for him." In our current world, "helper" is commonly associated with the toddler in Sunday school who earns a gold star for picking up all the crayons. It's really no wonder that some women cringe when this verse is referenced from the pulpit, as our culture treats it as a marginal or subordinate position in a relationship: man as the delegator, woman as the delegated. Yet, to the original Old Testament Hebrew audience, it held a far greater importance as it pointed to the woman as a wise counselor, a person of power and strength.

The Hebrew word here is *ezer*, and it *never* refers to a subordinate or inferior anywhere in the Old Testament that Christ would have known. Not once. In fact, it can at times refer to a superior. Though it does translate to "one who helps," it's interesting to note that its prevailing use—*seventeen out of twenty-one times!*—is as a reference to God, Himself. David wrote in Psalm 121:1: "I will lift up mine eyes unto the hills, from whence cometh my *ezer*" (see also: Psalm 10:14, 30:10, 54:4, 70:5, 72:12, 121:2). Clearly, God is not subordinate or inferior in any way. In the context of Psalm 121, David is saying that he needs God and depends upon Him. When the Lord said, "It is not good that the man should be alone," and then followed it by creating an *ezer* for Adam, it was because man *needed* the power and strength of a woman who would "rule" or "have dominion" together with him—not rule or have dominion *over* him, but *with* him. (Note that one popular interpretation of the Fall narrative states the serpent specifically targeted Eve because she was the *ezer*, the "stronger" of the two. The logic follows the idea that if the serpent could convince the "stronger" sex, Eve, he knew the "weaker" sex, Adam, would follow. I don't buy this at all, as Scripture throughout this area is clear the two were created equal, and no evidence suggests that either was more powerful in spirit than the other...but the fact that such an interpretation is considered to be valid by so many scholars lends support for the actual power and weight of the word *ezer*.)

Need further proof of gender equality in the Creation order? "Fit" and "suitable" are translated from the Hebrew preposition *kenegdo*, which means "equal" and "corresponding to."[92] As such, Genesis documents that woman was made to be "an equal person of power and strength, corresponding to Adam." It is saddening that so many women are led to believe that they were made to be little more than cookie bakers or vacuumers in the Church because of the generations of men that have told them so after misinterpreting these texts to mean "cute little helper." Adam, himself, acknowledged equality when he said, "This [woman] is now bone of my bones, and flesh of my flesh" (Genesis 2:23).

And as stated in the previous chapter, the order of Creation (Adam first, then Eve) is not what establishes authority, or else the animals would have had authority over Adam. He would have had to bow to the whims of an insect or consider his own needs less than a tomato plant. Throughout the Bible we see that the Israelites gave special privileges, rights, and inheritances to first-born sons, and one comment I saw this past week on Facebook asserted that this was proof enough that "God's way" was to honor whichever male presence is first established within the household. But let's not forget that the Bible also proves that God deliberately reversed this several times, despite the familial tradition of the Hebrews, some of which were in *major* narratives: Jacob as father of Israel instead of Esau; David as king of Israel instead of all his older brothers; Moses as recipient of the Ten Commandments and deliverer of the Israelite slaves in Egypt instead of Aaron; and so on. The rule of authority and/or dominion should never be based on "who got there first."

As far as who was more at fault the day of the Fall, Paul makes it clear that Adam holds the greater share of responsibility (1 Timothy 2:14). But was the woman alone at the time of the serpent's temptation, as "the cartoons tell me so"?

Genesis 3:6 states that Adam was "with her": "And when the woman saw that the tree was good for food, and that it was pleasant to the eyes, and a tree to be desired to make one wise, she took of the fruit thereof, and did eat, and gave also unto her husband *with her*, and he did eat" (emphasis added). Some interpret this to mean that he was "with her" only when she offered the fruit, and others say that he was "with her" through the entire conversation with the serpent.

The former of these approaches depends upon the argument, "If Adam was with her the whole time, why didn't he intervene? Therefore, he could not have been 'with her' while she spoke with the serpent, because Adam knew better and would have said something. Clearly he followed her lead innocently." Although this argument makes a great deal of sense, it is an assumption—one that presumes Adam would have: a) done the right thing if he'd been within hearing distance of their conversation (which Paul's words debunked); and b) *not* recognized the fruit in her hand—that which he had walked by every day and noted as the food that would make him "die" if he partook of it. Likewise, Eve is referred to in Paul's epistles as the one who was "deceived," but if Adam had no clue as to what fruit he was about to bite into because his beautiful wife simply showed up with pretty food, then he, too, was "deceived" (tricked, duped) by Eve, as Eve had been by the serpent. The role of the "sinner" Adam is distinct from the role of the "deceived" Adam, thanks to Paul's assessment. The bottom line here is that Adam wasn't deceived at all. He sinned knowingly, which further supports the idea that he had been standing there the entire time.

Additionally, we must answer why the "with her" specification was mentioned by Moses (the author of Genesis) in the first place. If Adam was *only* "with her" while she "gave also unto her husband"—handing

Adam something with her hand in person—then Adam's presence during that exchange is already apparent, and there is no need for Moses to go out of his way to stipulate Adam's attendance in that part of the narrative. The sheer obviousness behind such an apparent calculation cancels out the necessity of mentioning it specifically. No, Moses would have had a reason to write that Adam was with her in this whole ordeal.

Lastly, the biblical account offers no conversation between Adam and Eve. So, if Adam was *not* "with her" while Eve spoke with the serpent, we either have to assume that Moses for some reason omitted what Eve said to tempt Adam when they met up later on, *or* that she walked up silently to Adam and held her hand out toward him, and that he then ate without asking questions (which, again, presumes that Adam would not have recognized the fruit *and* that he would have been duped).

The latter of these two interpretations (that Adam was "with her" during the whole conversation between Eve and the serpent) is the most logical and consistent with other biblical passages, and the Jews living at the time of Christ agreed. Some classical commentaries even document this as fact. From *Gill's Exposition*, we read; "*The Jews* infer from hence, that Adam was with her all the while, and *heard the discourse between the serpent and her*, yet did not interpose nor dissuade his wife from eating the fruit."[93] From *Ellicott's Commentary for English Readers*, we read: "She eats, therefore, and gives to her husband—so called here for the first time—and he eats with her. The demeanour of Adam throughout is extraordinary. It is the woman who is tempted—*not as though Adam was not present, as* [John] *Milton supposes, for she has not to seek him*—but he shares with her at once the gathered fruit. Rather, she is pictured to us as more quick and observant, more open to impressions, more curious and full of longings than the man, whose passive behaviour is as striking as the woman's eagerness and excitability."[94]

The Hebrew text, in its original form, also harmonizes with this interpretation. The word "you" spoken by the serpent to Eve is in plural form: "Though many translations lack the statement, the Hebrew literally says, 'She gave to her husband, who was with her.' Furthermore, the Hebrew text indicates that the serpent is speaking to both the man and the woman, for the plural form of the second person is used. The account infers that Adam and Eve were equally responsible."[95] From yet another source considering the Hebrew: "Something often overlooked is their [Adam and Eve's] apparent unity at the moment of their sin. When the serpent spoke to the woman, he asked, 'Did God really say, You must not...?' In English, you can refer to one or more than one. But Hebrew has two different words; the 'you' used here is plural. Eve also responded in plural, saying, 'We may....' The serpent's next words again used the plural you when he said, 'You will not surely die.' Even though we only hear the words of the serpent and Eve, the text suggests that Adam was standing there, too, a silent accomplice in the crime."[96]

As for the Septuagint translation (the Word at the time of Christ), the message is clear: "And the woman saw that the tree was good for food, and that it was pleasant to the eyes to look upon and beautiful to contemplate, and having taken of its fruit she ate, and *she gave to her husband also with her*, and they ate" (emphasis added). If the Jews believed that Adam was standing with Eve during the serpent's temptation, and if Jesus was Himself a Jew, then in all likeliness He also believed Adam was "with her" while the serpent spoke with her.

A rather unflattering moment in Adam's life occurs once he's been discovered. He blames Eve (and ultimately God) for his transgression instead of owning up to what he had done (Genesis 3:12). In the next verse, Eve also passes the blame, but her target was upon the serpent, not God or Adam.

Both Adam and Eve were guilty of the transgression in the garden. They lived together, walked together, sinned together, hid together, and played the blame game together. Neither of them were ever subordinate or superior to the other. There was full gender equality in the creation order.

And Jesus knew it.

This brings us to Genesis 3:16: "Unto the woman he [God] said, '… thy desire shall be to thy husband, and he shall rule over thee.'" Boy oh boy does the battle rage on with this one. Where do I start…?

First of all, man and woman, by order of God's ideal design, ruled together as one. He built even their physical bodies to intertwine and come together as one. Everything about the creation of humans as we know it from Genesis is formed around an optimum aim—a divine order—that man and woman would be as one, if we are to embrace God's original plan and not the accursed state that Adam and Eve generated in the Garden of Eden. Either of the genders "ruling over" the other wasn't even an issue until after the curse of sin, and it certainly wasn't what God wanted for them. It is here that we must ask the question: "Was God setting a new 'absolute and normative regulation' for all women in all times to be ruled over by their husbands, or was Genesis 3:16 a 'relative' circumstance pertaining to Adam and Eve only?" Let's assume for a moment that God, when He pronounced the curses their sin brought upon them in this vicinity of Scripture, was setting "absolute regulations" that must always be obeyed. Proximate to this "husbands ruling over wives" whammy are the following two accursed realities:

1. Pain for the woman during childbirth (3:16)
2. Pain and struggle for the man in working the soil of the field (3:17–18)

If "husbands ruling over wives" is, in this precise context, an "absolute regulation that must be obeyed at all times," then so, too, are these others within *the same context*, including the second item that now becomes an "absolute" for all men in all times. A woman is in sin if she opts for an epidural or any painkillers to lessen the pain her body is in while she's delivering a baby. A man is in sin if he doesn't a) work the field, and b) find it painful and exerting. Today, nobody has a problem considering the childbirth and field references as "circumstantial to

Adam and Eve" when a woman is getting an injection on the delivery bed or a man wants to pursue a pleasant career in business—but when the same question comes up for husbands ruling over wives, there is a nearly unanimous and resounding oh-no-you-don't reaction when anyone suggests that it's circumstantial. Why is this?

Let's stop and think about what just happened here in Eden…

This marital relationship is now marred for Adam and Eve. There is nothing praiseworthy or admirable about ruining what God made when His original plan was so pure. This is a product of the curse of sin. Is it not completely clear here that man's dominance over woman was the result of sin, and therefore *not* God's original intention for how men and women are supposed to interact?

Should such a superior/inferior relationship status be continuously adhered to as a law given by the same Creator who desired the opposite? Or should such a relationship status be avoided in the interest of returning to what the Creator desired? Which should we be striving toward today? Should we follow God's ideal, divine design? Or should we follow the product of the curse of sin?

Which of these would *Christ* choose?

Actually, we already know the answer to that…

When Jesus taught on the subject of marriage in Matthew 19:4–6, He chose to focus on the relationship that was established *prior* to the Fall when He quoted Genesis 2:24. He could have chosen instead to quote from the post-Fall relationship order (Genesis 3:16), but by realigning His listeners to the pre-Fall relationship, He was placing His own approval on the perfect design established before sin corrupted it. If we are allowing Christ to have the last word on this, then the conclusion is that we should strive to *avoid* the inferior/superior status.

Furthermore, if these childbirth and field curses were introduced to humanity *in general* as a result of sin's entrance into the world (meaning they didn't exist prior and now they're a reality, which is what I, and most Christians, believe)—*yet* the Christian Church at large believes in the humane act of alleviating these torments whenever possible—then it's a double standard to alleviate childbirth and field torments and not a marital relationship torment. The way our modern Church sees it, of these three curses, two are viewed as afflictions to be avoided when possible (taking painkillers, buying better field equipment, getting a different job, etc.), while the third curse on the list (husbands ruling over wives) is viewed as an "absolute" command that should be strictly adhered to.

Why on earth would living under the penalty of a curse be viewed as pleasing God?

Should a woman submit to her husband? Absolutely! The Bible is clear about that in several passages. But the submission is not to be demonstrated by her alone. The divine order is to be mutual submission, each to the other in a peaceful and efficient union. Should a man submit to his wife? Again, absolutely! Even Paul instructed this (1 Corinthians 7:3–5; Ephesians 5:21).

Should either the man or the woman "rule over" the other? Never! It's not what God designed!

God's words to Eve in Genesis should be read as, "Because you did this, you've introduced this issue into the world, and all women will suffer from this day forward because of what you've done; that is shameful." It should *not* be read as, "Because you, Eve, will be ruled over by Adam, all women throughout time should be ruled over by their husbands; I endorse this."

As for why a woman desiring her husband is seen as a curse, this one is simple: The Hebrew text depicts this kind of desire as a longing. A woman *should* long for her Lord more than anything. When sin entered the world, a layer of separation rose like a thick fog between God and humanity, and afterward, both men and women would depend more upon the provision of fellow humans than upon God...and that is most definitely a curse if there ever was one.

As Jesus Christ was reading Scripture in His youth, He would have known as He took in the Messianic promise of Genesis 3:15 (Eve's seed) that *He* was the answer to this problem. The fog can now be lifted on an individual basis through the New Covenant; men and women can once again long for and be fulfilled in a personal relationship with God—and Jesus knew it would happen just as Scripture says. Through such a relationship, men and women *together* can have dominion over the things of this earth. We should strive for a return to the original blessed relationship God made.

Women, you are not cute little "helpers" who bake cookies for the men at your church. Rise up as *ezers*! Be the wise, strong, and powerful *kenegdo* "equals" God created you to be!

Beyond Eve, Christ would have been familiar with the other women who populated the narratives of the Old Testament. We will not look at every one of them, but two that the Lord placed in substantially powerful positions were Deborah and Huldah.

Jesus Knew of Deborah

The story of Deborah can be read in the book of Judges, chapters 4 and 5. The backdrop is an exhausting one. The whole book of Judges documents a circular pattern that goes around and around the same cycle: "The Israelites did what was evil in the eyes of the Lord," followed by the Israelites' repentance and God's mercy, followed by, "The Israelites *again* did what was evil in the eyes of the Lord," and so on. It's a ceaseless "God we're sorry" then "Let's worship other gods and act wickedly" loop. No matter how many times the Israelites traveled around it, they landed back in the same old pattern of unwise decisions. Throughout this cycle, God appoints prophets and judges to act as the mouthpieces of His will:

Nevertheless the Lord raised up judges, which delivered them out of the hand of those that spoiled them. And yet they would not hearken unto their judges, but they went a whoring after other gods, and bowed themselves unto them: they turned quickly out of the way which their fathers walked in, obeying the commandments of the Lord; but they did not so. And when the Lord raised them up judges, then the Lord was with the judge, and delivered them out of the hand of their enemies all the days of the judge: for it repented the Lord because of their groanings by reason of them that oppressed them and vexed them. And it came to pass, when the judge was dead, that they returned, and corrupted themselves more than their fathers, in following other gods to serve them, and to bow down unto them; they ceased not from their own doings, nor from their stubborn way. (Judges 2:16–19)

Judge Othniel's post begins with, "And the children of Israel did evil in the sight of the Lord" (3:7); it ends with, "And the land had rest forty years" (3:11). Judge Ehud's post begins with, "And the children of Israel did evil again in the sight of the Lord" (3:12); it ends with, "And the land had rest fourscore years" (3:30). The next judge, Shamgar, has only one verse mentioning his role—"And after him was Shamgar the son of Anath, which slew of the Philistines six hundred men with an ox goad: and he also delivered Israel" (3:31)—and then we're back to the old drawing board in the next verse with, "And the children of Israel again did evil in the sight of the Lord" (4:1).

For twenty years during this interim, King Jabin of Canaan, with his nine hundred chariots of iron and his military commander, Sisera, oppressed the Israelites with cruelty. They once again cried out for help, and, once again, God raised up a judge over all His people.

This time, the judge was a *woman.*

The Word tells the following story: King Jabin is oppressing the nation of Israel. God calls Judge Deborah into service, and she calls for Barak, an Israelite general, to follow God's command to attack Sisera and his men. Barak tells her that he won't go without her, so she agrees to accompany him—but she warns him that because of his hesitation in following the Lord's command, he would not have honor in the fight, and the final victory blow will be dealt by a woman's hand: "I will surely go with thee: notwithstanding the journey that thou takest shall not be for thine honour; for the Lord shall sell Sisera into the hand of a woman" (4:9). *Together with Deborah*, Barak goes to the battle lines with ten thousand men. At this moment, Barak is either lacking in confidence or waiting for his judge to give the order to fight, because it's not until *after* Deborah tells him to get up and go that he leads the Israelite army against Sisera's men: "And Deborah said unto Barak, 'Up! for this is the day in which the Lord hath delivered Sisera into thine hand: is not the Lord gone out before thee?' So Barak went down from mount Tabor, and ten thousand men after him" (4:14). Sisera proves to be a coward and flees the scene, leaving every last one of his men behind to die by the hands of the Israelites. He arrives at a tent on the plain of Zaanaim and seeks refuge with a woman inside, who then waits until he's asleep to drive a tent peg through his head, bringing the fulfillment of Deborah's prophecy that Sisera would be killed by a woman.

Chapter 5, known as the "Song of Deborah," repeats the same story in poetic form.

I can't begin to tell you how often, while digging through research on the subject of women in Church leadership positions, Judge Deborah is considered only "kind of" a judge. Arguments for this line of thinking state that, unlike the other judges, she "didn't lead any victorious battles" or "bring defeat to any enemy rulers," or that she is irrelevant to the women-as-leaders issue because she "bowed to the command of another" and "didn't speak out in public; she just sat around under a tree." Another popular opinion is that God only chose a woman because "the men weren't doing their jobs," so "a man was not available."

All of these assertions are *wildly* inaccurate, and they strip God's sovereignty out of the picture entirely. Those who marginalize Deborah's role as a judge over God's people can't possibly be doing so because they truly believe she was a lesser judge, because the facts of the story are glaringly clear. Those people are either doing so because they're misinformed or because they're looking for reason to prove that women aren't supposed to rule over or teach men. Deborah, however, did *both* of these things, and she did so with a higher level of excellence and morality than did many of the men who were called before and after her (consider the humiliations of David, the controversial decisions of Samson, and the revolting acts of all the numerous Israelite kings on the "wicked" list).

But whether or not she served her role better than many of the men, it's *crucial* to remember that the holder of the judge's seat was not chosen by human election or lineage. It didn't matter who the *people* liked, and it didn't matter what family you were born into. A judge was chosen by God, and by God alone. He chose Deborah, a woman and prophetess, to judge *His entire nation.* Some say that Deborah is irrelevant to the women-as-church-leaders argument because she wasn't a priest or a preacher. Again, that's humanity's "title" game, not God's. If the God of the Israelites is the same God of Christianity, and He is, then His choice to appoint a female judge over the whole of His people is *extremely* relevant to the argument of women leaders in the Christian Church today. Or are we Christians, God's current nation, going to tell Him He's not allowed to do that?

The Hebrew word for "judge" is *shaphat* (sometimes *shofet*), and it means "to judge, i.e. pronounce sentence (for or against)…to vindicate or punish…to govern…[and to] rule."[97] Earlier in this book, we discussed the role of a prophet or prophetess, which means to give the word of the Lord to the people, and has less to do with law directly. Put more simply, a judge enforced the laws (Mosaic as well as ethical) while the prophet delivered the will of God. Deborah was both judge *and* prophetess! She was the central governing authority—and deliverer of God's bidding—at the same time, over all the children of Israel, including the men.

What a powerful woman God chose to speak in the "Church" of her day!

Scripture tells us: "And she [Deborah] dwelt under the palm tree of Deborah between Ramah and Bethel in mount Ephraim: and the children of Israel came up to her for judgment" (4:5; the tree was named after her). This verse continues to stock the arsenal for biased researchers who say Deborah couldn't have been a true judge because she "didn't speak in public." But if we take something as menial as "she sat under a tree" to mean that she didn't speak in public, we're grasping at straws. There is no evidence anywhere that says Deborah kept her mouth shut at all times unless she was asked to speak while under her tree out in the boondocks. If we read the Bible without a bias, *all* the judges over Israel spoke loud and clear, and Deborah is no exception just because she liked the outdoors.

As for her only being chosen because "men weren't doing their jobs" so "no man was available," that logic, when applied to the fullest extent of its potential meaning, is even worse than the palm-tree argument. First, God had an entire nation to choose from if He wanted to select a man. He also has all the power in the universe if He had wanted to empower a weaker man into service, like He did with Moses. And while we're on the subject of Moses, had God felt that a woman shouldn't speak, He could have chosen Deborah to be judge and positioned a man to do all the speaking for her so that she wouldn't be guilty of "ruling over" male Israelites, but as we all know, that's not what He chose to do. God didn't pick from the "leftovers," and those who say He did are placing unfounded and unscriptural limitations on His supremacy. Second, this argument has backfired and actually has fueled the aggressive and religious "women's-lib" agitators in several recorded debates, because there are those who feel that Church leadership today is failing the lost, so the "men weren't doing their jobs in Deborah's day" claim only leads the more determined women to say that we're facing such a time again, and women need to get loud like Deborah did. (*Under no circumstances* should this be seen as my own counter-argument. I do not, in any way, see linking Deborah to a women's lib movement as appropriate. I'm simply illustrating how quickly this logic fails in the ongoing debate.) But the most glaring error in this assumption is answered in the following questions: "Would God contradict Himself? Would He sin? Would He tell His people that something is wrong and then carry out that act on His own end?" The answer to these questions is an obvious "no." Therefore, if allowing a woman to teach men or have authority over men is scripturally wrong, as so many modern ministers believe, then would God have used Deborah to do this very thing? Again, the answer is "no."

However, before we wholly dismiss any merit in this conclusion, a few parallels are worthy of mention. Roberts Liardon, pastor of Embassy International Church and author of such historically minded works as *On Her Knees* and *The Great Azusa Street Revival*, took a deeper look at what was being said in Judges 5. His conclusion, as shared from a pulpit during a sermon on Deborah, was as follows:

> Throughout biblical and world history, there have always been women who have broken the barrier of cultural [and religious] regulation...and fulfilled a destiny role of leadership that changed the course of nations, and history, and the Church. In this book of Judges, we have one of those great women. Her name is Deborah... She is a very unusual character, because when she first starts coming on the scene, she had no plans to do what she ended up doing.... She was looking for the leaders of Israel to give themselves willingly among the people...and she found that they were all "busy," "distracted," moved [toward other goals] besides the ambition of making Israel a great, productive, and prosperous nation. It sounds a little bit like what we're going through *today* in our world.[98]

Liardon then reads from Deborah's own words in Judges 5:6–9: "In the days of Shamgar the son of Anath, in the days of Jael, the highways were unoccupied, and the travelers walked through byways. The inhabitants of the villages ceased, they ceased in Israel, until that I Deborah arose, that I arose a mother in Israel. They chose new gods; then was war in the gates: was there a shield or spear seen among forty thousand in Israel? My heart is toward the governors of Israel, that offered themselves willingly among the people. Bless ye the Lord." Yes, these issues were in regard to an earthly condition that had spread throughout Israel, but the earthly condition was a symptom of a *spiritual disease*: The people had forsaken their God.

Have we done this today?

Liardon continues: "She describes what the nation of Israel was like when there were no strong leaders. She articulates so well, [that] if she were to live today and look at the Western democracy, she could almost [say] the same thing. She lists about five things here…and because of the vacancy of strong, bold…leaders, [this is] what it was like."[99]

The first thing Deborah speaks of, as Liardon points out, was the highways. People of Israel were so vulnerable under their enemies' oppression that, during travel, they were forced to go from place to place via the obscure side roads. Without a strong leader in Israel, the highways belonged to the enemy. Not only do we have this reality today in a literal sense between warring social factions—and some major US streets are dangerous to travel upon—Liardon makes the link in a figurative sense as well: When the Church is vulnerable in its function because of the enemy's grip upon our spiritual welfare, then the enemy "occupies the highways" and causes the people of God to carry out their ministerial calling through the less-efficient side roads. Young people who are just being called into their positions of leadership don't have a significant understanding of the gifts of the Spirit or the armor of God because they've been kept from the "highways." Their only hope of understanding the fullness of God's providence in ministry is via the outskirt roads appropriately named "human reasoning," "intellect," "talent," or "popularity" instead of "anointing."

The second item on Deborah's list is the decrease in the population of Israel's villages and towns. Liardon links this to the mass exodus of the Church today. Without the blessing and anointing of God upon His people, the Church is simply producing apathetic social clubs. (I spoke on this topic at length in my previous book, *Radicals.*) The lost hear the name of Christ, the Holy Spirit draws them in, they attend a church service for guidance toward an enriching faith life, and they leave shortly thereafter when they discover that "church" is an establishment or institution of routine.

Third, Deborah addresses how the Israelites were choosing new gods. Liardon said of this: "If there's ever been a moment when this seems to be happening again, it is *now* in the Western democracies! The populations of our country seem to tolerate *every* religion but the one that made them great!"[100] When the Israelites inherited the Promised Land, they had everything, including prosperity and the blessing of God upon their every need. Likewise, they had an incredible healthcare plan, because there "was not one sick or feeble among them" (Psalm 105:37). They traded this, as the Word documents, for "whoring after other gods" (Judges 2:17). Today, America has forgotten all we inherited when we were freed from our own pharaoh. We have traded freedom in Christ and the worship that made us great for a revival of pagan religion.

Fourth parallel: Deborah notes that there were wars throughout the land, and the "swords" and "shields" of Israel had all vanished. Today, as Liardon connects, it appears that our radical Christian leaders—those who will stop at nothing to fight for the truth of Christ above all else—have all but vanished. Where are our faith warriors? Where are our soldiers who will dig so deeply into Scripture that they understand the *intent* of the Word instead of memorizing pulpit-zingers for the self-righteous, one-two-punch, verse-dropping attacks of intimidation and control?

The last item on Deborah's list is a praise offering to Yahweh for those leaders who *did* stand up to battle against the condition Israel had found itself in. However, the fact that she conveys this overwhelming gratitude for the minority who responded points to the majority who didn't. The words, "My heart is toward the governors of Israel, that offered themselves willingly among the people" could be reworded contemporarily to say, "My heart goes out to those few Israelites who actually stepped up and did something about the state our people were in." But ultimately, the boldest of these responders can be found in 5:7: "I Deborah arose, that I arose a mother in Israel." Liardon rewords this: "I, Deborah, got up! You can't do something sittin' down!"[101] He goes on to describe her nature: She didn't "arise" like a queen or princess who lives to bedazzle with costly array or exotic dancing, and she didn't "arise" halfway like one who is obedient but stunted by her own lack of confidence. She arose as a *mother!* Liardon's sermon got the highest level of reaction from his audience when he said, "When *mama* gets up, *somethin's gonna happen!* Amen? When *mama* gets up, even Lucifer gets nervous! There's something inside of a *mother* that no matter how tough it is, how big the mountain is, it's going to get conquered!"[102]

Whereas I would never say that Deborah was chosen just because "men weren't doing their jobs" or because "a man wasn't available," the biblical narrative of Deborah shows without a doubt that sometimes, God's people need a *woman* to get things done. It's not a matter of God choosing from the weaker sex because the males were demoralized. God's appointing Deborah was not a last resort. She was precisely the kind of feminine voice that was needed for such a time as this. If God saw fit to bring a *woman* into leadership of all His people, there is every reason to believe He would do it again, and every circumstance, as Liardon preached, is spiritually paralleled in our Western world today.

Where are you, ladies? Don't let the archaic and false interpretations of only *two* sections of Scripture (1 Corinthians 14 and 1 Timothy 2) cancel out the hundreds of others that are calling you to action right at this moment.

Let's get back to our list of reasons some ministers refer to Deborah as only "kind of" a judge… Those who claim that she "bowed to the authority of another"—or that she "obeyed a *man*"—are referring to how she "obeyed" Barak when he "ordered her" to go with him to battle. I offer this answer: She *chose* to go with him; she was not coerced to do so. She was the judge over all Israel, and she was a *woman*. Nobody in his or her right minds in those days would have expected a woman to go to battle, or even go near it. Let's look at Barak's actual "order": "If thou wilt go with me, then I will go: but if thou wilt not go with me, then I will not go" (4:8). This isn't an "order" at all. Surely there is an ultimatum here, but this is not an order. Barak was not commanding her. He was telling her that he needed her for strength. Had she refused him, her refusal would have been acceptable on two grounds: 1) women didn't fight; and 2) as the judge, she was ruler over him. This is not a scene of a meek and gentle woman bowing under the authority of a man, although many ministers today wish to think it was; it's a scene of a woman so confident in the sovereign power of the Almighty God that she harnesses every bold and fearless bone in her body and rages to the enemy lines like a mad hornet shouting, "Get up! The Lord is already out there on the field! The battle is already won!" Only those following a bias to dilute her influence would say that Deborah was subordinate to Barak.

However, for balance, I believe now is a good time to address a popular misconception about Barak's "cowardice." Many derogatory things have been said of Barak. I heard a sermon over the Internet that actually went as far as to say that Barak asked Deborah to go with him because he "needed his mommy in battle" (this sermon was preached by a man, by the way). I personally believe that if Barak had asked a *man* to go with him, comments about his being a sissy or a wimp wouldn't be handed out as easily. Only because he needed a woman is he remembered this way. Consider this: You don't become the commander or general of tens of thousands of men unless you're brave, strong, and have shown trustworthy character. Barak didn't ask Deborah to go because he was a scared puppy hiding behind a skirt. If we take the whole two chapters of Judges in context, it's clear that he asked her to go because he recognized the authority of God within her. God had appointed her as both judge and prophetess. She was the *mouthpiece of God's will.* Who wouldn't want that power at the battle lines? Barak may have lost some of his honor when Sisera fell to a woman because he hesitated in his mission, but he should be remembered not as a coward, but as the strong soldier who felt an extra hedge of protection when the mouthpiece of God was present.

Remember that if you ever preach about Deborah, ladies... If you take your stage and use it to emasculate the men God has called to work alongside you (as equal to you in their calling), you will be guilty of joining the same mud-flinging contest that started this whole thing in the first place, and if you *truly* want the anointing of God on your life, you won't find it by stirring up dirt.

Finally, for those who say Deborah "didn't lead any victorious battles" or "bring defeat to any enemy rulers," I honestly can't even dignify this claim with a lengthy or analytical answer. It's all there in chapter 4 of the book of Judges. These folks can read it for themselves. She absolutely did lead that victory, and it's blatantly clear that it couldn't have happened without her. People who want to argue about whether or not she killed thousands of men are, again, only looking for reasons to downplay her as the judge God appointed her to be.

And the result of her influence as judge over Israel? Forty years of peace...

As a final thought on Deborah: The Israelites were a strictly patriarchal society. The *last* person they would have chosen to be judge was a female. But *God* chose her because He saw a leader within her. Today's Church is largely under the power of a patriarchal order. But *God* will choose women to stand up today and preach the message of the great Messiah, because He sees leaders within the women He calls to serve.

The Deborah *we* know, thanks to generations of biased teaching, is one who sat around under a tree and followed the orders of men. The Deborah

Jesus knew was a fearless trailblazer. Jesus came into this world studying Deborah and, like His Father and the Holy Spirit, He saw *kenegdo* equality in the gifts God gives to the *ezer* women for a Kingdom use.

Jesus Knew of Huldah

While we're on the subject of women who are only seen as "kind of" what they were called to be, I would like to briefly tackle the subject of the prophetess Huldah.

The Word documents the following story, beginning in 2 Kings 22: Josiah becomes king at the age of eight. Following the mentorship of his elders and ancestors, he begins to reform the nation of Israel back toward Yahweh. After he has reigned ten years and has shown to be a righteous king in the eyes of the Lord, Josiah orders the rebuilding of the Temple. During the reconstruction, Hilkiah, the high priest, uncovers the Book of the Law that the Israelites have been without for some time. When the document is brought to the king and read aloud, King Josiah tears his clothes in grief that Israel has not followed the word of God. He sends the Book of the Law, along with his highest officials, to Prophetess Huldah, who verifies its authenticity. She proclaims that devastating judgment will fall upon Judah as a result of their provoking God's anger, but she adds that because Josiah's heart was repentant upon hearing God's word, the judgment will not come within his lifetime, and he will be given the grace to die peacefully. Josiah oversees the completion of the Temple restoration and the sacrifices, and restores the covenant with God as well as the Jewish feasts; meanwhile, he removes all the troublemakers and crushes all the old idols.

Then, suddenly, we read that Josiah dies violently instead of peacefully…

This is the reason that Huldah is remembered as a "kind of" prophetess, because it's easy to simply chalk this up to, "She got it wrong."

Support for this conclusion is found in Deuteronomy 18:22: "When a prophet [or prophetess] speaketh in the name of the Lord, if the thing follow not, nor come to pass, that is the thing which the Lord hath not spoken, but the prophet hath spoken it presumptuously."

If Huldah was a true prophetess, her words would have come true; since they did not come to pass, she must have been a false prophetess. Right?

Unfortunately, this thinking links back to that age-old idea that a prophet or prophetess is merely a "fortuneteller for God," and everything he or she says must come true. As a result, many today write off Huldah as a woman who made a mistake—or worse, as a "false prophetess." But these same folks would not question for a second whether Jonah was a false prophet, even though he, too, "got it wrong" if we hold him to the same standard of logic. Jonah prophesied that the city of Nineveh would be destroyed in forty days, but the book of Jonah documents that the people of the city turned from their wicked ways and God showed them mercy; He did *not* destroy the city as the prophet had said He would (Jonah 3:4, 10). Nor would anyone question that Isaiah was a true prophet, even though he also "got it wrong" when he told King Hezekiah that he was going to die and that he would "not recover" from his illness (Isaiah 38:1, NIV); King Hezekiah repented, the Lord heard his prayers, and he did *not* die as Isaiah had prophesied. In fact, God added fifteen years to Hezekiah's life and even delivered him out of the hands of the Assyrian king (Isaiah 38:5–6).

The outcome of a prophecy is contingent upon the God-fearing response of its recipient. That has always been the case, and it can be proven repeatedly throughout Scripture. Just as we are reading about Josiah's non-peaceful death in 2 Kings 23:28–30, we stumble upon this redirect: "Now the rest of the acts of Josiah, and all that he did, are they not written in the book of the chronicles of the kings of Judah?" The author of 2 Kings gave us a clue as to where to find the explanation behind Josiah's death. Turning to 2 Chronicles 35:20–21, we read:

"After all this, when Josiah had prepared the temple, Necho king of Egypt came up to fight against Charchemish by Euphrates: and Josiah went out against him. But he sent ambassadors to him, saying, 'What have I to do with thee, thou king of Judah? I come not against thee this day, but against the house wherewith I have war: for God commanded me to make haste: forbear thee from meddling with God, who is with me, that he destroy thee not.'"

So far, we see that King Necho of Egypt has been sent *by God* to fight against Charchemish. Josiah takes it upon himself to clash with King Necho, so Necho sends out ambassadors to deliver the following message (in my own modern rewording): "King Josiah, my issue is not with you. What do you have to do with my war? I'm not even bothering you. God has sent me to fight against Charchemish, and quickly. Don't get in the way and meddle with God's affairs. God is on *my* side in this, and He doesn't want to destroy you. However, if you get in the middle of this—if you meddle with the affairs of God—He *will* destroy you! I'm warning you now to back off…"

After being given a warning by God through King Necho, we read of Josiah's response in the following verses, 2 Chronicles 35:22–27 (emphasis added):

> Nevertheless Josiah would not turn his face from him [Josiah deliberately disobeyed God's order not to meddle], but disguised himself, that he might fight with him [he snuck in and did it anyway], and hearkened not unto the words of Necho *from the mouth of God*, and came to fight in the valley of Megiddo.
>
> And the archers shot at king Josiah; and the king said to his servants, "Have me away; for I am sore wounded." His servants therefore took him out of that chariot, and put him in the second chariot that he had; and they brought him to Jerusalem, and he died [he was destroyed just as King Necho warned], and was buried in one of the sepulchres of his fathers.

And all Judah and Jerusalem mourned for Josiah. And Jeremiah lamented for Josiah: and all the singing men and the singing women spake of Josiah in their lamentations to this day, and made them an ordinance in Israel: and, behold, they are written in the lamentations.

Now the rest of the acts of Josiah, and his goodness, according to that which was written in the law of the Lord, And his deeds, first and last, behold, they are written in the book of the kings of Israel and Judah.

Josiah certainly *would have* been given the peaceful death he was promised, but he chose to go against God. The first word of God, as given through the mouth of Huldah, said he would live and die peacefully. The second word of God, as given through the Lord's servant Necho, said he would be destroyed if he stood in Necho's way. It could be, perhaps, that Josiah was so confident in the words of Huldah that he thought he was invincible when he disguised himself and went out on the field against Necho. It could be that he didn't care and was driven by pride or rage, or who knows what else… But the fact remains: The Lord told Josiah he would be killed if he meddled in God's affairs, and then Josiah meddled in God's affairs, so he was killed.

Was Huldah wrong? If we consider a prophet to be a fortuneteller for God, then, yes, she was. If we consider a prophet to be one who delivers the wisdom, word, and will of God (which is what a prophet truly is), then no, she wasn't wrong by any stretch. God had the will to see Josiah to a peaceful end, and He even cared enough to send Josiah a message that he could avoid his own painful death if he remained neutral to the Charchemish/Necho feud. It is nowhere close to Huldah's fault that Josiah brought on his own death by disobeying God's final warning.

To some today, Huldah was a "false prophetess" because she "got it wrong." These readers don't consider how Josiah threw himself into the target zone of God's war, because they get to the sudden death of Josiah in 2 Kings and don't flip over to the rest of the details in 2 Chronicles.

But to *Jesus*, Huldah was to be revered as the one who authenticated the Book of the Law and confirmed to all of Judah that God's Word was once again with them. Through her validation of the Book found amidst the rubble of the Temple reconstruction, all of Judah could, for a season, be properly restored to glory.

Other prominent women throughout the Old Testament, such as Miriam (sister of Aaron and Moses), Isaiah's wife, Ruth, Naomi, and others, had bold and womanly voices that made a paramount stamp on the biblical role of women throughout time. However, I have centered the focus up to now only upon women who have been misunderstood, and whose names have been dragged through the "women as church leaders" debate with erroneous understanding. Let us now turn to the women Jesus knew in the New Testament, starting with His mother. For centuries, Mary has been remembered as meek, mild, quiet, gentle, and saintly. However, the Mary *Jesus* knew was far different.

Jesus Knew Mary

Christ was raised by a very powerful and bold woman. Joseph is no longer mentioned by the time Christ reaches His ministry years, as the last time we hear of him is when Jesus, age twelve, is conversing with the holy men in the Temple of Jerusalem. When Christ was on the cross, He charged Apostle John to care for His mother, which He wouldn't have done had Joseph still been alive. Jewish custom during the era of Roman crucifixion was for fathers to be responsible for the bodies of the victims, but in the case of Christ, the duty to care for His remains fell to another: Joseph of Arimathea. Additionally, whenever the Gospels refer to Jesus' living family (Matthew 12:46; Mark 3:31; Luke 8:19; John 7:3), Christ's siblings and mother are mentioned, but Joseph is not. As discussed earlier in the reflection on Priscilla and Aquila, a man was always the first to be mentioned both in person as well as in classic literature of this era, so the fact that Joseph is missing from the text here relates that he is likewise gone from the narrative by this point. Thus, we know that Jesus had an influential earthly father figure during His earliest developmental years, but somewhere between the ages of twelve and approximately thirty, Joseph died, leaving Mary a widow to care for her children alone. We may never know how old Christ was when His adopted/legal father died, or what other influential male presence may have stepped in upon Joseph's death to assist Mary with her children, but we can safely assume that, at some point after Joseph's earthly departure, Christ was gently guided by the maternal instincts of a woman.

We know for certain that Christ obeyed and honored His mother. If He hadn't, He would have been found guilty of sin by disobeying the fifth commandment, which, from His own mouth, was a commandment that must be followed (Matthew 15:4; Mark 7:10). Indeed, He was without sin (Hebrews 4:15), so we know He honored His mother and listened to her counsel.

As to why Mary should be considered powerful or bold as opposed to the "meek" or "mild" woman that pops into our mental imagery today, let's imagine what she faced in her early years. Who was she as a girl? How did she feel about Gabriel's task? What were her thoughts prior to such the drastic shift in her life's responsibilities the angel's message revealed?

Picture this possible scenario…

A young, innocent Jewish girl is carrying out her daily chores and helping her household in a way any girl would in those days (washing, cooking, etc.) when her father pulls her aside to tell her the news: "Mary, you are now engaged to be married to Joseph, the carpenter." Obediently, she accepts the contract of her engagement and returns to her work, but as soon as she is once again alone, she raises her hand over her mouth in disbelief. She has always known this moment would come, but now that it's upon her, it feels all too surreal.

In the following days, her mind is reeling with thoughts of her future. Soon, she will no longer be just a little girl; she will be a woman, in every sense of the word. Her husband will take her hand and lead her into a new role as a mother.

Everything she ever knew her life to be is about to change.

As she is walking through town on an errand, her eyes flicker over to the carpentry shop in hopes of catching a glimpse of her betrothed at work. She rounds the corner of the building and sees him hammering away on a table. He stands to wipe the sweat from his brow, and from his peripheral vision, her robe catches his eye. He straightens his posture and nods a warm greeting to her. Her eyes momentarily linger on his muscular hands and forearms as she feels nervous butterflies swarming about her stomach. Nodding back, she timidly turns her focus to the road in front of her, unable to hide the colorful evidence of the heat that has landed in her cheeks. It's the blush of a chaste girl who has never known a man, and soon she will be his. They will stand together in the assembly of witnesses and vow to carry out their devotion to one another for the rest of their lives, and then he will take her unto him upon the marital bed, and she will carry his child.

Shortly thereafter, she is going about her business when suddenly she hears the voice of Gabriel, the archangel of Yahweh. His greeting is immediate and intense: "Hail, thou that art highly favoured, the Lord is with thee: blessed art thou among women" (Luke 1:28). As soon as she spots her otherworldly visitor, she becomes terrified and her head starts to swim in wonder at the implications of what this messenger is about to reveal (1:29). Gabriel, aware of the young girl's panic, continues: "Fear not, Mary: for thou hast found favour with God. And, behold, thou shalt conceive in thy womb, and bring forth a son, and shalt call his name Jesus. He shall be great, and shall be called the Son of the Highest: and the Lord God shall give unto him the throne of his father David:

And he shall reign over the house of Jacob for ever; and of his kingdom there shall be no end" (1:30–33). The frightened Mary finds her voice long enough to ask how this will be possible, since she has not lain with a man. Gabriel explains, "The Holy Ghost shall come upon thee, and the power of the Highest shall overshadow thee: therefore also that holy thing which shall be born of thee shall be called the Son of God" (1:35).

The Son of God!? The one and only Son of Yahweh!?

What a moment in history!

No human alive could imagine the explosion of responsibility…

If we let the weight of what just occurred in Mary's life settle within our thoughts, the bravery and boldness of this young woman at this moment in time is extraordinary, if not unfathomable. In an instant, Mary transforms from a scared little girl to a spiritual warrior with a determination that would make Joan of Arc pale in comparison. She responds with tenacious heroism: "Behold the handmaid of the Lord; be it unto me according to thy word" (1:38).

Christians have read and celebrated this narrative for so long in a culture that paints her as a quiet, gentle, and mild-mannered saint that the authority Mary shows in her words here has been traded for the image of a woman bowing her head in docile servitude. Yes, servitude was an enormous part of the big picture regarding Mary, absolutely. By accepting such an inconceivable task as carrying the Son of God into the world in a day and age when a premarital pregnancy would have likely resulted in the death penalty by stoning or, at the very least, banishment from her family and the rest of her people, Mary was no doubt an illustrious servant—first and foremost. Everything stable in her life was now at risk, and she accepted the mission of the Lord despite that. However, it is *because of* such factors, as well as the obedience and humility in her response, that we can catch a glimpse of the warrior within. Her submission to the messenger of God does not relate weakness, but *tenacity!* She had every reason to be afraid of the earthly, societal repercussions of being pregnant before marriage—thousands of unimaginably awful hardships undoubtedly lay ahead of her—but she didn't waver for an instant. This is not to say that she didn't feel fear, as Luke 1:29 states that she did. But it is to say that she did not allow the fear to rule her. She immediately cast away all concepts of leading a normal life and did the bravest, most warrior-like thing any human in her position could have done: She submitted herself to being the mother of the most important Man this world has ever known, and she did so without any experience whatsoever. She didn't just agree with Gabriel's decree, she *owned* her role bravely despite all human reasoning.

Had she been selfish, she might have said, "But wait! What about my betrothed? What about the people in town? What about my parents? Everyone will think I am tainted by indiscretion! I will be killed, or made to leave my people and wander the world alone. I am chaste. This is not a fair thing to ask of me!" Had she lacked confidence, she might have said, "Surely not I, messenger. I am a girl of humble means. Joseph is only a carpenter. I cannot give the King of kings a full life. I have never raised a child, and I cannot possibly know how to guide this Child, the Son of God." Had she allowed any one normal, human emotion to lead her response, she would have revealed that she was still only a child—perhaps more befitting of the modern ideas we have of the "meek and mild" Mary. Instead, she said, "Behold the handmaid of the Lord; be it unto me according to thy word." It's as if she downloaded ten lifetimes' worth of maturity in a matter of seconds.

What bravery! What valor!…

What *leadership*!

We all know what happened next, but rarely do we pause and reflect upon the enormity of it.

When Joseph discovers she is pregnant, he plans to discreetly divorce her, believing that she has given herself to the temptation of promiscuity, but he is halted by an angel in a dream who tells him that Mary has, in fact, been impregnated by the power of God. The angel instructs Joseph to support her, and the carpenter obeys (Matthew 1:19–25).

Don't miss this: God chose a *woman* for a very important role, and He commanded a *man* to support her in that role. One might argue, "Of course He chose a woman. Only females can bear children." Whereas that argument is true within our finite comprehension of the human body's capabilities, it limits God—the Creator of the universe—to say that there was no other way. Consider what God did *not* choose as the method to bring Christ into the world. He didn't use the "blessed" or "undefiled" sperm of a man, no sudden "poof" appearance of a baby in a manger, no glowing fusion of flesh particles in the air hovering above a fully-clothed Mary as she symbolically experienced birth pains, no lightning-bolt delivery, no angel-holding-a-baby visitations, nor any stork with a cotton bundle-bag. The Almighty *could have* chosen from billions of delivery options, but when that precious Savior arrived, it was through the body of a simple, innocent girl who, in seconds, became a dynamic woman of brute-force tenacity in the face of all odds—and she followed through with her task alongside a man whom God sent to *help her.*

And Jesus, as I said previously, obeyed her. Reflect upon that for a moment. Jesus—God, *Himself*—respected the counsel, as well as the *authority,* of a woman… The very Deity our entire belief system is built upon acknowledged the leadership qualities of a female. Again, if God the Father could have chosen from limitless alternative ways to bring Jesus into the world, He could have likewise placed Jesus in a position where He wouldn't be "under the authority of a female." We could have been left with a narrative describing Jesus appearing outside the temple and being raised only by nurturing holy men, or this story could have taken any number of other directions, just to ensure that God in the flesh was never "obeying a woman." Yet, Scripture tells us plainly that Mary was always a part of Jesus' life, and He *always* obeyed her and respected her parental headship.

And the list grows even longer regarding Mary's womanly strength. Once the Son of God was born to her, Mary left home with her new husband and traveled more than two hundred miles within the first few years—Nazareth to Bethlehem, seventy miles; Bethlehem to Jerusalem round-trip, twelve miles; Bethlehem to Egypt, more than forty miles; and Egypt to Nazareth, one hundred-plus miles—all without the modern conveniences of a vehicle or paved roads. Far from any concept of a home-body female plucking chickens near a stove and squeezing fresh fig juice, Mary was a voyager. A journeywoman! She fearlessly packed up the family's mule and carried their belongings—as well as her infant (and later toddler)—from place to place as the Lord directed, regardless of potentially harsh weather conditions, dangers of the road, marauders by nightfall, or any other concerns that might have made another woman long for baking bread and sweeping the floor. It's likely that Mary knew how to tie sailor's knots, build fires, assemble a tent, and locate nearby food and water sources. What a resourceful woman she must have been.

But the greatest challenge was ahead of her, and it was one she met with equal grit and determination.

When the Christ child grew up and Joseph was gone, Mary willingly went to the foot of the cross and revealed a whole new level of bold heroism as she watched her boy bleed to death slowly and painfully. Her little boy… Her little *Yeshua.* The babe who had moved inside her belly. The babe whose knee boo-boos she had kissed and whose smile she would only ever see in memory until her journey through the Paradise Gate. The boy whose knowledge of Scripture was so impressive that He held His own amidst the intellects in the Temple. How proud she must have been of Him, the sweet and loving Messiah…and how unwaveringly fearless she was to remain by His side while He suffered.

Mary was as much a servant as any human could possibly be, but she was more than that. Far more. Mary was a dauntless, unflinching *fortress* of strength.

This was the woman who raised Jesus Christ, and her example teaches much for those women who have been called by the Holy Spirit to preach the Word of God.

Jesus (Likely) Knew of Anna

There are only three verses about the prophetess Anna: "And there was one Anna, a prophetess, the daughter of Phanuel, of the tribe of Aser: she was of a great age, and had lived with an husband seven years from her virginity; And she was a widow of about fourscore and four years, which departed not from the temple, but served God with fastings and prayers night and day. And she coming in that instant gave thanks likewise unto the Lord, and spake of him to all them that looked for redemption in Jerusalem" (Luke 2:36–38).

Here we have a woman who was only married for seven years before her husband died, and she remained a widow for the rest of her life. We meet up with her at the age of eighty-four as she spends every moment of her life ("night and day") at the Temple of Jerusalem. Baby Jesus is brought to the Temple to be presented to the Lord, and a man named Simeon instantly recognizes the child as the Messiah. He gives his glorious blessing over the Holy Family, and then Anna enters the scene. She, too, immediately recognizes the Messiah and gives thanks to the Lord that the day of salvation has finally arrived.

It wasn't uncommon that a reputable prophet or prophetess of the Lord would be given living quarters within the Temple. (A similar situation was set up for Huldah [2 Chronicles 34:22].) As Anna was a prophetess in Jerusalem, we can likely take the words "departed not from the temple" in a literal way, understanding that the Temple was probably her home. Like any other Jew of her generation and locality, Anna was waiting daily in anticipation for the promised Messiah to arrive. When He did, Anna tells everyone she meets, "all them…in Jerusalem," that the Savior has arrived, and that anyone who wants to be saved can be through belief in the blessed Babe.

The Good News of Christ is meant to be shared, and Anna was not silent. In fact, she was one of the first to hit the information highways of her day and make sure that every soul she came into contact with who was "looking for redemption" had the answers he or she sought. The Word does not say that Jesus knew Anna personally in His youth, but it is probable that Mary and Joseph would have told Him about their trip to the Temple—and about the man and woman they met on that day who took one look at Him and knew precisely who He was.

One of the very earliest ministers of the Good News—just after the birth of the Savior—was a *woman*.

We may never know whether Jesus knew of Anna or conversed with her in His early years, but many souls in Jerusalem had her to thank for the acknowledgment of His arrival.

In His later years, however, He personally commissioned women to go and tell others about Him. It is to that supreme authority that we will now turn.

6

The Women Jesus *Sent*

Although there were exceptions to the rules regarding how women were treated in ancient times (especially in pagan cultures such as Ephesus and Corinth), women were frequently viewed as second-rate citizens. Their role in society—unless they were willing to exploit their sexuality and use seductive measures to socially overpower men in certain cultures—was unfortunate.

Treatment of Women in Christ's Day

Despite the fact that the Old Testament is clear on how and why women were created to be the powerful *ezer* alongside man, patriarchal hierarchy within both the public and home settings proved to change how women were to be valued. They were given very few rights, and the closer one got to Jewish traditions and customs, the more women were, by the time of the New Testament era, reduced to the rank of lesser sex. Equality, *within Judeo-Christian context*, was not to be found from any aspect, and this kind of social arrangement influenced the imprinting of the woman's role from thousands of years before Christ and onward.

Old Testament laws regarding women were set to protect the female gender, not to harm them or place them in uncomfortable positions. Just as one example, take Deuteronomy 24:1–2: "When a man hath taken a wife, and married her, and it come to pass that she find no favour in his eyes, because he hath found some uncleanness in her: then let him write her a bill of divorcement, and give it in her hand, and send her out of his house. And when she is departed out of his house, she may go and be another man's wife." This directive is for when the woman has committed some act that has made her "unclean" to her husband. It's not a matter of her being uncomely, old, barren, or any other factor she can't help or change. And even if she makes herself unclean, she is still eligible for remarriage. The law certainly protects the man from being unequally yoked, but the fact that the woman—despite being seen as "unclean"—can be married again actually shows the grace and provision that God is extending to the female population of His people. This law was never meant to be abused, but by the time of Christ, women were handed divorce papers for nearly any reason whatever. A man could grow weary of his dinner being five minutes late, the floor being too dirty in one corner, or his wife's looks and claim that "she [found] no favour in his eyes," and the marriage would be ended. The man was then free to take a younger, prettier bride and the woman was left hoping some kinsman redeemer would care for her. Marriage was viewed for centuries among the Hebrews as a business contract, the woman being property of the man: an object to own, not a person to be loved or valued.

A woman, on the other hand, *could not* divorce a man, and since men were behind the marital arrangements, women frequently found themselves bound to an unkind or disinterested husband and were trapped in that position until the man grew tired of the relationship and replaced her. This was not by any means how the original law was supposed to be implemented, and it was not how God designed relationships to be, but it was how the law eventually came to be abused. What began as an official law about how a woman was allowed to remarry and thus be cared for by another man became a law about how men could discard an inconvenient piece of property because ancient interpreters allowed their own "today's culture" to produce the final interpretation of Scripture. (Some things never change within the realm of human nature...)

This scenario painted above was a harsh reality, but it should not be assumed that every man in the ancient world treated women poorly. Some women were held in high honor within the household as businesswomen and patronesses, and *some* even within the synagogue! In fact, Bernadette Brooten has uncovered nineteen inscriptions within the remains of ancient synagogues that prove women were priests and elders even in places of Jewish worship. One of these inscriptions assigns a woman as "ruler of the synagogue," and another assigns "mother of the synagogue."[103] Ross Kraemer, professor of religious studies at Brown University, adds six epitaphs to this list proving women as religious elders and officers of the day.[104] One woman, Beruriah, was so profoundly respected as a correct scriptural interpreter that she is mentioned several times in the Talmud. So we have proof that women weren't always in abusive or subordinate positions within Jewish society, but we have far more proof in existence that they were tossed away like old trash whenever a man wanted a change of pace—and that the overall cultural attitude toward women was overwhelmingly negative. And this situation was exacerbated by the time we reach the New Testament.

The Old Testament documents a time when the Northern Kingdom of Israel was overthrown by Assyria and the Southern Kingdom (Judea) fell to Babylon. The Israelites were exiled from their land, and during the Intertestamental Period (the span of years between the last events recorded in the final book of the Old Testament and the first events recorded in the first book of the New Testament), only a small portion of them returned. So by the time of Christ, the Jews were no longer in supreme control as they lived under the influences of Greco-Roman cultures. As the Jews lived among these peoples, eventually their original religion, Yahwism, became a legalistic and cold religion, Judaism. The Judaic oral traditions bypassed the laws until the "Word of Yahweh" became the "word of Pharisees/Sadducees." Although the Pharisees and Sadducees have been given a terrible rap because of how Christ continuously denounced them (even going as far as to call them snakes and vipers), their intention was *initially* honorable. When Alexander the Great's prized Hellenism slowly began to infiltrate and replace Yahweh's divine orders with Greek philosophy, mythology, and pagan rituals, a stricter adherence to the Mosaic Law was a necessity. Pharisees and Sadducees reacted to the secularization by implementing new laws on top of the old ones, and over time, these became biasedly patriarchal and extremely exclusive of women. This warped revision of God's intent and design again polarized women as baby-makers and bread-bakers among men, so when Christ entered the scene, women were frequently kept indoors and required to remain silent on social or political issues. Some Jews were hard on women because of the Pharisaic traditions, and others were equally hard on women because of the influence of Greco-Roman culture, so women were faced with oppressive circumstances from both inside and outside the social norms of their own people groups.

Rome was an aggressive influence, paving its ways of life through violence, war, and brute force. Greece, on the other hand, though it had its time of conquering the world via Alexander the Great's leadership, had a greater longevity and wider spread in its influence over the ancient world due to the fact that the Greek ways of life were made via philosophy and intellect. The views the Greeks held about women in Greco-Roman times were largely that women, unless born into rich families who could afford to educate them (such as many of those in Ephesus), were inferior to men. Socrates, Plato, Aristotle, and hundreds of other Greek philosophers recorded such a view in their writing. If a mother delivered a female baby, it wasn't uncommon that the baby would either be abandoned on the ground outside the home where it would perish, or given away as a future slave or prostitute. Women weren't a~~llowed to~~ hold any kind of leadership positions in most mainstream religions, but as prostitutes in pagan cults, they thrived as oracles, diviners, mediums, and conduits of the gods. Roman culture was similar (unless the woman belonged to a noble or wealthy family), and many wives weren't out of their teens before they were joined to a forty-something year-old man and expected to have a baby every two years.

By the time we arrive at AD 550, it is clear by the writings of the Talmud that women were disproportionately subservient and inferior to men in every aspect. Let's look at a few examples from Jewish writings and sayings of the time.

Although Leviticus 15 discusses the cleanliness of both genders, the Talmud almost doesn't address the topic of men's uncleanness at all, though it devotes ten whole chapters to the subject of women's uncleanness, suggesting that men are generally cleaner than women. Many Mishnah writings openly revile the idea that a woman would be allowed to know the Law; in fact, it was seen as such a corrupt notion that the Jews would have rather burned their sacred writings than to allow a woman to be taught from them: "Rather should the words of the Torah be burned than entrusted to a woman" (Mishnah Sotah 3).[105] One writing even goes as far as to say a woman shouldn't hardly be spoken to under any circumstances, lest the man who converses with her be punished for it eternally: "Who speaks much with a woman draws down misfortune on himself, neglects the words of the law, and finally earns hell" (Mishnah Avot 1:5). A woman wasn't even allowed to pray in some circumstances: "Let a curse come upon the man who [allows] his wife or children say grace for him" (Talmud bBerakhoth 20b), and even the birth of a baby girl was supposed to be seen as a mournful event: "At the birth of a boy all are joyful, but at the birth of a girl all are sad; When a boy comes into the world, peace comes into the world; when a girl comes, nothing comes" (Talmud bNiddah 31). No woman could celebrate her virtue amidst Jewish men, for "even the most virtuous of women is a witch" (Mishnah Terum 15). And some writings and sayings at the time were so derogatory against women that it's hard to believe men claiming to belong to Yahweh would have ever uttered them, such as: "A woman is a pitcher of filth with its mouth full of blood, yet all run after her" (Talmud bShabbath 152a).

These postbiblical sayings, writings, and oral laws were so effectively implemented amidst the Jews that: "In the daily prayers prescribed for Jewish males there [was] a threefold thanksgiving which graphically illustrated where women stood in Rabbinic Judaism: 'Praised be God that he has not created me a gentile; praised be God that he has not created me a woman; praised be God that he has not created me an ignorant man'" (Tosephta Berakhoth 7, 8).[106] And this prayer is not simply the product of one misogynist Jew, as it is repeated in two other central rabbinic collections (Talmud pBerakhoth 13b and Talmud bMenakhoth 43b).

The Jewish men *daily* praised God for not making them a woman!

Some of the traditional beliefs were not just "add-to" laws birthed from the concern of Hellenism, but were completely invented imaginings of Judaizers—such as the idea that because Adam was the first lifeblood of humanity and Eve was the reason he fell, the curse of monthly menstruation blood was now upon women (Talmud pShabbath 2, 5b, 34). (Many statements in this section can be traced back to Ben Sira, circa 180 BC, author of the apocryphal *Ecclesiasticus*, who likely played a crucial role in influencing the Pharisees and Sadducees. It is from this document that we read: "Any iniquity is small compared to a woman's iniquity; may a sinner's lot befall her!" [*Ecclesiasticus* 25:19]. In other words, any man's sin, no matter how bad, is insignificant when compared to any woman's sin, no matter how small.)

These are only a few examples of how women were viewed in Jewish circles closer to the time of Christ. They rarely left home, they weren't allowed to be educated, and they weren't considered in any numbering when men were present, such as in the congregations of the synagogues or even in the Gospel account of the crowds who were fed by the loaves and fish: "And they that had eaten were about five thousand men, beside women and children" (Matthew 14:21).

But then, along came Jesus…the Radical of radicals who challenged these cultural and societal norms, honoring women privately and publicly, even when doing so guaranteed controversy.

How Christ Interacted with Women

In Luke 7:36–50, we run across this beautiful narrative:

And one of the Pharisees desired him that he would eat with him. And he went into the Pharisee's house, and sat down to meat. And, behold, a woman in the city, which was a sinner, when she knew that Jesus sat at meat in the Pharisee's house, brought an alabaster box of ointment, And stood at his feet behind him weeping, and began to wash his feet with tears, and did wipe them with the hairs of her head, and kissed his feet, and anointed them with the ointment. Now when the Pharisee which had bidden him saw it, he spake within himself, saying, "This man, if he were a prophet, would have known who and what manner of woman this is that toucheth him: for she is a sinner."

And Jesus answering said unto him, "Simon, I have somewhat to say unto thee."

And he saith, "Master, say on."

"There was a certain creditor which had two debtors: the one owed five hundred pence, and the other fifty. And when they had nothing to pay, he frankly forgave them both. Tell me therefore, which of them will love him most?"

Simon answered and said, "I suppose that he, to whom he forgave most."

And he said unto him, "Thou hast rightly judged." And he turned to the woman, and said unto Simon, "Seest thou this woman? I entered into thine house, thou gavest me no water for my feet: but she hath washed my feet with tears, and wiped them with the hairs of her head. Thou gavest me no kiss: but this woman since the time I came in hath not ceased to kiss my feet. My head with oil thou didst not anoint: but this woman hath anointed my feet with ointment. Wherefore I say unto thee, Her sins, which are many, are forgiven; for she loved much: but to whom little is forgiven, the same loveth little." And [Jesus continued] unto her, "Thy sins are forgiven."

And they that sat at meat with him began to say within themselves, "Who is this that forgiveth sins also?"

And [Jesus] said to the woman, "Thy faith hath saved thee; go in peace."

Students of the Bible admire Jesus' boldness when the woman caught in the act of adultery was brought before Christ (John 8:2–11). It is perhaps the second most controversial moment in His ministry involving women, just behind the woman at the well (which we will address later in this chapter). Again, the holy men attempted to trap Jesus in a public challenge. If Christ agreed to allow this woman to be stoned, He couldn't be the loving rabbi He had painted Himself to be. If He opposed her stoning, He would be guilty of marginalizing the Jewish Law that elsewhere He claimed to fulfill to the letter. It was a lose-lose trap set by the same holy men that would go on to produce such dogmas about women as those found in the Mishnah. This woman was an adulteress.

Honor meant everything at the time of Christ. Seminary professor of New Testament and Greek studies, David deSilva, wrote the amazing book, *Honor, Patronage, Kinship, & Purity: Unlocking New Testament Culture.* This book stands alone as one of the most well-researched resources I have read regarding what the world was like in the days of the early Church, but it also happens to be used as a textbook for many religious universities. DeSilva begins his first chapter with the statement: "The culture of the first-century world was built on the foundational social values of honor and dishonor."[107] He goes on to say: "Honor…is viewed as the first and foremost consideration.… [W]hile honor with pleasure was a great good, pleasure without honor was the worst evil. Those who put pleasure ahead of honor were considered to be more animal-like than human.… In the first century B.C. a teacher of public speakers held up honor and security as the two primary considerations when trying to win an audience over to support the course of action the speaker promoted…[and] successful orators were the ones who could demonstrate that the course of action they advocated led to the greatest honor."[108]

Again, honor meant *everything* to the people groups of the New Testament culture, and one of the biggest slams on honor fathomable was a woman who desecrated her own body in pursuit of the most illicit of worldly pleasures whilst potentially wrecking the marriage of another man! To the Pharisees who stood there holding stones, it didn't appear to matter where the *man* was who held equal shame in the act of adultery. The woman would have been seen as the seductress, the home-wrecker, and the man would have been viewed as the victim of her wily desires, regardless of whether it had been the man who initiated the immoral rendezvous (which we have no way of knowing). Mosaic Law, culture, social standards, ethics, politics, the constant striving toward purity—all of these standards would have justified Christ's approval of this woman's death. He could have easily shown love repeatedly throughout His ministry and in this one moment made an exception. It certainly would have made the Pharisees happy… Instead, however, He met their challenge with another: "He that is without sin among you, let him first cast a stone at her" (John 8:7).

What an unbelievable response! We skim straight past it today, but when I close my eyes and imagine this moment in history, I can almost hear the murmuring of the crowd; I can see the quick exchange of desperate glances; I can appreciate the blast of Christ's words as they settled in the stomachs of the bloodthirsty crowd while hands released stones to the ground and sandaled feet meandered away in defeat.

They—the crowd—saw a harlot. A dog. A "pitcher of filth" whose blood on the temple floor would have hardly been worth cleaning up after.

Christ saw a *person*. He took *her* side over the leaders of the "Church" of that day.

And it was a radical move that changed history forever.

Those who oppose women being leaders in the Body of Christ frequently ask the following: "If Christ was all for women, then why didn't He choose a woman to be among His disciples?" In conversations I've witnessed in person wherein the recipients haven't done their research, the question falls in the air as a final-word stamp, for who can argue with such a statement? However, in response, I ask a question of my own: Why do so many people think there *weren't* women disciples? Haven't they read the Word? Don't they see all the verses that straightforwardly list women as disciples (for example, Luke 8:1–3, 10:38–42; Mark 15:40–42)?

Jesus taught His ways to both men and women. Our English word "disciple" comes from the Latin *discipulus*, "pupil, learner, student, follower." Prior to that, the word was from the Greek *mathetes*: "pupil, apprentice to master craftsman, student, learner." Our current understanding of the word "disciple" is that it was a title given to the twelve men who followed Christ in His ministry travels and who later became the Twelve Apostles. This is an errant understanding of the original Greek that would have applied to anyone, male or female, who learned from Christ in person (or, as it applies today, those who followed His teachings after His earthly departure). In His day, women weren't allowed in the inner court of Israel at the temple, so what did Christ do? He took his teaching to the women's court![109] He didn't just "allow them" to learn from Him if they happened to be standing around; He specifically sought them out and *went to* them to ensure that they were included in His teaching—despite that His contemporaries believed teaching a woman the Law or anything religious was like training them in the ways of "lechery" (Mishnah Sotah 3:4), or that speaking "much" with a woman would cause a man to "earn hell" (Mishnah Avot 1:5)! (These writings are postbiblical, but they represent the mentality of the Palestinian social customs that existed in Christ's day.) We cannot board a time machine and experience in person how intensely the holy men of this era reviled the idea of engaging women in conversation, *especially* as that related to theological discourse, but Jesus did so regularly, and even when such women were despised (Matthew 9:18–26; Luke 10:38–42; John 4:7, 27).

Jesus included women and men equally in His deliverance, healing, and miracles (Matthew 8:14–15, 9:18–26, 15:21–28; Mark 5:25–34; Luke 13:10–17, 8:40–56), and even defied social and cultural mores when He touched not only a woman, but a woman's *corpse* to raise her from the dead (Mark 5:41). Women were "unclean" during their menstrual cycle or during postpartum bleeding, and the Law said that anyone who touched them during those times would also be unclean. But when the woman who had been bleeding for twelve straight years reached out and touched Christ's clothing (considered at that time to still be "contact"), the taboo issue of blood wasn't even mentioned. Instead, Christ said "thy faith hath made thee whole; go in peace" (Luke 8:43–48). He frequently told women to "go in peace." He cared about the peacefulness within a woman's soul. Instead of praising the men for the heaps of money they were donating to the temple's treasury, to His disciples He commended the one poor woman who only contributed two coins because it was all she had (Mark 12:41–44). Whereas the men around Jesus treated women as marginal or worse, expecting them to maintain their place in the kitchen, *He* treated them as people and loved on them even when His own standing with the holy men was at stake. Consider when Martha wanted her sister, Mary, to help her serve the men rather than sitting at Christ's feet to learn from His teaching. After Martha said, "Lord, dost thou not care that my sister hath left me to serve alone? bid her therefore that she help me," Christ's radically countercultural answer was, "Martha, Martha, thou art careful and troubled about many things: But one thing is needful: and Mary hath chosen that good part, which shall not be taken away from her" (Luke 10:38–42).

Jesus actually preferred Mary to sit and be taught than to serve the men.

The Bible makes it perfectly clear that women were present while Christ taught, and that makes them disciples. If we consider the thousands of people who were in the company of Christ at any given time (such as during the loaves and fish event), we can assume that at least hundreds of those crowd members were women. For that matter, hundreds or thousands were children disciples as well. So why do so many people mistakenly assume there were no women disciples? Furthermore, why do so many people use this false claim to suggest that Christ only chose men because He believed only men could be leaders in the future Church of Christianity?

This is not to say that the Twelve were not distinct in role and purpose, however. Even Peter acknowledged that it was important to bring the number of the chief disciples (apostles) back to twelve after the suicide of Judas (Acts 1:15–26). So why weren't there any women within the chief Twelve?

Linda Belleville, author of *Women Leaders and the Church: Three Crucial Questions*, suggests that it was Christ's fulfillment of symbolism:

Twelve Jewish males…represent the twelve tribes and their patriarchal heads. It is the twelve apostles who will sit on thrones, judging the twelve tribes of Israel (Matt. 19:28; Luke 22:30). The new Jerusalem will have twelve gates, twelve angels, twelve foundations, and on them the names of the twelve apostles (Rev. 21:12, 14). It is important not to make a leap from the twelve apostles to male leadership in the church. The leap, instead, should be from twelve apostles to the [entire] church of Jesus Christ. It is not male leaders who will serve as judges in the future, nor, for that matter, is it female leaders. "Do you not know," Paul says, "that *the saints* will judge the world?... Do you not know that we will judge angels?" (1 Cor. 6:2–3).[110] (Emphasis in original)

This view has been adopted by many scholars and remains a mainstream explanation of why Christ didn't choose a woman to be one of the Twelve. However, even if this is only a theory, scores of Jewish cultural reasons also support why women wouldn't have been among the Twelve:

1. Women were given in marriage or engaged at an early age and, once promised to a man, would have likely been forbidden by their betrothed to even hold conversation with a man, let alone keep company with men as they traveled around and slept in groups. The very thought of that would have been seen as an illicit act for a married woman. Christ might have been a radical, but He wouldn't have ordered any woman to defy her husband, so we can rule out any Jewish matrons.
2. Likewise, any woman who had children would be needed at home to care for them, and Christ would not have wanted any mother to abandon her children, so we can rule out any mothers.
3. If a woman or young girl was not married, she was still under the authority of her fatherly figure. Fathers of unmarried Jewish girls would have never allowed their daughters to travel around with men who a) stayed together in groups even overnight and b) talked about theology. Remember, Jewish girls weren't allowed to learn, because it was believed to be immoral. Christ would not have ordered any young Jewish female to defy her father,

so we can rule out most young Jewish girls or unmarried young women.

4. Lastly, following eons of sociocultural and ethical imprinting that the Jews held so firmly, calling a woman to follow Christ would have placed her in a vulnerable position, because she would have had to defy her entire community and deal with the backlash.

Once we consider the culture, the reason women were not called to be part of the Twelve disciples is clear based on the disobedience it would have required her to demonstrate in order to participate in Christ's mobile and theologically rich ministry. Any woman who followed Him and learned from Him would have had to do so at her own will, *not* because she was called to or told to by Christ (as were the men who followed Him), since that would put her under the authority of a man other than her patriarch. As for whether women who were free from the authority of a male figure at home decided to hold company with these men and their Savior, we already know several of them did. The most widely referenced is the female disciple Mary Magdalene.

People can continue to argue that Christ opting for twelve men equates His preference for men as Church leaders, but that doesn't make it true. And these people are ignoring—either innocently or deliberately—that it wasn't only *women* Christ excluded in the Twelve… He also excluded anyone who was not a *Jewish* man. He did not choose Gentiles, even though His ministry was at the cusp of breaking down the social and religious barriers between Jew and Gentile, and there isn't a range of ethnicities, either. Yet, today, we do not deny leadership in our churches to those who would fit the description of a modern Gentile (anyone belonging to a different religion prior to conversion), nor do we prohibit as leaders anyone who isn't of a Jewish bloodline. If we use the men Christ chose for the Twelve as a model for leaders today, we would have to exclude these men. But sadly, the standard is only applied to women. Such a narrow approach to the subject refuses to consider the culture at the time of Christ—as well as the mainstream "symbolism" interpretation discussed prior—and it also makes a blatantly unfounded assumption that just because women weren't in the Twelve, Christ was setting a new rule: Jesus didn't choose women, so women can't be Church leaders. The absence of women in the group does not prove this, no matter how hard one tries to arm-wrestle that dogma into the picture. This logic is, at best, grasping.

Dr. James B. Hurley, professor of marriage and family therapy and author of *Man and Woman in Biblical Perspective*, wrote: "The most striking thing about the role of women in the life and teaching of Jesus is the simple fact that they are there. Although the gospel texts contain no special sayings repudiating the views of the day about women, their uniform testimony to the presence of women among the followers of Jesus and to his serious teaching of them constitutes a break with tradition which has been described as being 'without precedent in [then] contemporary Judaism.'"[111] The ministry of Christ, as extended through Paul, was to form a new community of believers that broke tradition: "There is neither Jew nor Greek, there is neither bond nor free, there is neither male nor female: for ye are all one in Christ Jesus" (Galatians 3:28).

If we begin down the trail of omitting anyone or anything from ministry based on what method or who Christ did *not* choose to use, then all we would be allowed to do now is travel on foot from city to city, sleeping in tents or patron houses. For example: Christ didn't use dogs, horses, or any other animals in His primary strategies for ministry, either, so all ministries that use animals have to go. Why? Because Jesus didn't choose them. This list could go on perpetually. We can't simply "pick" that Christ stood against women leaders based only on the fact that He didn't choose them for the Twelve, especially if there is evidence that He personally inspired them to go and preach.

But is there evidence of such a thing?

Irrefutably.

The Woman at the Well (John 4)

The story we are about to discuss, in my opinion, holds the ultimate power over the entire debate about the role of women in today's Church. It's the final word on the subject, because it is birthed straight from the actions of God in human form. Let's review the Scriptures as a refresher about what occurred that day: "When therefore the Lord knew how the Pharisees had heard that Jesus made and baptized more disciples than John… He left Judaea, and departed again into Galilee. And he must needs go through Samaria" (John 4:1–4).

Stop right there for a moment. This is the first clue relevant to Christ's mission regarding the woman at the well. The Samaritans were natural enemies of the Jews. As a result of the Assyrian exile as recorded in the Old Testament, the Samaritans were a group of people with mixed bloodlines and blended beliefs. They had roots in paganism as well as Judaism, so at the time of the exile, their worship was innately syncretic. This was often viewed as being even worse than pagan faith systems, because it merged the monotheistic (only one God) Yahwism religion of the Jews (those who were taught to "know better") with the polytheistic (many gods) pagan religions. By the time of Christ, the Samaritans were staunchly monotheistic (they had returned to only one God, and in some ways they were even stricter than the Jews in Judea where the Mosaic Law was concerned), but their mixed ancestry (they had pagans in their bloodline—a big "no-no" to the rest of the Jews) and the evolution of their theology and sociocultural norms drastically differed from the Jews of Judea. For instance, they held to the belief that only the Pentateuch (the first five books of the Old Testament) were canonical, rejecting the Psalms, the prophets, and the wisdom texts; their temple was not at Mt. Zion in Jerusalem but at Mt. Gerazim; and they freely spoke the divine name of Yahweh, which the traditional Jew found too sacred to say aloud. As such, the Samaritans were despised as disgraceful blasphemers, as they were seen practicing Yahwism erroneously. To even pass through their land was to taint oneself. Samaritans were "unclean," so anyone dealing with them risked making himself or herself "unclean" as well. Jews traveling from Judea to Galilee made a substantial effort to go around Samaria by crossing the Jordan River (which was well out of their way). To readers of our day, it's easy to read straight past what was just said in John 4:4: "he [Christ] must needs go through Samaria."

Christ wasn't just passing through. His culture and the leaders of the religion He was raised in taught that He must avoid that area of land at all costs. Yet Scripture tells us He "must needs" (or "had to") go through Samaria. The Greek word for Christ's "need" is *dei*: "the necessity of law and command, of duty, of equity."[112] Why did Christ "have to" or "need to" go through Samaria? Because He had a divine appointment with a very special woman. He trekked through forbidden lands just to meet her, because He knew what was about to happen:

> Then cometh he to a city of Samaria, which is called Sychar, near to the parcel of ground that Jacob gave to his son Joseph. Now Jacob's well was there. Jesus therefore, being wearied with his journey, sat thus on the well: and it was about the sixth hour. There cometh a woman of Samaria to draw water:
>
> Jesus saith unto her, "Give me to drink." (For his disciples were gone away unto the city to buy meat.)
>
> Then saith the woman of Samaria unto him, "How is it that thou, being a Jew, askest drink of me, which am a woman of Samaria? for the Jews have no dealings with the Samaritans." (John 4:5–9)

Stop once more. Look at the implications of this exchange. First, Christ was a Jew, so He was not supposed to speak to a Samaritan. Second, Christ was a Jewish *man*, so He really wasn't supposed to speak to a woman. Third, Samaritans were "unclean," so accepting a drink of water from a Samaritan would have certainly, by tradition of the Jews, made Him ceremoniously "unclean" as well. The price to be paid for that drink of water, had Christ intended to follow it up with customary "cleansing" rituals and all that entails, would have been huge. Christ was determined at all costs to see this woman's upcoming ministry carried to full fruition. Let's continue:

> Jesus answered and said unto her, "If thou knewest the gift of God, and who it is that saith to thee, Give me to drink; thou wouldest have asked of him, and he would have given thee living water." [Uh-oh… *Now* Christ is even going as far as to discuss theology with a woman.]
>
> The woman saith unto him, "Sir, thou hast nothing to draw with, and the well is deep: from whence then hast thou that living water? Art thou greater than our father Jacob, which gave us the well, and drank thereof himself, and his children, and his cattle?"
>
> Jesus answered and said unto her, "Whosoever drinketh of this water [the literal water from Jacob's well] shall thirst again: But whosoever drinketh of the water that I shall give him [spiritual water provided only by Christ] shall never thirst; but the water that I shall give him shall be in him a well of water springing up into everlasting life."
>
> The woman saith unto him, "Sir, give me this water, that I thirst not, neither come hither to draw." [She didn't understand the spiritual nature of Christ's words; at that time, "living water" meant water that moved, like from a stream or river.]
>
> Jesus saith unto her, "Go, call thy husband, and come hither."
>
> The woman answered and said, "I have no husband."
>
> Jesus said unto her, "Thou hast well said, 'I have no husband': For thou hast had five husbands; and he whom thou now hast is not thy husband: in that saidst thou truly." (John 4:10–18)

Let's pause here; this moment is crucial. Most members of the Church today misunderstand this woman who had been married five times. Because of all her marriages and divorces, we assume she was a "loose" woman who has chosen to "shack up" with her sixth man. Remember that, in those days, *women were not allowed to divorce their husbands.* This woman had been used by five previous husbands who made covenant, marital vows to care for her. Then they either divorced her (we can't know their reasons why, but might presume they simply became tired of her), or they died, which is even *less* a reason to blame her as a five-time divorcee whom Jesus saved from a "life of sin." We find her at the well, living with man number six. Even in today's culture, two God-fearing "partners" living together is controversial, so at this time, the practice would have been much more of a shock. We assume now, as we have for centuries, that this woman had a *choice* in the matter of whether man number six was going to be her husband. We paint her in this scene as if she is in resistance to a marriage proposal from the sixth man, even though Scripture doesn't say a word about the man's interest in making her his wife. In that culture, women were likely never going to arrange their own marriage regardless of whether they were Jew, Gentile, *or* Samaritan. But even if she was refusing to marry (and agreeing to "shack up," as we like to believe), she was probably scared witless that if she agreed to marry him, she would be tossed away or widowed again. Furthermore, why do we find ourselves justified in assuming man number six is a romantic partner anyway? The Bible doesn't specify that the man she was living with at the time was involved with her romantically, and scholars have repeatedly noted this. It's true, when all evidence is weighed, that she was visiting the well at a time of day when most other women wouldn't have been there, likely out of social shame, but we take that to mean more than it does when we suggest the *only* reason for her shame would be her current living situation. If five men in her past had talked about how undesirable she had been as a wife before they divorced her, that is shame enough to want to avoid the well when the other women (and their whispers) are present. We often assume that man number six is sharing a bed with her, based on the fact that she had five previous husbands, but researchers and scholars have pointed out that this woman may have been living with a kinsman redeemer: a brother, cousin, or uncle, etc. Common thinking within our Church turns her into a flaky, selfish, "easy" woman who went through men like some "husband of the month" club founder. The injustice of this is unfortunate. Let's see what happened next:

> The woman saith unto him, "Sir, I perceive that thou art a prophet. Our fathers worshipped in this mountain; and ye say, that in Jerusalem is the place where men ought to worship." [Without being able to hear the vocal fluctuations of this conversation, we can't be sure whether she was attempting to gain true insight by this, or whether she was testing Christ in the Jew-versus-Samaritan arena to see how He would react. What we do know is that she's still stuck in the present, corporeal condition; her focus remains upon the Samaritan issue, and not upon the everlasting Gospel truth Jesus is attempting to tell her about.]
>
> Jesus saith unto her, "Woman, believe me, the hour cometh, when ye shall neither in this mountain, nor yet at Jerusalem, worship the Father. Ye worship ye know not what: we know what we worship: for salvation is of the Jews. But the hour cometh, and now is, when the true worshippers shall worship the Father in spirit and in truth: for the Father seeketh such to worship him. God is a Spirit: and they that worship him must worship him in spirit and in truth." [He was telling her that "the time is now" for the New Covenant through the Messiah, which, by her next words, we see she finally begins to understand.]
>
> The woman saith unto him, "I know that Messiah cometh, which is called Christ: when he is come, he will tell us all things."
>
> Jesus saith unto her, "I that speak unto thee am he." (John 4:19–26)

Stop one last time. Please, I beseech you, readers, do no[t]
just took place… Prior to this moment, Christ had not yet revealed that
He was the Messiah. This was the *first* announcement of His identity
as the promised Son of God and Savior of the world, and He bestowed
the honor of hearing His proclamation not only upon a Samaritan, but
upon a *woman*! The *very first time* Christ revealed His Messiahship was
to this woman at the well. Yet He even goes beyond stating that He was
the Messiah. Scholars have analyzed this sentence against the authentic
Greek, and the word "he" in the phrase "I that speak unto thee am he"
is not present in the original. Translators included it to smooth out what
might have been an ambiguity. So what was Christ saying here, exactly?
Consider Exodus 3:14, where it's recorded that God told Moses to tell
the Israelites he had been sent by "I AM." Many scholars take Jesus'
(original Greek) sentence, "I that speak unto thee am," to be the same
Old Testament identifier as the "I AM" the preincarnate Christ gave to
Moses. Without the "he," Christ openly said, "I…am." Period, end of
sentence. If this interpretation of the Greek is correct, then not only is
Jesus claiming to be the long-awaited Messiah, He is openly admitting
to this woman, this Samaritan female, that He is also God, Himself.
What a revelation! And what does she do with this information?

> And upon this came his disciples, and marvelled that he talked
> with the woman [they, too, were surprised to find Christ talking
> to a Samaritan female]: yet no man said, "What seekest thou?"
> or, "Why talkest thou with her?" The woman then left her water-
> pot, and went her way into the city, and saith to the men [did
> you catch that she was telling the men here?], "Come, see a man,
> which told me all things that ever I did: is not this the Christ?"
>   Then they went out of the city, and came unto him…..
> And many of the Samaritans of that city believed on him for
> the saying of the woman, which testified, "He told me all that
> ever I did." So when the Samaritans were come unto him, they
> besought him that he would tarry with them: and he abode

there two days. And many more believed because of his own word; And said unto the woman, "Now we believe, not because of thy saying: for we have heard him ourselves, and know that this is indeed the Christ, the Saviour of the world." (John 4:27–30, 39–42).

Christ first revealed His position in the Trinity, as God Himself, to a *woman* in *the longest recorded personal conversation that Christ had anywhere in Scripture with another human being.* This woman immediately left the well in such haste that she abandoned her waterpot and headed straight for the men in her city, and proclaimed to them all that she had a personal experience with the Messiah. The men of the city listened to her testimony, and went back with her to hear Christ for themselves. After being in His presence and hearing His words, they, too, believed.

What does it mean to "preach/evangelize the Gospel"? To a) have a personal experience with and relationship with Christ, b) proclaim of this experience and relationship, c) lead listeners to Christ, so that, d) they can experience Him personally, and then, e) they, too, will believe.

This Samaritan woman was the first preacher/evangelist of the Messianic Gospel message recorded in the entire Bible and she converted the whole city of Sychar—including the men—to belief in the saving message of God's love.

Let that sink in for a moment…

The first sermon about Christ—ever—was delivered by a woman. The first Christian revival—ever—was started by a woman. Author Mark Raburn wrote, "In preaching the Gospel, this woman brought about what Jesus had just told her could happen. She received the living water Jesus offered her and then immediately she became a well, gushing the living water of Jesus onto everyone in her reach.… We should all aspire to be preachers like this woman."[113] Yet most in our modern-day Church don't think of her as a preacher, we think of her as "the woman with five husbands." We remain stuck on that one detail instead of seeing her work for what it was. Reverend Judith VanOsdol of the Latin American Council of Churches agrees: "She lived in brutal solitude; loneliness enforced through guilt, shame, and humiliation. To this day we continue to judge and blame her, rather than recognize her gifts and celebrate her importance and transformation as the first preacher of Jesus, the Christ."[114]

Every person who is against women being preachers, teachers, and evangelists eventually has to tackle the Samaritan woman narrative. Reasons for dismissing the manifest evidence of Christianity's first preacher/evangelist being a *woman* usually trickle back to something like this: "Jesus didn't *personally commission her* to go and preach, so we don't have it from the mouth of God that this woman was called to be a preacher/evangelist. She merely went running into the city as a witness, and women are allowed to do that, so there's no discrepancy here. If women feel called to do the same thing the Samaritan woman did, they can go out and witness as well, but they have no place in Church leadership as preachers, teachers, or pastors." Whereas this statement holds some truth (that Christ did not personally commission the Samaritan woman to do what she did), it ignores the fact that Christ personally *inspired* her to do what she did—having chosen to travel specifically through the "unclean" route because He "must needs" to inspire her in such a way—then remained in Samaria for two days personally *watching her do what she did!*

We can't conclude that Christ was opposed to this woman suddenly feeling called to convert an entire city of the Jews' greatest enemies through the words of her mouth, or that He was unaware of it. He watched it happen (John 4:40). Let's look at the facts:

1. Christ, Himself, went to the "forbidden" territory because He had a divine appointment with an "unclean" *woman.*
2. Christ, Himself, inspired her to go preach the Good News of the Messiah.

3. Christ, Himself, remained in Samaria and observed this woman's actions.
4. Christ had every opportunity to chastise her and tell her she was supposed to "leave the teaching to the men," but He didn't.
5. When the Samaritans heard the woman at the well's message, they sought Christ and asked Him to "tarry with them," and He agreed to do so. Instead of using His time to refute a woman's role in stirring up (translation: leading) her city to Him, He used His time to tell them who He really was.

By choosing not to silence her, Christ showed His approval of what the woman was doing when she ran all over the city preaching the message of the Messiah's arrival—and based on His travel plans in the first place, He knew what was going to happen before it happened and sanctioned the entire event by His attendance. Passages and passages of Scripture show how and when Christ opposed the teaching of those He saw fit to rebuke (Pharisees, Sadducees, holy men in robes, etc.), so we already know He was predisposed to reprimand teaching that wasn't carried out in a way that would please the Father and coincide with His will. Yet regarding the Samaritan woman, He not only allowed her to preach, He watched it…and then responded to it when the crowds appeared for more.

That sounds like a "personal commissioning" to me. As a Samaritan, she was despised by traditional Jews; as a woman, she was oppressed by men who used her and then discarded her (if her previous husbands had, in fact, divorced her); as a potential multiple divorcee who was currently living with a man who wasn't her husband, she was shunned by other women.[115] Then Jesus arrived on the scene as the seventh Man in her life, showed her what a real man looked like, turned her into a preacher, and then watched as the Samarian harvest flocked in. He didn't run after her and remind her that she was a woman; He *commissioned* her by inspiring her and supporting her afterward. Why do so many people play the "potayto/potahto" game about whether Christ used the literal words, "Go preach to Samaria"? Is it that hard to believe that Christ would approve of a woman's preaching if it resulted in leading an entire city to Him? She was a product of *His* making! (Don't forget that He even permitted women to participate in His very own ministry [Luke 8:1–3]!)

After the town turns to Christ, the Samaritan woman falls out of the biblical narrative. Have you ever wondered what became of her? Did she remain faithful to Christ? Or did she fall away after the "honeymoon phase" was over? Does any historical data follow her ministry further?

Perhaps…

Photini

According to Eastern Orthodox tradition, the Church Fathers, Byzantine hagiographers, and ancient Greek sermons from the fourth to the fourteenth century, the Samaritan woman—whose name is admittedly unknown at the time she spoke with Christ—went on to be baptized in water by the apostles, then in the Spirit, on the Day of Pentecost. A new name was then given to her: "Photini" (often "Photina")—in Russian, Svetlana; in Western languages, Claire; and in Celtic languages, Fiona. Each of these names means "light" or "the enlightened one." Following is her story according to the aforementioned historical sources:

Photini had achieved victory in leading her whole city to Christ. Fervently, she continued to tell all she met that the prophesied Messiah had arrived, and—in the midst of her interactions within the community of fellow believers while Christ was tried, murdered, and resurrected—she made a solid connection with the apostles. At her water baptism on the Day of Pentecost in the midst of Christ's closest devotees, she was joined by her five sisters—Anatole, Photo, Photis, Paraskeve, and Kyriake—each of whom also received the baptism of the Holy Spirit and went out into the world to preach.

Time passed, and following the martyrs of Peter and Paul, Photini left the region surrounding Samaria on a missionary journey, making stops at many cities across the ancient world to preach the resurrected Christ every place her foot trod. As Roman Emperor Nero directed a sharp increase in the number of Christians persecuted and saw fit to murder any one of them he could find in horrible and painful ways, Photini and her son, Joseph, were in Carthage, Africa. Photini went to sleep one night like any other, and awoke with a new mission. Jesus Christ, she said, had come to her in a dream. Her next destination was to be Rome...

Meanwhile, in Attalia (Asia Minor), another of Photini's sons, Victor, was rising in status as a military commander in the Roman army. He was a well-respected soldier amidst his peers, and his reputation as a devout man of the sword for Rome resulted in Roman Emperor Nero's summoning him to work with Sebastian, an official in Italy. There, Victor's central duty to his emperor as an official informant was to track down early Christians, a duty about which he felt great conviction. He had heard the story of how his mother had met this Messiah in person, and he had also come to believe in this Yeshua as the Son of God.

After he and Sebastian had formed a friendship, and Sebastian learned the truth about Victor's mother and brother, Sebastian advised Victor to submit to the authority of the emperor lest he face the same terrifying deaths as Christians all around them. He promised Victor that he would be allowed to keep any monies belonging to the Christians he handed over to the authorities, and that he would write to Photini and Joseph, warning them to keep their faith a secret. Despite the offer of reward and the attempt to ensure the safety of his evangelist mother and brother, Victor unexpectedly responded that he, too, wanted to preach the Gospel. Shocked, yet resigned, Sebastian woefully admitted that such defiance against the emperor would only end in the death of all three of them, along with Photini's five sisters.

Upon uttering these words, Sebastian felt a searing pain in his eyes, and when he opened them again, he discovered that he was blind. For several days, he lay in complete silence on his bed, contemplating the Christ while his servants stood helplessly nearby. When he finally spoke again on the fourth day, he declared that Christ was the true God, expressed his desire to be baptized in the faith, and revealed that Christ was calling him to help spread the Gospel. Immediately after he emerged from the baptismal waters, Sebastian regained his eyesight. His servants witnessed the miracle, converted on the spot, and were also baptized. Emperor Nero caught wind of the event and commanded that Victor, Sebastian, and the servants be brought to him to answer for their defiance in person.

Around this time, Photini arrived in Rome with her son Joseph, her sisters, and many other Christians from Africa. She had been informed that Nero was in possession of her son Victor and that the emperor was looking to arrest her, so before he could make his move, she led her entourage straight to his gates, preaching to crowds of people along the way who were awed and amazed by her willingness to proclaim a forbidden name in a city where such an act guaranteed execution. When Photoni and those accompanying her were led to Nero's throne, he asked them, astounded at their boldness, why they had come. Photini answered that her purpose was to openly tell Nero about Christ. Without hesitation, the emperor asked the Christians if they were willing to die for their faith. Photini answered that, yes, they were happy to die for the sake of their beloved Christ.

Nero, incensed by the failure of his attempted intimidation, ordered the Christians' hands to be smashed by iron rods for an hour. The order was carried out while Photini calmly quoted from the Psalms, and by the end of the hour, not one of the believers had been injured, nor did any of them feel any pain in the process. Nero ordered a second hour of torture, and it, too, failed. A third hour was charged to the soldiers, and still, no harm befell the believers. Mystified, Nero sent the men to prison and the women to the imperial court, where the emperor appointed his daughter, Domnina, to tempt Photini and the rest of the women in her company to deny their Lord in exchange for riches. A denial of faith for worldly gain by the most faithful and supernaturally shielded Christians would send a strongly demoralizing message to followers everywhere.

Domnina led the group to a royal chamber, where they were seated upon thrones of pure gold. In front of them was a table with beautiful dresses, jewels, and all the money they would need to live lavishly for the rest of their lives. It was all free for the taking. The only price they had to pay was a denouncement of the Christ. As Photini explained why these luxuries were not a temptation in light of what she had been called to do, Domnina responded with further questions. Her servants, numbering a hundred, likewise stood nearby to hear the testimony of the Samaritan woman at the well. Before long, a sorceress was brought into the assembly to serve the guests food that had been secretly poisoned. In that setting, Photini, her sisters, and the other believing women with her led Domnina, her hundred servants, and the sorceress all to Christ. They carried out baptisms for the whole assembly, and afterward, Domnina commanded her servants to take the riches upon the table and distribute them to the poor throughout Rome.

Outraged by this development, Nero had his men heat up the furnace and throw in Photini and the other women. For seven days, the fire raged on, but not a hair upon their heads was singed. When the doors were opened on the seventh day and the believers emerged unharmed, Nero lined them up for poisoning. Photini stepped forward and offered to be the first to drink the poison so that the power of God could be shown through her once more. Her companions followed suit, and though they drank the poison to the last drop, each one survived.

Beaten at his own game, Nero demanded that the believers be thrown into the prison and remain there with Victor, Sebastian, Joseph, and the men who had come to Rome with Photini. She and the women with her went willingly, and dwelt there for three years. During her incarceration, word spread that believers of Christ were being held there whom no one could harm, and curious Romans flocked to the cells to hear their preaching in person. Each time a man or woman came to believe in the Messiah and Son of God through Photini's prison ministry, praise broke out within the walls of the prison, and before long, the building dedicated to isolation and misery became no less than a church where Romans could hear the Gospel from the mouth of the woman whose life had been forever changed when she met the Christ in Sychar.

Nero's anger rose like never before by the end of the third year as he saw residents of his own city giving their lives over to the work of Jesus Christ. He summoned all his prisoners and ordered all but Photini beheaded.[116] That day, after the stamp of God's glory had already been placed upon the city, everyone in Photini's troupe was martyred. Photini was brought to Nero and given one last chance to deny her Lord after seeing his success in beheading everyone she loved. Photini, considering her loved ones' martyrdom as a crown of glory, refused.

In a final, wrathful act of irony, Nero told his men to throw the famous "living water" preacher into a deep well.

Photini had met Christ at a well in Sychar. She met Him again via a well in Rome, circa AD 66, as her earthly life at last came to an end.

As a result of her spiritual strength and determination, Photini was referred by historians and Church Fathers in the first four centuries as *isapostolos*, "equal to the apostles," and she is frequently listed alongside the preeminent Peter, James, and John.

As stated prior, the account of Photini outside the Johannine narrative is extrabiblical and noncanonical, so it should not be considered to hold the same authority as Scripture. However, to a Christian, *no* historical writing holds the same authority as Scripture, yet many historical documents are true. Regardless of whether or not a person decides to believe what the historians and Church Fathers wrote about Photini, nobody can take away the truth of John 4, wherein the Samaritan woman was documented as the *first* preacher, evangelist, and revivalist of Christ—and it was Christ, Himself, who transformed her into that role.

Despite the naysayers, the Word is clear: Women *can* be preachers! Christ created one.

Yet, the woman in Sychar wasn't the only woman Christ sent. Why does Mary of Magdala so often get overlooked? Was she not also *sent* by the Messiah?

In fact, she was.

Mary Magdalene: "Bearer," Not "Prostitute"

Mary Magdalene was known to the semi-early Church (after the tenth century) by the title "Apostle of the Apostles," due in part to her being the central messenger (present with other women) commissioned by Christ to inform the apostles of His rising in Luke 24:10 and John 20:10–18. Other more obvious reasons for this entitlement have to do with the function she performed for Christ in person.

This title was not the norm until around the twelfth century, but it appeared as early as the writings of Hippolytus of Rome (AD 170–235). To this day, in Catholic churches, she is still known as an "apostle." Many voices on the supporting side of the "women as leaders" discussion from Protestant denominations have, in recent years, called Mary Magdalene an "apostle" as well. The reasoning behind this is due to the meaning of the Greek *apostolos*: literally "one [who is] sent." In New Testament application, the "one sent" refers to a person commissioned by Christ to go and tell others that He, the Son of God, has risen. In John 20:10–18, we read the following:

> Then the disciples went away again unto their own home. But Mary stood without at the sepulchre weeping: and as she wept, she stooped down, and looked into the sepulchre, And seeth two angels in white sitting, the one at the head, and the other at the feet, where the body of Jesus had lain. And they say unto her,

"Woman, why weepest thou?"

She saith unto them, "Because they have taken away my Lord, and I know not where they have laid him."

And when she had thus said, she turned herself back, and saw Jesus standing, and knew not that it was Jesus. Jesus saith unto her, "Woman, why weepest thou? whom seekest thou?"

She, supposing him to be the gardener, saith unto him, "Sir, if thou have borne him hence, tell me where thou hast laid him, and I will take him away."

Jesus saith unto her, "Mary."

She turned herself, and saith unto him, "Rabboni"; which is to say, "Master."

Jesus saith unto her, "Touch me not; for I am not yet ascended to my Father: but go to my brethren, and say unto them, I ascend unto my Father, and your Father; and to my God, and your God."

Mary Magdalene came and told the disciples that she had seen the Lord, and that he had spoken these things unto her.

Jesus, after His death and in the flesh, sent Mary Magdalene to go and tell the apostles that He had risen. Pope John Paul II said of this momentous charge (italics in original):

From the beginning of Christ's mission, women show to him and to his mystery a special *sensitivity which is characteristic* of their *femininity.…* The women *are the first at the tomb.* They are the first to find it empty. They are the first to hear "He is not here. *He has risen,* as he said." They are the first to embrace his feet. The women are also the first to be called to announce this truth to the Apostles. The Gospel of John emphasizes *the special role of Mary Magdalene.* She is the first to meet the Risen Christ.…

Hence she came to be called "the apostle of the Apostles." Mary Magdalene was the first eyewitness of the Risen Christ, and for this reason she was also *the first to bear witness to him before the Apostles*. This event, in a sense, crowns all that has been said previously about Christ entrusting divine truths to women as well as men. One can say that this fulfilled the words of the Prophet: *"I will pour out my spirit on all flesh; your sons and your daughters shall prophesy"* [Joel 2:28]. On the fiftieth day after Christ's Resurrection, these words are confirmed once more in the Upper Room in Jerusalem, at the descent of the Holy Spirit, the Paraclete (cf. Acts 2:17). [117]

Pope John Paul II is certainly not the only one to make this connection. There is a revival of Mary Magdalene's "Apostle of the Apostles" title within Protestant churches all over the US. However, in order to fully appreciate this outstanding label, we need to address who Mary Magdalene really was.

To the mass population of today's Church, Mary Magdalene is viewed as a repentant prostitute. In almost every movie made about Christ's ministry years, she is the woman caught in the act of adultery reported in John 8:1–11. Christ told *that* woman—who is unnamed in the Johannine account and not by any stretch of the imagination identified as Mary Magdalene—to "go, and sin no more," the emphasis for this study being the word "go." Mary Magdalene was heavily involved in Christ's ministry and kept company with Him frequently, so the idea that Christ would suddenly send her off on her way, though gently so, doesn't add up if He's speaking to someone He regularly walks *beside*. Likewise, there is no shred of evidence anywhere in Scripture that Mary Magdalene was a prostitute, a harlot, a loose woman, or anything else of this sort.

Another mistake frequently presented in movies, educational materials, and sermons is that Mary Magdalene and the woman who washed

Jesus' feet and dried them with her hair is the same wo
woman—also unnamed and known only as "a woman in the city, which
was a sinner" in Luke 7:37—has a reputation of being a prostitute as
well. Here, too, Christ says, "go in peace" (verse 50). (Another instance
of this is in John 12, and that woman is named Mary of *Bethany*, not
Mary of Magdala.) Why that reputation exists for this anonymous
woman is a whole other issue we won't address herein, but because that
is her reputation, and because so many in the past have asserted (incorrectly so) that she is the same person as Mary Magdalene, Mary has been
deemed a prostitute.

Mary Magdalene is *not* the same woman as these two others, even
if "the cartoons tell me so," and the proof of that is how she is referenced elsewhere. Scripturally, she is known by name (a *great* honor for
a woman in that day, by the way, since so many women were never
directly identified), and these other two women are not. Mary Magdalene's name appears more often in the New Testament than any other
female except for Mary, the mother of Christ. Furthermore, the title
"Mary of Magdala" says a lot. Most men and women in the Bible are
referenced by whom they're related to ("son of," "daughter of," "sister
of," and so on), not by the city or town they come from, *unless* they are
prominent, well-known, and *respected* patrons within the social community of that city or region. The fact that the Gospel writers included
her name in connection with "Magdala" insinuates that she was likely a
highly esteemed patroness or business woman in the fishing commerce
"on the northeast bank of the Sea of Galilee. She left her home to follow Jesus, and it is believed she was among several well-off, independent women who financially supported Jesus' ministry."[118] Because of
the importance of Mary Magdalene's role in Christ's earthly ministry,
the writers of the Gospel would have every reason to clarify her identity
in these two other scenes had they been her. Yet the Church has turned
her into a woman of the street. (This is most likely due to the infamous
twenty-third homily delivered by Pope Gregory the Great on September

14, 1591—which pointed to Mary Magdalene's ointments at the tomb as proof that she used expensive perfumes during promiscuous activities prior to meeting Jesus. These ointments also associated her with the foot-washing scenes. The fact that she had expensive perfumes could simply mean that she was a wealthy patroness, a woman of upright earnings who enjoyed pretty smells. It's amazing the leaps we make...)

Another interesting cultural fact *finally* being taught today is that women were not allowed to be legal witnesses at that time (which explains why the disciples didn't initially believe Mary Magdalene when she told them what she had seen). A woman's word at the scene of a significant event was immediately disregarded. So this not only shows a radical move on Christ's part in choosing a woman as His first witness (He could have appeared anywhere and to anyone in His first appearance), it also argues for the authenticity of the Gospels that the story was documented to have women in this position, because if the Gospel writers were attempting to invent a credible story, they would have said that Christ appeared to a man. Luke 8:2 tells us that Christ cast seven demons out of Mary Magdalene at the start of their association, which adds a layer of credibility as well, because again, if the Gospel writers wanted to devise a brilliant resurrection tale out of thin air, they probably wouldn't have chosen to assign a witness who had previously been demon-possessed.

Though one might find a case of demon possession as a reason to flinch away from Mary Magdalene as the first "bearer" of the Good News, it's actually her reputation as a prostitute that does the most damage for women today, as Professor Barbara Bowe relates: "Women looking to the Bible for inspiration already have limited choices of female role models. When we suddenly cut Mary Magdalene off at the knees and turn her into some kind of evil sex pervert, we deprive men and women, but especially women, of a figure with whom they can identify."[119]

The next logical question, once we remove Mary Magdalene's muddied reputation, is what she and the other women in Christ's company would have been doing for Him. Many have the idea that these women were cooking or cleaning for their Lord and His disciples. As much as this imagery may paint a derogatory picture in the minds of most contemporary feminists, it's not an inappropriate assumption, simply because that was the role women were given at this time. However, I assure you, there is more to the women in Christ's circle than brooms and cookies.

Let's look at Scripture: "And it came to pass afterward, that he went throughout every city and village, preaching and shewing the glad tidings of the kingdom of God: and the twelve were with him, And certain women, which had been healed of evil spirits and infirmities, Mary called Magdalene, out of whom went seven devils, And Joanna the wife of Chuza Herod's steward, and Susanna, and many others, which ministered unto him of their substance" (Luke 8:1–3). The word "ministered" here is translated from the Greek *diekonoun*. In various instances throughout the New Testament when this word is used in reference to the actions of the apostles, it can mean serving a table, but it can also mean, as deacons, *diakonos*, the ministry of the spoken word. Christ, Himself, uses this word in Luke 22:27, when He refers to *Himself*, "I am among you as he that serveth." Luke specifies that these women were "dieko-nating" ("ministering," "supporting"), if you will, to Christ from "their substance" (*hyparchonton*), meaning their own financial resources. These women, if we visit the words *diekonoun* and *hyparchonton* to the fullest extent of their potential meaning, were monetarily sponsoring Christ, and assisting Him with words, possibly even teaching in His absence what they had learned from Him.

If Mary Magdalene was a prostitute earning money from a forbidden bed, we can be assured that Christ wouldn't allow that tainted money to sponsor His ministry. Let it be known, once and for all, that *Mary Magdalene was not a prostitute*. I know that the account of "harlot Mary" has immense profundity as a story of redemption, but we don't need to add that brand of sin to her to appreciate the seven demons that held her steadfastly before Christ delivered her. She was still redeemed by Him, and she went on to be known as an apostle to the early Church as well as today's Church in many Christian sects.

But the central reason I mentioned Mary Magdalene is not for the celebrated title others have given her throughout history. I want to funnel what we've discussed so far into a better understanding of what Christ did the day He appeared to her at the tomb.

As stated earlier, women in Christ's day were not recognized as legitimate witnesses. So when Christ appeared to Mary Magdalene, making her the first person to see and experience His resurrected presence, He was directly challenging this cultural norm. He did not choose to appear to a man, nor did He tell the women to track down a man for Him. He simply told the *women* to go and tell the *men*. He trusted the message of His resurrection, the foundation of the Gospel, to a woman first.

Jesus Christ, the Radical of radicals, in this moment, reversed and dispelled forever the notion that a woman can't be trusted with His message, and that she can't deliver it to a man.

Those who oppose women teaching in a church might argue that Christ didn't explicitly order Mary and the women to run through the streets preaching, but He wouldn't have done that anyway, because all the disciples and apostles were told to wait for the Holy Spirit's outpouring (Luke 24:49). When that occurred on the Day of Pentecost, the women *did* run through the streets preaching. So no, He didn't turn them into preachers at that moment, and it would be at the least a desperate claim to say that He did. It's not about whether Jesus suddenly transformed these women into preachers, teachers, or pastors. It's about the fact that the very first humans on the planet entrusted by God, Himself, in person with the "Christ is risen" message were *women*.

Why did He choose to appear first to women? Perhaps He was making the statement—setting a new precedent—that Jesus Christ trusts *women* with the truth of His story. Add to this the reality of women preachers on the Day of Pentecost, and the identity of each woman as

God the Father made her in her mother's womb with unique gifts, and we have the entire Trinity working together to release women ministers upon the earth in these last days, as Joel 2:28 prophesies!

This prophecy was, as Peter identified, fulfilled on the Day of Pentecost, and the time has come for this truth to be applied to the modern Church. God the Father, the Holy Spirit, and Jesus Christ, Himself, has equipped women for such a time as this.

Arise, women. Leave your waterpots behind at the well and go forward into your own Sychar. Lost souls are depending on it.

7

Created He *Them*

Genesis 1:27 says: "So God created man in his own image…male and female created he *them*."

When God created humankind, He did so by instilling His image in both genders. Since the dawn of time, God has not withheld power or entitlement, even to the extent of His very *image*, from the woman. This passage suggests—even *proves*—that since the beginning, He has endowed women with the same privileges granted to man. However, we should not assume that this means He made women as carbon copies of men. He took woman from the side of man and created an equal counterpart. She *was* equal, but she was also *different*.

Women and men often tease around about their differences, and it is no secret that the two sexes approach things from diverse angles. In an ideal relationship, this can be quite fun: Paula jokes about how many college degrees she could have earned while waiting for Stephen to pull over and ask for directions to their dinner party. Stephen grumbles that he could have built the Taj Mahal in the time it took Paula took to put on her makeup. When they arrive at the party, Stephen's hilarious "Paula took an hour on her eyeshadow" story is met with, "Yes, but how lovely she looks tonight!" He beams with pride in the fact that her appearance relayed the message that she cared enough about the event to present herself accordingly. Paula's "You wouldn't believe how many times we turned around" story inspires, "Yeah, but these roads are insane, and only a brilliant mind like Stephen's could have worked all that out without a map!" She likewise feels proud of his ingenuity.

 If the innate differences between male and female can be seen for what they are, then neither is ever "better," because both are proportionately resourceful and creative—their greatest weaknesses are often their greatest strengths—and the two genders complement and complete each other, just as God designed.

Up to this point in the book, we have reflected on the evidence that women are called to do anything a man can do within the Church by considering the original Greek and Hebrew texts. Passages like this one in Genesis go so far in confirming that, even beyond the scope of ministry, woman has been equal to man in every way since Creation.

Before we move on, let's review a quick bullet list of those conclusions:

- Woman was created as *kenegdo ezer*, a powerful equal to man— not a weak "helper." God created both man *and* woman in His image with the intent of holding a blessed communion with *both* genders even as early as the Garden of Eden. The promised Seed, the Christ Messiah, of Genesis 3:15 provided restoration of this relationship when He died and rose again.
- Women prophetesses (as well as Judge Deborah) in the Old Testament were chosen by God to fulfill spiritual leadership roles, not only over men, but over the entire nation of Israel.
- On the Day of Pentecost, the Holy Spirit fell upon both genders in the Upper Room, and women were sent by God to preach throughout the land.
- Women in the New Testament began churches in their homes and maintained leadership positions within these gatherings.

- Paul, the "silencer" of women in the Church, served along-side prominent women leaders in the early Church—several of whom he personally commissioned, all of whom he openly commended, and at least two of whom were considered "apos-tles" (three, if we count Photini) before the patriarchal hierarchy in the Church changed how these women would be known.
- Jesus Christ enlisted women in His own ministry, turned one woman into a preacher in Samaria, and entrusted the very first delivery of His post-resurrection Gospel message to a woman. A study of His radically countercultural and positive treatment of women shows His own view of leadership equality regarding them.

But it is here that we reach a conundrum: How does this all apply to women today? How does a woman practically utilize these liberties and channel them into effective ministry outlets such as teaching or preach-ing in a way that preserves her feminine strength as a woman, while preventing her from becoming a target of attack?

Act Like a Lady; Think Like a Boss

Many women (myself included) who dare to step behind the pulpit can become associated with imbalanced and inaccurate terms such as "man-haters," "feminists," "martyrs of gender oppression," and so on. There certainly must be a healthy middle ground where a woman is able to keep on track with her calling, following God's promptings within her life, without those around her assuming *she* is the aggressor…isn't there?

Sadly, the truth is, sincere servanthood often can be uncomfortable. Persecution lurks around many corners like a predator you can almost always detect but of whose assault you can't always prevent. Anytime we follow God's prompting, we have an enemy who retaliates. He doesn't like God's plan, and he can't stand to see us willing to walk in that plan in the face of all odds. This is true for anyone—as television evangelist and Bible teacher Joyce Meyer always says, "New levels, new devils." The minute we think we've been promoted to new enlightenment in God's perfect will, a fresh layer of struggles comes to greet us. You don't have to be a "woman behind a pulpit" to know this is simply the way it works. Christ, Himself, met incredible resistance from the very people He sought to save, and He is the ultimate example for us to follow while we "fight the good fight of faith" (1 Timothy 6:12). The good news for women is that we do not have to suffer the way He did, we're not expected to accomplish what He did (we couldn't if we tried), and we have the tools that can help us see what our challenges will be beforehand. Preparing our radars to detect the incoming missiles will help us react calmly later on.

We can do some things to alleviate these attacks; we will discuss those later in this chapter. But for now, I wish to stick to the question at hand: How does a woman transition to firm and steady leadership while retaining her feminine gentility?

When I was putting the finishing touches on the book you now hold in your hand, I kept a tradition that I started early on in my writing: I met with SkyWatch administrator Allie Anderson, and we went through it from start to finish. I was confident about the finished product until I reached the beginning of this chapter. My work up to that point felt solid, and an occasional, "Amen!" or "Preach it!" from Allie reminded me that I was indeed on the right track. But as I delved into this chapter, I noticed that Allie began to write many notes. She so often furiously scribbled on the page that more than once I stopped reading to let her catch up. Obviously, she shared my opinion that this particular chapter was missing something. When the read-through was completed, I asked her thoughts. While she had taken down two full pages of reflections, she could only really tell me what I already knew: This chapter was "missing something." She said she would give it more thought and call me later. I took her to lunch and then we went our separate ways.

As I arrived home and checked my mail, I pulled a piece of junk mail out of the mailbox that almost made me laugh out loud. Herein was my answer, as if God, Himself, had tucked it there where I could find it. Splashed with pink and black stripes and clad in various pictures of women's wallets, coffee mugs, and other women-targeting paraphernalia for sale, here was a brochure that sported the phrase, "Act like a lady. Think like a boss."

In a world where gender roles are confusing and women fight to be equal to men, we so often forget who we are inherently created to be: *ladies*. We have spent so much time shedding and burning feminine undergarments and fighting to accomplish all the roles that men so regularly complete that we forget that *we are not actually men*. When we do remember this fact, we chide ourselves for what we immediately own as a "weakness."

I was raised in a "no nonsense" household where emotions were, by requirement, channeled into productive activity and certainly not wallowed in; it was a rare occasion indeed when I would actually sit down and cry. (I have *zero* regret for being raised this way; let me make that very clear. My siblings and I were allowed to have feelings and process them, but as soon as a solution to the problem was identified, we were expected to act upon that solution and move on. As a human, this was great advice. As a *girl*—and with all the emotional implications that holds—this was priceless counsel that I would spend the rest of my earthly life thanking my parents for. We were encouraged to "let it out" on occasion, but most of the time my household strongly rejected walking around with "the face" [a generic, yet humorous, euphemism we coined to describe that self-pitying, wallowing, weepy expression].) The very words "acting like a girl" hung in my gullet like bitter castor oil anytime they were used in association with "feelings." I almost had to swallow twice before attempting to pronounce that phrase. "Acting like a girl"… It was naturally an insult. I might be a redhead, but I was never going to be that Anne of Green Gables who constantly found herself "in the depths of despair."

I didn't think there was anything wrong with having been born female; I enjoyed my femininity in a healthy and modest way. But when it came to those ugly little "psyche-viruses called emotions," as I identified them, I would sooner wax my legs than to get caught "acting like a girl."

I remember a time in my early adulthood when I was crying about some trouble at work. I don't remember the circumstances, but I'll never forget my friend and coworker—one we referred to as "Crazy Molly" on account of her ceaseless laughter and unparalleled wit—who came to check on me.

"What's wrong?" Molly asked. "You seem really upset…"

"Oh, I'm fine. I'm just being ridiculous." I wiped my tears away and readied myself to apply the "brave mask."

"Nah, come on. Don't do that. You never cry. Don't be a turd. What's the real deal?" When I didn't respond, she held her wrist close to her mouth. "If you don't tell me, I'm gonna bite my arm. This arm right here. I'm gonna do it…"

As her mouth slowly opened over her skinny limb, I let out a chuckle and shook my head. "I'll get over it, Molly. I'm just being a *girl*." The last of these words fell out of my mouth like poison. I felt like I had just divulged my darkest, most sinful secret.

I was *weak*…and I had been caught.

She dropped her arm, blinked…blinked again…and wrinkled her brow.

"Donna," she said, a smile toying with the edge of her mouth, "you *are* a girl."

I can't describe why this was such an epiphany for me. I knew it was a fact, but I had never had anyone respond to me that way. I had many times admitted this vile, "girlish" tendency to occasionally cry when I was having a rough day, but it was normally followed up with a lengthy psycho-analysis by my companion that began with how it's "okay to cry sometimes," or why "everyone needs to let it out," or how "it's not good to bottle it up." I had trained myself to respond to each of these with logic that reasoned away any "excuse for wallowing."

But then, Molly's point-blank bullet through every wall of retort stopped me in my tracks. She didn't have to analyze anything. I simply *was* a girl. Molly had made the simplest and most obvious statement ever, and by golly, it was actually true!

It's unfortunate, however, that this basic truth actually had to be pointed out to me in the first place. We women are born into a position that requires us to fight daily toward the goal of being equal in strength to men (a common fact that the world—*not my father*—impressed upon me). But by denying our intrinsic, female nature, we are actually placing our own femininity under attack. We keep forgetting: "Equal to a man" doesn't mean "identical to a man." It is necessary to remember that God created *both man and woman in His image.*

Christians tend to assign God a gender, and that's understandable since Scripture refers to Him with male pronouns such as "He," and when Christ came, He was a male. But it's important to remember that, as a Spirit and the Creator of *both genders* made in *His image*, God is not limited to the confines of any earthly language and its pronouns. God even said of Himself: "I am God, *and not man*" (Hosea 11:9; emphasis added), so His identity as Deity over humankind is above any humanized concept we may have. It might surprise some to see that God is even associated with feminine imagery in many Scriptures, such as Psalm 22:9, which beautifully portrays God in the role of midwife: "But thou art he that took me out of the womb: thou didst make me hope when I was upon my mother's breasts." The prophet Isaiah relayed God's personal sentiments in the following terminology: "I have long time holden my peace; I have been still, and refrained myself: now will I cry like a travailing woman [Hebrew language here depicts a woman in the pain of childbirth]" (Isaiah 42:14). Even Christ described Himself as a "hen [who] gathereth her chickens under her wings" (Matthew 23:37).

Yet my purpose here is *not* to prove that God is "as much female as He is male." My purpose is to illustrate that God is so far above our partial and inadequate comprehension that He should not be placed in any gender-specific box whatsoever.

Look at God's nature throughout the Bible. There are times when He is swift and firm in His actions (masculine traits). Other times He is gentle and gracious (feminine traits). Yet with *all* of these actions, He loves. Consider the differences between how men and women are wired using biblical examples: When the Roman soldiers came to arrest Jesus, Peter acted with bravery, ready to fight. He grabbed a sword and lopped off the nearest Roman soldier's ear (John 18:10). Although a vicious battle outbreak was not what Jesus wanted in that moment (because He knew His arrest had to be carried out), Peter's gallantry—his fundamental nature as a man—was undeniable and heroic. The women in Jesus' life were also very brave during this event, though they showed their courage in a nurturing way. They stayed near His side all night. Surely, these women must have known they could be in danger as well, but they remained beside Him until the bitter, *bitter* end. After the horrible deed was done and Jesus was placed in a tomb, it was *the women* who had the presence of mind to return with ointments and spices for His body. They weren't there to change fate or cut off ears. They were there to *nurture* their loved one and Master, even after Jesus had died. Men and women handled this situation differently, but both genders took action in loyalty and defense of their beloved Jesus.

When men and women are considered together in ministry to our Lord and Savior as a whole—with both male and female attributes experiencing full freedom to contribute—a better representation of God's image is displayed. When we, as women, give up our gentility, our innate femininity, in the quest to "be equal to a man," we are abandoning our God-given image traits in trade for an imitation of those given to the opposite gender. This only results in becoming counterfeit copies of the other.

Have you ever gone to the copy machine and made a copy of a copy of a copy? Each time the image is rendered anew from another copy, the clarity of the original is increasingly lost. With each copy, the machine produces a blurrier picture, and eventually the result is nothing but a fuzzy blob on a page. Generations of women attempting to be "copies" of men presents a hazard to the original God-image we bear. Additionally, we have the right to compare apples to oranges, and we likewise have the right to argue about which of these two flavors we prefer, but nothing we do will ever make these fruits the same as they provide nutrition to the body. Comparatively, we can continue to compare men to women, wasting valuable time arguing over who is stronger in ministry, but nothing we do will ever make these genders the same as they provide spiritual nutrients to the Body of Christ.

God's image is more complete than *only* what a man holds, or *only* what a woman holds. *Together* we create a fuller image of God, and by that, when we make room for each gender and that gender's natural traits, we fulfill a more complete ministry. When a woman preaches, teaches, or ministers, her nurturing point of view *affirms* and *encourages.* Her reassuring and faithful presence is like that of Mary, who refused to leave her suffering Savior. When a man approaches the pulpit, his *decisive* and *no-holds-barred* willingness to be truthful in the face of adversity can be just the ear-lopping that the Roman soldier of controversy needs. But whether the listener on that pew is a man or a woman, he or she can gain more insight about the role God and His precious Son play in the spiritual realm during this human condition called "life" when both aspects of His image are at liberty to work together harmoniously.

So how does a strong, spirit-filled woman who feels led to minister embrace her femininity? I will be honest, I'm still working on this myself. I am reminded of a conversation I had several years ago with Allie Anderson when I had found out that the baby I was carrying at the time was a girl. I had called her to give her the news that we decided to name the baby after her. Once Allie had calmed down from the excitement of learning she would have a namesake, I remember confiding in her that I was actually scared.

"Why on earth are you scared?" she asked.

"You know me, Allie. I've never been a 'girly girl.' I've always been a tomboy and I don't really 'act like a girl' most of the time. I don't do the big 'emotional' thing, I don't do the 'makeup and hair' thing, and I sometimes have a hard time connecting with other women who do that 'let's all go to the bathroom together and try on lipstick' thing." I considered for a moment what my true fear was. "What if she's a girly girl? How will I be able to set an example for her as a feminine woman when I'm not very feminine myself? Please tell me I don't have to start stumbling into the makeup counter every morning or give up my video games in exchange for tea parties in order to provide balance for her..."

I remember Allie telling me that I would know when the time came how to direct my daughter based on her characteristics and what she seemed to like. As her needs surfaced, my answers would come.

Truth be told, this still baffles me sometimes—because I *did* give birth to the girliest of all girls. But watching her embrace her own femininity has taught me a lot about my own. I have learned that sometimes it's as simple as Molly's answer: "Donna, you *are* a girl..." My daughter is still little, but she does her makeup almost every day, and before she donated her hair to a cancer foundation (it's now incredibly short), she was constantly trying out new hairdos. Hardly a day goes by when she doesn't make the family run late because she has to consider each dress in her collection before making that perfect wardrobe decision. She loves to sing, *must* dance—everywhere!—and yes, she gets her feelings hurt easily. On the other hand, however, she is constantly coming home from school with reports from her teacher that when another student feels down, my adorable Sissypoodle—her favorite nickname—is the first to nurture that student with encouraging words. She doesn't just "have" baby dolls, she tucks them into bed at night, tells them stories, prays with them, and sings them to sleep. I hear her telling her older brother all the time that he's smart and handsome when he comes home feeling sad. There is a beautiful woman developing in her tiny heart, and her nurturing instinct is active. Strangely, though, I haven't had to try very hard to instill any of that within her. The feminine side of God's image bestowed upon humanity in the Garden of Eden is manifesting within my daughter because it's what God ordained and designed, not because I have taught her how to "act like a girl." She "*is* a girl."

As for myself, I may not head for the makeup counter first thing every morning, and I can still totally blow away the average guy in a video game tournament, but as a reassuring spirit who looks after and cares for those around me like Mary did at the tomb, I am a woman…who "acts like a girl." My relationship with my daughter has taught me that this side of me has always been there, and I couldn't remove it if I tried. When it comes to ministry, when it comes to obeying the Lord, I have extreme strength to face whatever is coming against me in the interest of Kingdom work. I am dedicated to being "at His side" for the sake of the Gospel, regardless of resistance or fear. (More on this in the next chapter.)

Act like a lady. Think like a boss.

What does that look like? I'll tell you what I've learned: Not all strength comes through muscle or masculinity. The loudest in the room is sometimes the quietest. My mother-in-law, Joyce, was one of the strongest women I ever knew, and yet one of the most feminine. She may never have stepped behind a pulpit, but with only an expression she could preach an entire sermon. At her memorial service, countless testimonies were given that showed this to be a fact. One woman walked with Joyce daily and gossiped about everyone in the neighborhood. Joyce never once scolded her for this as she didn't feel it was her place to; she never tried to fix the other woman's bad habit. Over time, however, Joyce's sweet silence during the exchange was a witness, and through her quiet, gentle, nurturing nature, this other woman felt convicted to put a stop to the slander. This experience changed that woman's life forever, and every relationship she's held since has been healthier as a result of Joyce's influence.

Joyce was a warrior. She was strong *because of* her femininity, not in spite of it.

Ladies Acting Like Ladies in Church Leadership

I believe this book has made a solid argument for why women can be equal to men, both in marriage as well as in the Church. However, in the fight for equality, feminists have risen up in the wrong ways, causing more harm than good to the ongoing debate. In order to be equal to men, many women have sometimes been misled to believe they must assert themselves aggressively or "act like a man" in order to achieve equality. It is *crucial*, then, for a woman who believes she is called to a position of authority to act like a lady—she may have been called to do some of the same things that men do, but she was never called to *be a man*. Today's impressionable youth—the same young people who are surrounded by gender-identification confusion in certain communities—*do not* need even one more example of a masculine woman, whether that is portrayed externally or internally. (Nor do they need a mousey man who has been whipped into submission by a domineering wife.)

The word "authority" simply means the right to be in control of someone or something. Sometimes authority is inherited, but most often it is delegated or earned. In the case of a woman minister, the only way her role as a leader over the church can be successful is if the majority of the congregation finds such an arrangement agreeable. A woman who stomps into her pastor's office and demands that she be given authority in a church that is accustomed to male-only leadership will be viewed as being just as impertinent as a man who stomps into a women-only conference and demands to preach a sermon to a congregation who came to hear women. Nothing about either of these scenarios is agreeable, and their very nature goes against everything the Gospel message of love and peace stands for. Even if a woman's attempt at a power move by force were to be accepted, she would not retain the respect of her listeners beyond the glorified arm-wrestling match she won. A "leader" is only a leader if followers trail behind him or her *voluntarily*. Only a woman imbued with charisma and who has a charitable and gentle spirit will be equipped to bring about change to a male-only governing power. Because of this, it's important for a woman called into ministry to either find an outlet that welcomes her, or proceed with patience and caution to help reform a church built upon male dominance—knowing she will face significant challenges and resistance and she must always respond in love in the process.

One of the greatest atrocities of American history, in my opinion, was when the 1960s–'70s introduced the idea that there is no difference between men and women other than the external formation of their bodies and their reproductive functions. Science has repeatedly proven this wrong, based on studies related to chromosomes and the hormonal development of males and females even well before birth. Women and men are distinct, and it's to the benefit of both genders that they are, as one serves to balance the other. A woman should never feel pressured to deny her own femininity in order to be used by God in a position of authority, nor should she use her pulpit (literal or figurative) to debase men. Women are in no way better than men, and we are, whether we all want to admit it or not, very different from them. The word "authority" or "leadership" should never be confused with "power," because the journey to power leads to control over others, and that has never been the goal of Jesus Christ. It's about the lost. It always has been. The Church as a Body is everywhere we go (Walmart, the ballfield, schools, work, etc.), and the church as a building is a result of the Church Body, not the other way around. Although numerous mission endeavor reach the already-saved, Christ's central mission—and it should be ours, too—is to reach the lost. If that concept can remain at the forefront of our minds as we interact with the Church Body, then bickering within the church building would never be a priority.

Leaders of the Church Body, then, have one goal: to serve. Whether they are serving in a position that ministers to believers or nonbelievers, the mission remains the same. They are appointed by God to *serve*

(Mark 10:42–45; Luke 22:24–27), not to fight; the only exception is that they are called to fight against a common enemy, which we all know is not a male pastor who believes women shouldn't teach in a church.

By leading with agreeability and gentility, a woman can empower others (both male and female) to support her mission. But once a woman rises as a leader, she absolutely *must* treat that position delicately. Women can be just as power-hungry and conniving as men from every angle, because we are *all* fallen. A woman leader is accountable to respecting the gift of ministry that God has given her.

This leads to my next point: There are a few classic, no-brainer rules any woman in ministry *must* follow, no matter how "old-fashioned" they seem. The following pointers are not shared because we care what other people think, but because we should protect the ministry God has entrusted to us.

1. Never be in a room with a man other than your husband or son if the door is closed.

Not everyone out there is our enemy, and I don't want anyone to think I'm promoting paranoia, but as female ministers, we are already a walking controversy to some, and to the extremists, we may even be unfairly tagged as a "Jezebel," thanks to those who interpret Revelation 2:20 as representing *any* woman teacher: "I have a few things against thee, because thou sufferest that woman Jezebel, which calleth herself a prophetess, to teach and to seduce my servants to commit fornication, and to eat things sacrificed unto idols." Additionally, since so many male preachers associate *all* women with Eve as the "deceived," a closed door in the presence of another man could easily perpetuate a wave of whispers about what's going on behind it. This simple rule is recommended in many denominations as prudent for all in ministry of any type, regardless of gender, and is wise for anyone to follow.

Extremists aside, we don't have to be considered a "Jezebel" or a "deceivable Eve" to be seen as someone who may use our positions in ministry inappropriately. The simple truth is that nobody in ministry—male or female—should be in a room alone with a member of the opposite sex. It's sad, but many churchgoers thrive on gossip, and even some of the sweetest, kindest-acting congregants become bored if they're not stirring up one big, juicy tale or another. The defense, "There was nothing going on, I promise," might be believed if we're lucky and have a spotless reputation, but why go there if we don't have to? Let's keep all doors open if we're speaking to a man.

As to how to handle the special situations (such as counseling, one of those "May I speak to you privately?" moments, etc.), when you are not permitted to bring someone with you, ask the man if he would be willing to bring his wife or a buddy along. Always, *always* have a witness present at all times if at all possible. However, if you have a counselee who insists on full privacy, consult your board and ask how your church or the church's organization would like for you to handle it. If you belong to a large organization, policies are likely already in place to handle this. Security cameras that record audio are considered by some organizations to be the fix for this, whereas others simply state that the woman minister must refer the counselee to a respected male staff member. Whichever you choose, be smart and careful. A person can speak somewhere outdoors in view, but out of earshot as an option as well.

2. Restrict physical contact with other men, and while interacting with them, act like a lady, not a giggly girl.

For some women, it's natural to hug everybody as a greeting. I advise against this for a woman minister. A full-frontal hug that presses a woman's chest against a man's might be fine in the secular world, but it can give the wrong impression in church. If a man reaches out to hug you and there's no getting out of it, pivot your waist and respond with only one arm; turn it into one of those evangelistic side hugs we do in church.

Handshakes are fine, as long as they are followed with a quick break, lest you be seen as intentionally prolonging the contact. Never do that thing we all see in movies when a man is pouring his heart out to a woman and she strokes his upper arm as an offering of comfort. If you do this, you're just begging for someone to accuse you of flirting.

A woman minister must show that she's intelligent. If you're in the presence of *only women*, then you can giggle with the best of them. But an overly perky, bubbly woman who socializes with other men like a teenager who is continuously flattered, enamored with her speaker, and laughs at all his jokes with a high-pitched titter will label you an "airhead" or worse (a flirt, etc.). It also sends a red alert out to other women present and raises suspicion. Your body language will likely be under constant scrutiny, so don't move in a way that could be viewed as suggestive (head to the side with a sway, or the upper body inclined too far forward, etc.). Avoid doing anything that might make you appear suspect, such as leaning over to whisper in a man's ear.

3. Dress modestly, and keep your attire feminine.

When I preach, I wear whatever is comfortable. I delivered my most recent sermon while I was wearing bell bottoms, a bohemian-chic top, and sandals. I am the poster child for comfort. So by "modest" and "feminine," I'm not talking about a potato sack dress that goes to your ankles, and I don't believe that it even needs to be a dress (depending on one's denominational interpretations of a female's appropriate attire). But steer clear of dressing like a man. Some couture fashions are trending right now that, although cutting edge on the walkway of a fashion show, would appear to those in the pews as a woman who is struggling with her birth gender. Wearing something that looks like a man's suit and tie, even if it is tailored for a woman (think Ellen DeGeneres), could cause some old-fashioned folks to wonder if you're trying to say more about your identity than you really are.

Keep your hemlines below the knees. You don't want a rumor started that you're only taking the stage to show off your legs, and if you're on a raised platform, a skirt any shorter than that could result in an accidental flash of thigh (or worse). Keep your collars high enough that you can safely bend over to pick something up off the floor without inadvertently giving anyone a "down the shirt" show. This is especially true for a woman who intends to pray for others at the altar. Don't allow your midriff to show under any circumstances either, because even though the majority of the world might see it and think it's just a belly, some people in the Church might a) think you're displaying an area that's inappropriate to bare in church, or b) like what they're seeing for the wrong reasons (which is far worse). Other good rules of thumb are: No skin-tight clothing that accentuates every curve, no wrap dresses that might come untied and open suddenly, and no garments with peek-a-boo slits.

Lastly, I know it seems silly to discuss shoes, but a few high-heel styles out there are made to look a little too sexy. Some of those candy-apple red, high-gloss, six-inch heels may appear suggestive.

As unfair as it is to say this, and it really *is* unfair, all these rules should be followed even more strictly if you're physically attractive. The prettier a woman minister is, the more finger-pointing sharks will have to talk about if she slips in her wardrobe choices even once. Do not let the purity of your ministry be spotted by something as menial as inappropriate clothing.

4. Be a good example to youth.

Younger girls will be watching how you dress and interact. With certain gender-bending communities at large today you need to not only be a modest woman, you need to be a Christ-like woman. Teach young women how to be strong, but show them how to be righteous and feminine as well. Your style doesn't have to involve fancy hair and makeup, but your influence needs to be womanly and chaste.

Don't use your pulpit to talk about your husband's bad habits, even if it seems like a funny topic. Younger ears might hear this and repeat it later without the discernment you may possess for correct timing and context. Let young girls see you as their own shining example of how a woman should love, honor, respect, and submit to the man she's married. Teach them from a godly woman's perspective what they should be looking for—and what they should avoid—in the opposite sex. Empower them to feel worthy of a great guy, but help them understand that their central pursuit should be first and foremost Christ.

Let your reputation be one that speaks to young men as they are learning what it means to respect and care for women. Be an example of what a real woman looks like—not a raging feminist who challenges the male species at every turn, but a gentle voice that welcomes understanding, growth, and maturity. By this, they might just approach the next girl in their life with a higher level of regard for the person inside the pretty shell.

There are many young girls who don't have fatherly figures in their lives, and there are many young men who don't have motherly figures in their lives. Take this into consideration when you minister.

5. Do not—under *any* circumstances—gossip.

People, including women, are already horrible about this in church, and the worst, in my opinion, is that many times, personal information that should be kept confidential and slanderous stories are disguised as "prayer requests." If you have a congregation, you will hear concerns that are brought to you. Some will be sincere; others will only be given by those who want to be the first to deliver you the juicy news. If a person comes to you with "in-the-know" information, listen politely, tuck it in the back of your head, and never mention it again unless the situation gets so out of hand that you're forced to intervene. If the speaker is a repeat gossip, find a polite way of letting him or her know that *your* church will not be a place of slander.

Nothing can topple a ministry faster than a bunch of senseless rumors, and no woman's pulpit can crumble faster than when she allows herself to get in the middle of those rumors. Nothing can be so efficiently divided as when it happens from the inside out.

6. Have the support of your spouse.

If you are married, this is the most important of any of these rules. It may seem unfair if you feel called and your husband isn't on board. But while understanding that marriage is the most sacred of institutions ordained by God, He will not call a woman into ministry that would pull apart her marriage. Consider the "open-door" rule I mentioned prior. One rumor could subsequently wreak havoc upon a marriage and ruin a ministry as well. The last thing a woman minister should be known for is having disregarded her husband's convictions and disobeyed his wishes because she felt called to do what so many men today already interpret as Paul's explicit prohibition in Scripture. If your spouse doesn't agree with the direction you feel drawn toward, keep praying that God will either make His will known to your husband or reveal His more perfect will for you. If God wants you involved, rest assured that He will communicate with your spouse in time. On the other hand, God just might be using your husband as a sounding board to keep you from a path that isn't the right one for you at this time.

One thing is certain, a house divided will fall. A marriage that stands in disagreement with a ministry will be set up for failure from the beginning. Not only will a woman preacher be heading into murky waters without the support of her husband as it affects her reputation, but her closest and most important support system will be missing from the get-go.

That brings me to the next key point of this chapter on gender roles.

What does a biblical marriage look like? If today's culture makes no difference in "normative" and "absolute" regulations from Scripture, then what are women supposed to do when met with resistance against what they feel God has called them to do? What happens when a woman is married to a nonbeliever, or when she is challenged by a male church leader? When does she submit, and when does she obey God despite the confrontation of other humans? Where is the line between a woman who is only being obedient to God's will versus the woman who is a feminist agitator?

This is a touchy subject, but the answer always—*always*—comes back to two words: "prayer" and "balance." My publisher asked that I write a little about my own experience, as he believes my relationship with my husband, James, is a good example of what God intended marriage to be. I don't share the following as any kind of formula women should follow. I share it because one person's history can be another person's refinement.

My Story and Application

Anyone who knows me in person will know that I continuously and explicitly obey my husband. I respect his word over my own, and if there is ever a moment he tells me not to go in a specific direction, I submit to his authority. This is easy for me, because I followed the advice my mama gave me: "Be careful who you marry. Make sure the man you link yourself with for the rest of your life is one whom you can respect, and one who will respect you and the life God has called you to live." Before I ever tied the knot with James, I dated…a *lot*! I was not a promiscuous girl, and I was by no means a "player," but it ended up taking a lot of time and many relationships before I knew myself well enough to know what I needed for me. A common problem with the concept of women as the "submitters" is that a young woman can easily be misled into thinking that the man she is dating at the time is more in touch with God than she is, so when he pops the question—sometimes dropping a line that infers God has given him the green light on their union—she believes it is her place to accept. Add to this all those flittery and glowing "feelings" of a romantic relationship, and these girls are also led by their "hearts," which sounds like a beautiful thing until they realize that being led by the "heart" is not truly the same thing as being led by their impulsive "feelings" or "emotions."

Being "unequally yoked" (2 Corinthians 6:14) is a notion that has been preached about for so long and so heavily that it has lost some of its potency. A yoke is a wooden bar that joins two oxen and supports the weight of the load they pull. If one ox is large, strong, and muscular while the other is small and weak, the larger one is constantly moving ahead of the smaller one, slowing down the journey. In an extreme situation, if the smaller ox is either so weak it won't walk at all, or if it is belligerent and stands still, the larger ox will be resigned to walking around in circles or dragging the smaller ox where it does not want to go. When Paul wrote of this scenario with a spiritual application, he was warning that we do not bind ourselves in marriage to a weak or stubborn mate who will later place us in the position of spiritually walking around him in circles perpetually or force him to go somewhere he doesn't want to go (coercing him to attend church, begging him to accept Christ—and settling for a half-hearted and insincere "conversion sinner's prayer" said only to hush the spouse's persistence). Whereas God is almighty in power and can make one spouse strong and willing to walk in the same direction as the other, it is unwise to proceed in a relationship with the idea that God will "fix him or her later." This principle is true for both men and women. If you are not yet married and are still considering all those proverbial fish in the sea, make this warning a priority as you go. However, do not limit this verse to refer to spiritual passion or a belief in Christ. There is also the matter of *direction*. For anyone still single, this is perhaps the most important aspect of choosing a mate, just under their zeal for the Lord.

I dated many godly men who sought God and His approval before they pursued me or my approval. As we went out to various events, I always had a strange gut feeling that although they were equal to me in fervor (in fact, several of them were far more mature than I was at the time, spiritually speaking), the direction they were headed was different. I took the yoke warning seriously, knowing that even if both of us were large, strong, muscular oxen who believed wholeheartedly in Christ and wished to please Him with our lives, we would both be met with delay in our calling if we weren't headed in the same direction on the road of life. Submission, then, might actually become a means of relationship disintegration instead of a pleasant mutual show of respect and admiration: If he felt called one way and I the other, both of us evenly convinced of our calling, and yet both of us evenly submissive to the other (as per Ephesians 5:21), then who submits to the other—the wife to the husband or the husband to the wife? One has to submit, and as I am the female, it was even more important for me to avoid this situation as the verses about wives submitting to their husbands are heavily abused.

As such, I made sure that the way I advertised myself was in every way true to who I was, even before I really knew who that person was. It started with physical appearance, because the depth of the "real me" as a wife—the woman I had no experience in knowing yet—was obscured in naivety until I had interacted enough with young men to know my own strengths.

I remember the average first date: I would put on makeup, wear some chic thing from my closet, do my hair up with a bunch of chemicals and sprays, and perfume myself—the reasoning for this preparation up front instead of later was because I didn't want to bombard my dates with the idea that I was a slob who couldn't "act the part" when I was required to care about my appearance. Then, after the "you look nice" compliment, I knew I had an open door to describe who I normally was. I would sweetly accept the kind words, and then explain that, yes, the "makeup" version of Donna was my best face forward, and I wanted them to see I was capable of this and would return to it if ever a situation called for it, but that the "real me" was one who almost refused to "doll up" for any reason whatsoever, save for extremely special occasions. The "real me," I often explained, was a heavyset, redheaded tomboy who preferred to live, eat, and dress comfortably. I wasn't a slob, but I wasn't Donna Reed either, and I was going to make sure that precedent had been set. If we were to go on another date, these young men needed to be prepared to see a girl with fresh skin, a T-shirt, pajama pants, and sneakers who cared about health, but didn't obsessively count calories. Some might assume that such an explanation would discourage a suitor, but I assure you, it did the opposite. I knew who I was (when it came to the whole "delicate lady" routine), and I was determined to be *real*. I didn't believe in drawing a man in with eyeliner and mascara and then being accused of "letting the gut hang out" after the vows.

One after another, I watched as this approach got reactions such as: "Finally! A girl I can take out to pizza!"; "You mean you aren't going to always be twenty minutes late because of your eyeshadow? Awesome..."; "Fine by me. I'd rather you be real from the beginning than entice me with a physical appearance you don't plan to maintain." It surprised me that so many young men were actually *more* interested in me once they knew I had zero plans to impress them. It made me more independent because I didn't rely on their positive opinions of my appearance, which also made their pursuit more intriguing. Right away, I was not the "clingy girl" they attempted to avoid.

On the second date, and most thereafter, I would go along just as promised: no makeup, no big hairdo, no heels, no perfume, nothing dazzling. Just me, myself, and I, in the cozy way I carried myself on a daily basis. As a redhead, my eyelashes and eyebrows are almost exactly the same color as my skin, so they "disappear" if I'm not wearing makeup. The change from "dolled up" Donna to "natural" Donna has always been a dramatic one indeed (and it's a changeover that many women will never understand; a brunette or blonde still "has" eyebrows and eyelashes even when they're not enhanced, but some redheads like myself look as if we've shaved them off entirely because they blend in with the complexion). Again and again, this bold move proved to increase a young man's interest in me. I was what I was, take it or leave it.

Only twice, this was the point when I was dropped. Ryan and Isaac. Both were disenchanted with the idea of me as a mate when the face I was born with was the face that greeted them at the door. When their interest fizzled, I considered it a relief that their true feelings were revealed. Both of these young men were solidly God-fearing, but to them, a woman's *brain* came second to her face, and I knew that as a Christian girl I was always vulnerable to becoming some man's arm-candy if I wasn't careful—and that was a deep fear from the beginning.

It wasn't that I was playing mind games or attempting to pull a switcheroo on anyone. I had even warned my dates that I would be appearing in subsequent outings *au naturel.* I was just disgusted with the dating game as I saw it play out amidst my peers, and I was always anxious to have the already awkward "what's your favorite movie" routine over with so we could get to the real meat of this "getting to know you" game—which, for me, involved knowing not what they *wanted* in a woman as much as what they *expected* from her: I couldn't be what they wanted if I could never live up to what they expected, so that always had to be figured out first. I had grown up in church, and I had seen the way some women were pressured to present themselves perfectly on the outside, participate in every bake sale, make crafts for each fundraiser, attend all social functions, organize potlucks, raise amazing children, and cook delicious meals for their husbands (meals they couldn't possibly indulge in themselves lest they put on a little extra girth around the middle). It was a stifling life for some of these women, who appeared perfect on the outside but who were unfulfilled and secretly lost on the inside, and I wanted no part of that life for myself or my future husband or children.

One of my closest older friends once told me while I was in my teens: "Don't be in a hurry, Donna. Know who you really are and what you really want before you promise your life to someone. You'll regret it all your days if you do what I did and tie the knot before you've worked all that out." I took her advice to heart (thank goodness!), but the problem was, I didn't know who I was, and I didn't know how to "work that out." I was a teenager with a hearty laugh and an aggressively independent spirit, but how would that transfer into womanhood?

Looking back, I can see that all the strange quirks of my true nature—the personality that God instilled within me—were manifesting in this "no makeup" creed. It would have been difficult to find a way of announcing that I didn't want to be the same kind of wife as some of those I had observed around me in church on a first date, so my psyche took that anxiety and channeled it into a stance on physical appearance. If I didn't *look like* "wifey," I was distanced from "wifey" even on some subliminal level.

Then, one night at youth group, I heard the pastor's son, Brandon (he was about seventeen years old, and single at the time), sharing his opinion about what "real men" ought to be in a casual conversation before service started: "Where has our chivalry gone? Is this how we practice acting like men? We see a pretty face, experience a biological reaction, date her until we find out the pretty face didn't come with all the features *we* want, and then we dump her for the next one in line?" I don't know what he had recently gone through or witnessed to make him explode like this, because usually if Brandon was going to explode, it would be with smiles and side hugs. On this occasion, he was outraged. Others around me were shocked as well, and even the youth pastor looked over to listen to the impromptu mini-sermon that had begun:

> Young men, you are never going to find the godly woman that you dream about unless you become the man *they* dream about. Don't just talk to girls, learn them. Get a feel for what God has called *them* to do. Ask them about *their* ministry ideas. It's not all about *you*, bros! It's also about her! The kind of support your future wife will give to you will depend on the calling God has given her first. We have to let go of this concept that we, the

men, are the only ones God speaks to while our wives follow us around having babies. Don't just date to see how well they fit you, date to see how well your skills fit them. No, they are not better than you, and they are not more in touch with God than you, but you must stop thinking you're their superior.

If you're truly and sincerely a real man, you're not going to play the dating game with the idea that you're out there to find a leaf that will blow in your own wind. You will care deeply about their passions and opinions, and below all those hormonal or butterflies-in-the-stomach reactions, you will want to protect her and support her. You will want to make sure no harm ever falls upon her. You will look at this gentle, feminine face and your thoughts will be for her well-being, not your future marital bed and the skirt attached to your arm. *That's* how we practice being real men, bros.

It hadn't occurred to me until I heard this guy going on and on about a "real man" that I had been overlooking chivalry as a crucial factor in a relationship. Mind you, I'm not talking about a man opening a door for a woman, putting down his coat out over puddles so her heels don't get muddy, stooping down to retrieve her dropped handkerchief, or even earning a lot of money so he can buy her diamonds and fancy gifts. All those classical concepts of chivalry are romantic and beautiful, but any man can do these things and still have wrong intentions—and Brandon's outburst covered that as well. I'm talking about chivalry of heart.

A "real man" enters a relationship with a priority of protecting and providing for a woman what he can provide within his own means. A "real man" appreciates a woman's chastity and purity, never intending to defile her. A "real man" understands that any woman he marries is going to have a call upon her life that is unique to her, and he will endeavor to support her in that process. A "real man" cares for a woman's well-being and happiness over his own.

And a "real woman" would do the same on all these counts for her man.

What an exquisite example of the relationship God intended us to have!

As obvious as that should have been for me, I had been so busy making my own statements of independence (often making the first move, paying for meals, opening the door for men, wearing sneakers, and doing anything I could to distance myself from the "weak female" label), that it never occurred to me how important it was to let myself be a lady and let my date be the gentleman. I was so busy trying to exert myself as an equal that I was acting as if I thought I were *identical.* Instilled within me, deeply to the point that I didn't recognize it well enough to uproot it, had been this concept that I was only dating men to show them what I could offer for their future. After all my efforts to avoid being one of the women whom I had seen struggle in their wifely role, I had inadvertently picked up the idea that dating was my audition for them, instead of a mutual experience.

I was a child of the Church. I was slated to be the "submissive wife" for my time here on earth, and that biblical principle had been so distorted that even the teenage boys in my youth group had grown to believe they were superior to me, even though I wasn't in the lineup for becoming their future spouse. The thought of being trapped in a marriage that didn't honor the authentic relationship God designed terrified me, but I wasn't cognitively aware that this was my deepest fear.

Had these young men gone on dates with me because they valued my mind, my desires, and my true calling?

That's when it dawned on me. I wasn't finding a real man, because I hadn't been looking for a real man. I was going to movies and eating pizza and playing a "dating game." But what did a real man look like on the outside? How would I know when I had found one?

All those years when I had prioritized being the "natural Donna" were not lost. (Many women—who would never dream of leaving their house without their makeup on or until they lose five more pounds—

have told me that my honest self-acceptance of appearing on TV and behind pulpits without a stitch of makeup and comfortable in my own one-hundred-eighty-plus-pound body has inspired them to love and accept themselves just the way God made them.) These experiences played a huge role in developing me for my marriage with James. Many other dates occurred before James, but when *that* relationship came along, I recognized something refreshing...

I'll never forget the early days. I went on my first real date as usual: makeup, hairdo, chic clothing, and so on at a nice dinner place near home. When James complimented me, I made sure he knew this was only one side of me, to which he responded positively. The restaurant had live music and a patio where we talked for hours about life, religion, philosophy, and our own feelings and beliefs on all those subjects. I wanted to know what was in his mind more than I wanted to know anything else about him, since I already knew he was a man of faith, and I was encouraged when he repeatedly began each conversation segue with, "What are your thoughts on [fill in the blank]?" You mean there was really a guy out there who cared what *I* thought about something? There was a man who valued a woman's opinion? Some man other than my dad? It wasn't until James started asking about my take on things that I realized how infrequently I had heard those questions from other men.

Our second date was breakfast at the Village Inn. We met at nine o'clock on a Saturday morning. My hair was in a messy bun, and I was wearing pajama pants, flip-flops, and a red T-shirt. Again, we talked of many deep things, and he didn't treat me any differently than he had when I had been in the "dolled up" version of myself. On our third date, when the subject of women's rights and religious leadership came up, I made sure he knew that was an essential factor from the start: I didn't know what my calling was yet, but I needed to insist that when I figured it out, I would be allowed to fulfill that role; that needed to be said before I got serious with anyone. His answer was balanced, and it showed a lot about him as a person. Additionally, it became what I now believe should be the stance of any Christian man considering a wife: James said he would not allow himself to become a slave to any woman, because he had his own direction in life, but he would remain devoted to supporting a woman in any role she believed God gave her, even when that support required attention or action from him. He didn't believe that it was his place to continually assess or assert himself over a woman's role or calling, but if he should ever marry, he believed a gentle criticism along the way may be required from him to her, and he hoped to find himself an open-minded woman who showed a willingness to grow— and who didn't believe she had the answers to everything. Why would any woman want to yoke herself to a man in the first place if she only needed him for cuddling? If that were the case, a woman could buy a cat, James said, but any person entering into a marital relationship needs to do so with the understanding that growth is mutual, marriage is interdependent, and the whole purpose of the sacred union is, through joining into one, to become better individuals in the process. That puts both husband and wife in the position to accept gentle critiques from one another. Furthermore, he said, he believed that women could do anything men could do, but women should never attempt to take over or dominate men in the process; nor should a man attempt to rule over his woman, because it's simply not the ideal relationship that God designed.

Wow! So *that's* what a "real man" looked like...

James was quickly earning my trust. He respected me, treated me like a gem, cared more about my mind than my mascara—and above all, he truly cared about my happiness and God-given calling upon my life. Whether he would have used the words of Paul at the time or not, James was aware that women are the "glory of man" (1 Corinthians 11:7).

We had other dates, certainly, but this conversation was the one that did it for me. I assure you that I did not tell him at this time, but I knew in this moment that James would be my husband. I knew this because I had trusted the Lord to bring me someone who would complement my life, including my own future role in ministry, whilst also expecting the same from me. I knew James wouldn't let me become a domineering female (which hadn't been my goal anyway, but I have a strong personality and I *am* human, so that was a possibility in the wrong relationship), yet he had no plans to rule over me like a king to a servant. He didn't just *love* me, he *liked* who I was and wanted to be a part of making me better—and I felt the same way toward him. Neither of us knew what the future held, but it wasn't long before he casually told me he would be honored if I would be his wife, and the rest is history.

Since the day I married James, we have locked horns occasionally, but overall, we have had a loving, *mutual* respect and submission to each other. I obey him always, but that should not be taken to mean that there is always a rule I must obey. For instance, James does not want me to travel alone, for safety purposes. He wants me to be protected, so if I go out of state, he wants me to have an appropriate travel partner. This is his role, as a husband, to see to the protection of his wife, and the Holy Spirit is guiding him to do so. Therefore, to respect and submit to his wishes in this area is to show respect, submission, and obedience to God, who gave me this man as provision.

However, the reason I can go forward in obedience to my husband so comfortably is because we established from the beginning what that obedience was going to look like. Had he said on our third date that his woman must "obey" by always baking him cookies and keeping the house clean, I wouldn't have married him in the first place. As for missed travel opportunities, I have put that in God's hands. I believe that it is *God, Himself,* steering James' provision over me. If someone wants me to go to California for a television interview, God will either provide me a traveling companion, or He will not...and if He doesn't, I trust that it wasn't an interview He wanted me to carry out anyway.

If you are still single, be sure to talk at length with your potential spouse about what "obedience" and "submission" look like in a marriage. It is *crucial* to discuss that deeply and with mutual respect, so that when an issue comes up you didn't plan for (such as traveling alone), the subject can be addressed in a way that benefits both husband and wife. Therefore, after the act of submission (in this case, myself submitting to James), both the husband's and the wife's prayers can go up together in a way that strengthens them even more and proves even greater reliance upon God (in this case, we pray that God provides a traveling companion if I am supposed to travel out of state).

By now, you might be wondering if I, too, have asked for my husband to submit to me at times. As a matter of fact, I have, and he respects me in those occasions very well. For instance, when he and I are having a conversation, I ask that we ignore our cellphones, because I don't like talking to someone who is staring at an electronic device any more than a husband would like to talk to the back of his wife's head. The dinner table, where our two children eat with us and hold a Bible study every night, is a no-cellphone zone, unless there is a justifiable reason to have it present (such as when my brother's wife was expected to go into labor any moment last year). There are certain conversations that I don't want to have around our kids until they're older, because little mouths may repeat certain words in the wrong context elsewhere, so when James wants to have a more mature conversation (such as the promiscuity or gender-bending in our nations' youth circles, political opinions we hold regarding our former president, etc.), he has agreed to wait until we're alone. I have asked that James not teach my children about a few aspects of Hell just yet, because both of them are still at the "nightmares" phase of life, and he has agreed to wait. If I ever have a gut feeling or what I perceive to be a word from the Lord, I expect that to be taken seriously, and it always is. All these "rules" could have been given to me, and I would have respected them as well.

But most of the time, our "rules" for each other are mutual: Neither of us goes anywhere alone with a member of the opposite sex; neither of us spends an unusually large sum of money without checking with the other; neither of us commits to host an event at our house without

.e other; neither of us obligates the other to attend a
..on without checking with the other; and so on. Probably 90
..nt of our "submission rules" apply to both of us equally, and none
requires subservience or the acknowledgment of superiority/inferiority.

I submit to my husband freely, of my own will, and he submits to
me freely, of his own will, on topics ranging from vocabulary words all
the way to intimacy. By this, we are holding high the biblical standards:

- "Let every man have his own wife, and let every woman have
  her own husband. Let the husband render unto the wife due
  benevolence: and likewise also the wife unto the husband. The
  wife hath not power of her own body, but the husband: and
  likewise also the husband hath not power of his own body, but
  the wife" (1 Corinthians 7:2–4).
- "Submitting yourselves one to another in the fear of God. Wives,
  submit yourselves unto your own husbands, as unto the Lord.
  For the husband is the head of the wife, even as Christ is the head
  of the church: and he is the saviour of the body. Therefore as the
  church is subject unto Christ, so let the wives be to their own husbands in every thing. Husbands, love your wives, even as Christ
  also loved the church, and gave himself for it; That he might
  sanctify and cleanse it with the washing of water by the word,
  That he might present it to himself a glorious church, not having
  spot, or wrinkle, or any such thing; but that it should be holy
  and without blemish. So ought men to love their wives as their
  own bodies. He that loveth his wife loveth himself.… For this
  cause shall a man leave his father and mother, and shall be joined
  unto his wife, and they two shall be one flesh.… [Note that if the
  two become one, as Paul states here, one is not "over" the other,
  because they are "one unit" together.] Nevertheless let every one
  of you in particular so love his wife even as himself; and the wife
  see that she reverence her husband" (Ephesians 5:21–33).

- A godly man must be "One that ruleth well his own house, having his children in subjection with all gravity" (1 Timothy 3:4), while a godly woman must "guide the house [and] give no occasion to the adversary to speak reproachfully" (1 Timothy 5:14).

I couldn't be luckier or happier in my marriage. And yes, it is a relationship that God put together, but it also required—on my part as well as that of James—to understand what we needed as individuals and what we were looking for in a mate well before we committed to someone in this life.

We see each other as a life mate God has given each of us to sharpen one other as individuals, and thus to His service. If God gives someone the gift of a spouse, He intends for that person to take care of that gift.

For those who are already in a marital relationship whose spouse may not be as respectful toward them as James is toward me, all hope is not lost. A truthful, open-minded study of these biblical passages has the power to restore a marriage to the union that God designed. If two people love God and each other so much that they place their own feelings aside for the other, then when a disagreement comes along, a sound answer can be found through love, support, and submission from both spouses. It is a recipe of restoration that ends without anyone ever having to "have the last word"—as long as it can be appropriately and practically applied. A wife should pray that God will help her want to go along with her husband's wishes; a husband should pray that God will help him want to go along with his wife's wishes; and *both* should pray for God to reveal His will in the matter, because, regardless of whatever each partner wants, His way is the best.

If two marriage partners are equally yoked, they will be attached to the same load, and heading the same direction.

This is my personal story, and the application that can be gleaned from sharing it. As a wrap-up of this section, I will share that I still don't wear makeup unless I absolutely must, I still wear whatever is comfortable,

I still prefer an intellectual conversation (especially regarding exegesis and Scripture) over most other activities, I still require a substantial amount of alone time, and I have become the grown-up version of the little bookworm nerd God created me to be—and my husband wouldn't change a thing. When I told him that I felt called to put myself through Bible school and obtain my ministerial credentials to become a reverend, I didn't dare proceed without his permission. Had he told me I was not allowed to preach or teach—to women, men, or both—I would have accepted that as God's way of telling me it wasn't the right path for me to be on, or that the timing wasn't right. I am in a position many women, regretfully, are not in, because I believe God sincerely speaks through my husband to help steer me on the correct path toward my greatest maturity and achievements. This, in our situation, is *true* submission via voluntary respect, as opposed to fulfilling a domestic role or putting up with being treated poorly via commanded subjection.

My story of achieving a healthy submission relationship aside, however, there remains one major theological hindrance for women on this subject.

The Man as the "Recipient" over His Family

I can't count how many sermons I have heard that suggest that God speaks first to the male presence in every household, some of which go as far as to say the man is "priest" over his household (a term that does not appear anywhere in Scripture). There may be biblical evidence that points to the idea that God delivers His instructions first to the man (Abraham, for example), but there is also biblical evidence that refutes this, such as when God spoke first to Samson's mother of His plans to raise up another judge over Israel, including all that was to be expected of her as she raised him. This was done even though we know that there was a husband in the picture whom God could have chosen to instruct first. And if Joseph was betrothed (engaged) to Mary, he would have been the legal male of their "household" (i.e., union, marriage) when the angel Gabriel gave instructions to Mary first, even though Mary and Joseph were not yet residing in the same home. This is a significant example, because Mary was young, and the instruction/revelation given to her regarded her carrying the very Son of God.

One reason this concept is held by so many Christians today is because of a misinterpretation of Paul's words: "Wives, submit yourselves unto your own husbands, as unto the Lord. For the husband is the head of the wife, even as Christ is the head of the church: and he is the saviour of the body. Therefore as the church is subject unto Christ, so let the wives be to their own husbands in every thing" (Ephesians 5:22–24). Yet, we should not assume that Paul's comparison holds an underlying insinuation that the man is a "type of Christ"—and therefore a *spiritual* authority—over his wife, as so many have done. More simply, Paul's words should be taken exactly as they were delivered, which could be rewritten in contemporary language as: "Wives, you must submit to the authority of your husbands, in the same way that the Church submits to the authority of Christ." Likewise, Paul says in verse 25, husbands are to love their wives, which, at times, will require their willingness to surrender their own desires or comforts to love them completely, just as Christ did: "Husbands, love your wives, even as Christ also loved the church, and gave himself for it." Yes, these verses address a wife's submission to her husband and the husband's love of the wife, but we need to accept that there is no hidden meaning about a man being the only recipient of God's instructions or will.

The first issue this "man as recipient" concept raises is how unfair that would be for the woman. However, let's not forget how unfair such a concept would be for a man! Imagine a home where the man is the sole receiver of truth. What man would want to bear that responsibility? If a woman or child in that family is given instruction by the husband or

267

father to do something, and that activity is later identified (even unintentionally) as a sinful or immoral act, then who is ultimately responsible for the sin? It would be the man's fault that the woman or child sinned. It may appeal to some men who seek more power and some women who wish to avoid responsibility, but ultimately, this arrangement produces huge problems. What if the man is internally corrupt and orders a member of his family to do something evil? If he is the recipient of God's instruction, then should that family member obey him in order to obey God, even though he's ordered something that goes against the Bible's instruction? Heaven forbid! Doesn't Acts 5:29 say, "We ought to obey God rather than men"? Weren't Ananias and Sapphira equally punished for their transgression in Acts 5:1–11? And don't get me started on how many angles this theology would *not* apply to the Adam and Eve account.

Or, as another example, what if the man is not stepping up to fulfill his duty as priest over his family, as *so many* families today face? These homes would not have any righteous teaching at all if a woman had to rely on her finite husband as the archetypal "Christ."

I know a godly woman whose husband began to migrate away from God's Word, teaching outlandish ideas to their children as he delved ever deeper into conspiratorial "fringe gospels." His beliefs became so corrupt and fantastical (God was really an alien, Paul was really a heretic planted by fallen angels to corrupt the early Church, etc.) that she felt she was given no choice but to insist that he no longer teach the children about God. Not only was she "usurping his 'priestly' authority" within the household, but she took this responsibility onto herself after stripping him of it. Was it right or wrong to do so? It was a hard line for her to draw, but her children were counting on her for accurate, biblical teaching. The bottom line, as made perfectly clear throughout the whole of Scripture, is that God speaks to individuals—male, female, slave, free, young, old, rich, poor, etc.—and each is held accountable for the instructions God gives through personal revelation as well as adherence to the Word, which openly assigns the word "priest" to anyone who follows Christ (1 Peter 2:9).

Nonbelieving Husbands

The issue of submission gets into muddy waters when a person's husband is not a believer of Christ. First, we must always remember that the top authority—well before that of any "man" or "woman"—is God. If a man tells his wife to do something outlined in Scripture as wrong, then by no means should the wife obey. She may answer to her husband, but she answers to the Lord above all else (which, in my opinion, answers the aforementioned question of the wife who limited her husband's ability to teach biblical issues to her children). If the issue is not a moral one, then, whenever possible, a wife should still humble herself and submit, assuming it doesn't place her in harm's way.

Paul and Peter, together, made it clear that a wife's faith, humility, modesty, fidelity, and "chaste conversation" have great influence over the conversion of a nonbelieving husband (1 Corinthians 7:14–17; 1 Peter 3:1–7). (Peter also said in this reference that a man's prayers could be hindered if he doesn't "honor" his wife with love and unity.)

If you are married to a nonbeliever, remember what was said earlier about the yoke. If you are spiritually the strong ox and your husband is the weak, pulling him along by force will not accomplish sincere conversion. There may be a few miracle stories in circulation regarding a woman begging her husband relentlessly to go to church, and then when he finally agrees in order to silence her, he finds the Lord in a radical intervention. This is not the norm—and, in many cases, pestering a man to go along with something he doesn't believe in is only going to *increase* his resistance to the faith. A man does not want to be "fixed," he wants to be desired! The greatest witness of Christ—no matter what the situation—is when a believer allows his or her choices, lifestyle, aura, and mannerisms throughout the day to shine through him or her like the light Christ spoke of (Matthew 5:14). If love is shown always and continually, eventually those around the believer—including the husband—will be inspired to ask, "What *is* that 'it factor' in her that makes her this way? How can she be so patient and kind at every turn?" It is then that she can tell her husband how much the Savior desires him.

Also consider how hopeless his situation might be. Believers have the Creator of the universe to talk to at all times, and if we belong to a church, we have a spiritual family at the ready whenever we need a listening ear. A man may have a group of friends, but his concepts about the afterlife may be incredibly bleak, especially if he is an atheist. Each time someone mentions death, he is reminded of how short his own existence is, and every time a loved one passes, he has zero hope for ever seeing that person again. Whom does he have to talk to? What a lonely life some people lead… A woman married to a nonbeliever will surely feel lonely, but if her husband is under the impression that she belongs to a family he can't belong to, his feelings of isolation may be even greater than hers. But by being available for questions and gentle in countenance—*without jerking him by the yoke around his neck*—he's likely to come around and ask his wife what she believes in these, and similar, situations.

If you have an unbelieving husband, try as hard as possible to see him in the same way God saw you before you surrendered your life to Christ: You were a lost soul in need of a Savior. It's not about getting a man to say words or attend a service, it's about reaching past the wall and loving the lost. A believing wife should never act as if she's more enlightened than her husband because she accepts the truth and her husband doesn't. Nor should she be motivated by the idea that he will finally come around to agree with her. A wife should always remember that her husband is as loved as she is by the Messiah she serves, and it's not about winning a debate or proving anything. It's a soul in the balance, and the central motivation should always be that the husband is so loved by the wife that she wishes for him to not only join her in eternity, but also live with the earthly joy and riches such faith can provide. After all, if we are to love our spouses the way that Christ first loved us, then this is how we would love them, is it not?

If you are married to a nonbeliever, pray that God will give you a love for your husband that is so profound it can't possibly originate from the human heart in its finite box of temporal emotions. Pray that the Holy Spirit will tug at your husband persistently, so that even if he doesn't admit it aloud, he feels the power each time Christ's name is spoken. The Holy Spirit does not need your husband's permission to bring the Name of Jesus to life each time he hears it.

Denying Female Leadership Actually Harms the Church

One final item on this list regarding gender roles that is necessary to address before we move on is the idea that by denying women leadership positions within the Church of Jesus Christ, only the women are affected. In fact, the gifts of the Spirit might be the same bestowed upon men and women alike, but the way they are used is not the same for men as it is for women, and when suppression of an entire gender population occurs, it harms the whole Body. Even Paul acknowledged this when he wrote, "And whether one member suffer, all the members suffer with it; or one member be honoured, all the members rejoice with it" (1 Corinthians 12:26).

When Pentecostal healing minister Katherine Kuhlman stepped up to the platform in her flowing gowns and pretty jewelry in the 1970s, the theology she delivered from a pulpit might be seen as similar to the theology a man would deliver, but it had a gentility, a *draw*, that no man could have imitated. She pulled in crowds by the hundreds, then thousands, then hundreds of thousands, and her ministry resulted in uncountable, medically documented healings. Who can deny such influence? Was it because she was a woman? No, because the Lord can use anyone. Did she reach specific people who would only respond to the kind of ministry this woman led? Absolutely, yes. And the same can be said for any woman. Women simply *can* reach people in a way that men cannot, having been endowed with different attributes of God's image, so every denomination or church that places male-only limitations on its ministry is stunting its own potential!

According to the Pew Research Center, the population of women attending Protestant Christian churches ("Mainline Protestant," "Evangelical Protestant," and "Historically Black Protestant," as the PRC has them listed) outweighs men by up to 59 percent.[120] In their overall summary, posted in the article "The Gender Gap in Religion around the World: Women Are Generally More Religious than Men, Particularly among Christians," they relay:

> In the United States, for example, women are more likely than men to say religion is "very important" in their lives (60% vs. 47%), according to a 2014 Pew Research Center survey. American women also are more likely than American men to say they pray daily (64% vs. 47%) and attend religious services at least once a week (40% vs. 32%).... [W]omen so outnumber men in the pews of many U.S. churches that some clergy have changed decor, music and worship styles to try to bring more men into their congregations....
>
> Based on these wide-ranging and comprehensive datasets, this study finds that, globally, women *are* more devout than men by several standard measures of religious commitment.[121] (Emphasis in original)

By disallowing women leadership roles, the Church is cutting down its ministerial capabilities and outreach potential by more than half the population of contributors!

Whereas I normally wouldn't engage in an argument related to which gender is more devoted to work, it is a well-known and documented fact that men generally see themselves as the harder-working gender, and this contemporary cultural concept contributes to why females wouldn't be viewed as productive in the ministry as males, as I have heard preached. According to governmental researchers (primarily the Bureau of Labor Statistics within the US Department of Labor) in various studies since 2003, and as reported by the *Washington Post*, "men have reported devoting more life to paid labor than their female counterparts...[while] unpaid labor [such as domestic chores] has long disproportionately fallen on women's shoulders. Women worldwide spend an average of 4.5 hours each day on unpaid work—cooking, cleaning, feeding the baby [in addition to their paid labor]. Men devote less than half that much time, according to the OECD."[122] So, yes: Men do often spend more time in "the workplace." This has contributed to the misunderstanding that men work harder than women. Really, though, it's because the fruit of their labor is quantified in monetary form so they have a tangible measurement of their productivity.

However, in our current culture, many marriages involve *both* the husband and wife in a full-time job at "the workplace," and the women are still the domestic sweethearts, as the article states: "In the United States, women now financially support 40 percent of homes *and* tend to take on more domestic chores."[123] I don't mean to suggest that this is always unfair, as many women enjoy coming home from work and cooking a meal for her family. In fact, I, *myself*, do this daily—as do my mother and sister. All three of us work well over forty hours per week at our jobs, we're all on salary pay (not hourly), and we still have smiles on our faces when we come home to whip up a nice meal for our families. (I will admit that my husband, *of his own will*, often helps with laundry and dishes in our home.) I approach this with an "if it's not broke, don't fix it" outlook. I am not setting out to prove that women are mistreated or that their labors of love are overlooked (although they sometimes are),

I am only attempting to show how hard-working most of us are. If a woman is fulfilled in this "full-time job plus domestic chores" position (*as I am!*), then that's wonderful.

Awesome. Great. Nobody's offended and everybody's happy. Including myself.

But—it becomes an insult to women when men stand behind a pulpit and proclaim that the ministry belongs to the men because they are "the working sex"; these men are dramatically inaccurate, considering statistics of the norm. Take the average woman's full-time job (forty hours) and add the average "4.5 hours each day on unpaid work" documented above (which also includes the weekends, since dishes, laundry, cooking, and cleaning duties never stop), and "the average woman" is working 71.5 hours every week!

What a hard-working breed women are!

Melinda Gates, wife of America's prized Microsoft entrepreneur Bill Gates, also looked at these statistics and responded in an open letter of her own:

> This isn't a global plot by men to oppress women [and I agree with her here…]. It's more subtle than that. The division of work depends on cultural norms, and we call them norms because they seem normal—so normal that many of us don't notice the assumptions we're making. But your generation can notice them—and keep pointing them out until the world pays attention.…
>
> In TV commercials you see, how often are men doing laundry, cooking, or running after kids? (The answer: 2 percent of the time.) How many of the women are advertising kitchen or cleaning products? (More than half.)[124]

The assumption that men work harder than women finds its genesis in the hours reported in the workplace, but even those numbers are starting to even out, which points to the fact that women are frequently—whether some want to admit it or not—working more than men today when they come home from a full-time job and begin their second job for their family. (Readers, do not take this as an all-encompassing statement! Bear with me. Keep reading…)

And we can't assume for a moment that men are better in the workplace and women are better at home, just because of how God designed our genders. If a church leadership position involved administrative duties as well, women are just as competent to be entrusted with that work, as studies have shown.

As one example: In 2012, a research study was conducted by the Ponemon Institute in conjunction with the company 3M, who developed the 3M Privacy Filters (panels that attach to the computer monitor and cut out external distractions, as well as increase the privacy of the worker's screen). The study involved 274 participants from five different companies, and the purpose of the two experiments (one with the filters, one without) was to show the increase of productivity for participants who had installed the 3M Privacy Filters. Though the study did not initially focus on gender-related data, a collection of interesting facts was compiled:

> Results of both experiments indicate a gender effect, wherein female subjects worked longer than male subjects…. [F]emale subjects whose computer had a 3M filter worked 4.9 minutes versus 4.3 minutes for male subjects. Similarly, without an installed filter, female subjects worked 2.5 minutes as compared to 2.1 minutes for males.
>
> Findings reveal an unexpected interaction between the gender of the researcher and subject. The average time worked was 4.0 minutes when both the researcher and the subject are female and 3.6 minutes when the researcher and the subject are male. In contrast, the combination of female researcher and male

subject worked, on average, 2.8 minutes during the 10-minute experimental period.

Gender also makes a difference with respect to the walk away versus continue working response during the experimental waiting period. Accordingly, 55 female subjects (38 percent) walked away rather than worked on their computer during a 10-minute waiting period. For male subjects, 67 (52 percent) walked away during the waiting period.[125]

Now, to use this one study as "proof" that women are more efficient than men in the workplace would be biased, immature, and ridiculous, to say the least. Please understand that I am not trying to form a feminist, "women are better" argument. That has not been my goal anywhere else in the book, and it certainly isn't my goal now. If it were, then I would quote from one or several of the hundreds of articles that claim science has proven women are of higher intelligence. (Google it for yourself… They are out there.)

Why don't I quote these articles and make a big statement about women's intellectual superiority over men?

Because I don't believe it for a second!

History has shown equality of intelligence between men and women based on their individual achievements (for example: theoretical physicist Albert Einstein, first female Noble Prize winner and physicist Marie Curie), not on science and research studies. History has also shown equality of leadership skills between men and women based on individual achievements (General Patton at Normandy, Joan of Arc of the Hundred Years' War). The minute someone in the Church Body grasps onto a single "proof study" that one gender is better, smarter, or predisposed to be more efficient leaders, our Christ-centered focus of reaching the lost is thrown off-course. I am simply attempting to show how great a loss it is that women are viewed as the cookie-bakers of the Body while only the men are viewed as the preachers and teachers.

That. Is. Not. What. God. Designed.

We are not created "the same"; we are created "equal"—and there's a difference.

Consider what is taking place when a man steps behind a pulpit. He is delivering God's Word the way a male brain interprets it, from a male's perspective, involving a male's system of logic and reasoning, influenced by the world and culture as a male sees it—which I can guarantee does not encompass the historical "Susie Homemaker baggage" the average woman faces—and he is accomplishing all of this in front of a congregation that the Pew Research Center has qualified as predominantly *women*.

What's wrong with this picture? Nothing. In fact, as iron sharpens iron, it has greatly benefitted me personally at times to hear a male perspective throughout the week at a church service, so nothing is innately wrong with a male preacher…

Until it is decided that a woman cannot deliver God's Word the way a female brain interprets it, from a female's perspective, involving a female's system of logic and reasoning, influenced by the world and culture as a female sees it. *Then* it becomes a tragedy that might very well have eternal implications: We're removing 50 percent of the faithful population's Holy-Spirit-given gifts that, like Katherine Kuhlman, may be even more effective in the Gospel commission to specific hearers who might be lost forever if the glorious truth of Christ isn't preached to its fullest potential among the saints! A man cannot always stand behind a pulpit and relate to what a woman in the pew is thinking or feeling. Likewise, if there are no women preachers or teachers, men can't gain the nurturing insight of women.

This harms the Church more than it helps the Church, folks! It's not a matter of feminism, women's lib movements, or proving anyone is better than anyone else. It's a matter of rejecting the equality that: 1) God the Father designed in the Garden of Eden when He created *both genders in His image*, 2) Jesus Christ inspired and supported throughout

His ministry on earth, and 3) the Holy Spirit equipped on the Day of Pentecost.

We have probably all heard someone ask, "How many potential scientists, warriors, presidents, and world leaders have been aborted by selfish or frightened women?" This question is thought-provoking, because it speaks to a "what might have been" curiosity we all occasionally ruminate. But I wonder: How many potential soul-winning ministries or churches have been aborted by the rejection of the biblical principles of equality in ministry?

I also once heard it said, "Anyone can count the seeds in a single apple, but only God can count the apples in a single seed." God *alone* knows the potential a woman has within her to draw the lost toward Him, but the "freedom to speak" seed must be planted within her for her full potential to materialize.

Ladies, with so many "gender identification" issues circulating the nation today, we have never needed your feminine voice of leadership more than now! We need women to show younger girls what a woman looks like, and we need women to show young men what to look for!

In conclusion: A minister should be appointed by God based on the qualifications He has bestowed, not based on one's gender, race, or anything else.

For women who sincerely feel called to respond, prepare yourself to minister. Nobody can complete the work God began in you but Him (Philippians 1:6).

8

"Prepare Yourself to Minister"

Do you feel it?" I asked my friends at a sleepover party nearly twenty years ago.

It was almost two o'clock in the morning. The room had been completely silent for approaching fifteen minutes. Nobody present had known that while they were drifting off to sleep in the dark with only a sliver of moonlight falling through the high window, I was on my back, fingers laced behind my head, listening to their breathing as each of them slowly took on that classic, deep rhythm of slumber.

When nobody answered, I tried again.

"Do you feel it?"

"What?!" one of them asked, slightly annoyed.

"The 'falling,'" I said. I raised up on one elbow with a serious expression, as if to suggest that my question was a perfectly reasonable one to offer at that moment.

"Oh my gosh, Donna! For crying out loud!"

At this, the room erupted in laughter. Those who had been asleep were elbowed awake and immediately told about my endearing lapse in judgment, everyone quite amused at my decision to disrupt the peace-fulness for such a ridiculous inquiry.

This "falling" to which I had been referring was that all-too-familiar sensation that creeps over the human body less than a minute before it is truly surrendered to sleep. I learned through this experience that not everyone—very few in fact—is aware of the "falling." I didn't know that this so-called human phenomenon had a name. Science refers to this as *hypnagogia*: the state between wakefulness and sleep. For some sleepers, it occurs while they are completely aware of the relationship between mind and body—the *hypnagogic* state of consciousness in those moments just before the mind begins to dream—and they can feel and sense things that defy our typical, physical, corporeal existence. Thoughts they wouldn't normally think and feelings they wouldn't normally feel are quickened within them as the body and mind coast to a different, almost transcen-dent, cognizance—an awareness prized by the world's most celebrated artists since the dawn of time, as it is within those precious seconds the greatest of human creativity has been reported to "unlock."

I remember the conversation I had with my friends earlier that day, well before bedtime.

"Hey, do you guys ever feel like you're *falling* right before you go to sleep?"

Wrinkled eyebrows told me I was not being understood.

"Come on, you know what I mean, right? It's like, you *know* you're falling asleep, but you're not asleep yet, but you're, um…it's like you feel you're gently drifting downward? Like you're falling on air? Like your room and the mattress aren't there anymore, and you're thinking about a million things at once, but you're still able to think about the falling sensation?"

No. They had no idea what I was talking about.

I have since learned that I am in the minority of people who expe-rience this often. For me, the phenomenon is frequently immediately followed by another I later learned was called the "hypnic jerk": an involuntary muscle spasm during or after *hypnagogia* that shocks a person to sudden and full awareness. As is the case for me, this hypnic jerk is recurrently accompanied by a quick, plotless dream wherein I am falling from the sky and jolt awake just as, or just before, I hit the ground. I am thankful that I have a second chance. Whereas almost everyone I have asked about this has answered that they have experienced the hypnic jerk, very few have said they were completely aware of mind and body during the preceding "falling" of *hypnagogia*.

But this phenomenon just took on fresh meaning to me…

Several years ago now, I started to feel uncomfortable about the world around me. Every day, all day, I was aware of a sensation I couldn't explain. It was like my spiritual skin was being prickled by the winds of change. I had written about it, I had spoken about it on episodes of SkyWatch TV, but I could not explain it. This time, however, I learned I wasn't alone in experiencing this enigmatic phenomenon. In fact, I noticed that even though it was possibly the most indescribably ambiguous sensation, it was also one of the most powerful—and inexplicably, people around me were being affected by it.

"Do you feel it?" I heard myself asking an acquaintance this question again two years ago, never considering the resemblance of my words to those voiced decades prior at the sleepover. "It's like something isn't right. Something *big* is coming in the world. Something huge. Something that's gonna turn the world on its head and redefine everything we know about life. The winds of change are blowing, you know?"

"Yes," she said. "I can't explain it either, but I feel it. I believe the Holy Spirit is telling me to get ready for it…" She paused for a moment, and then noted the obvious: "Get ready for *what*, though, seems to be the question of the day."

I shared with her that I, too, believed the Holy Spirit had recently given me a string of words: "Prepare yourself to minister."

This happened during the production and research phase of a book Tom Horn and I coauthored: *Redeemed Unredeemable: When America's*

Most Notorious Criminals Came Face to Face with God. The ceiling did not split open, no audible voice boomed in the room, and no great beams of light fell upon me through the clouds. But this was a calling; there is no doubt in my mind. From somewhere deep, somewhere quiet, a truth slowly dawned upon my psyche like a gentle but undeniable breeze, telling me that I needed to grow up, stop being a girl of "church," and become a woman of God. Within that puzzling message I somehow simply became aware in my mind, in my *spirit*, that I needed to "prepare myself to minister."

I tried with every ounce of strength to ignore it. When it came into my thoughts at work I found myself staring off into the distance, this calling prodding my mind and demanding my attention, and the only way to get rid of it was to physically shake my upper body and force my eyes back to my computer screen.

The gentle breeze was quickly gaining speed.

When it interrupted my conversations with others by forcing its way back into my brain and rendering anything else I had to say moot, I would blink and fill my lungs with air, apologize, and relinquish the floor so those I were talking with could speak in my mental absence.

The breeze had become a steady wind.

When it kept me awake at night and commanded me to listen when I would much prefer to be dreaming about dandelions and teddy bears, I had no choice but to get out of bed and wander about the house in frustration.

The wind was rapidly gaining energy.

When it got so bad that I couldn't function as a person anymore without constantly being coerced into a nearly catatonic and debilitating brain fog, I finally asked God what in the otherworld was going on with me, obediently emerging from my hiding place called denial, and faced the blur.

The wind had become a tornado, and I was standing in the center of a cyclone.

The only thing I could do was submit. My prayer had always been, "Here am I, Lord, send Aaron." Like a fearful Moses. Running to the wilderness. Knowing I was capable of use for the kingdom and willing to be obedient to the call as long as it meant I could serve in a back room where I could be ignored. I always knew that I was part of the Body of Christ, but I always assumed I was the appendix: that one body part nobody thinks about, and if it bursts or malfunctions, it can be removed with a quick surgery and the body continues to function without it. But after the wind...

The wind changed me.

I was later asked to write the history section of *Final Fire: Is the Next Great Awakening Right around the Corner?*, another inspiring work. One after another, I studied in great detail every Great Awakening and major revival known to the world, from the Protestant Reformation to the Jesus People of the American counterculture era. I learned—no, I *digested*—what these men and women went through when faced with opposition, how they gave everything including their lives to the cause of the Great Commission, and no person on earth with a beating heart could emerge from the immense depth of those stories without feeling intensely inspired. I read as some of them were martyred. I saw the anguish they suffered in the service of Almighty God. I believed their testimonies as they wrote of the millions whose souls would spend eternity in Christ's presence because of the work they obediently and diligently carried out. I observed over and over again the social, political, and spiritual turmoil that needled at these Christian pioneers and drove them to act...

And I saw identical social, political, and spiritual circumstances alive in our nation today.

That was when it finally hit me. Like a lightning bolt to the brain, the truth of this odd wind provided an answer that floored me, made me weep harder than I ever had in my life, and killed any resistance I had held prior:

The Church is in a state of "falling"—that all-too-familiar sensation that has historically crept over the Body of Christ just before it truly surrenders to sleep as it did in the days leading up to Jonathan Edwards, George Whitefield, James McGready, Dwight Moody, and the others.

Few are ever as aware of the "falling" as these leaders were, content to belong to a tired church of apathetic believers. These key activists, however, were completely conscious of the relationship between the sleepy mindset of the Church and the lackadaisical endeavors within the Body of Christ—the spiritually *hypnagogic* state of Body-consciousness in those moments just before the Church begins to drift into spiritual slumber—and they felt and sensed things that defied our typical, physical, corporeal existence. A willingness to serve they wouldn't normally demonstrate and a devotion to an at-all-costs mentality they wouldn't normally employ were quickened within them as they rose above the potential they formerly thought they had…and they welcomed a near-transcendent cognizance—an awareness that "unlocked" unstoppable revival and changed the world from that day forward.

Then, by the power of the Holy Spirit's mere finger-snap, the globe was thrust into a hypnic jerk. The Body's visions of the Church's falling were instantaneously more obvious and undeniable than ever as the proverbial Body's muscle spasm shocked them to full awareness. The Body was thankful it had a second chance.

We are now, beyond the shadow of any doubt, experiencing the spiritual hypnic jerk. God's nation is rising…

Once I stopped weeping and wrapped my brain around the enormous revelation, I asked the Lord, "God, might you be choosing *me* to play a role in the next Great Awakening?"

And the answer came immediately, but it wasn't necessarily all about me. I knew mine was not the only cyclone. I heard a still, small voice say, "Although God often chooses many voices to accomplish His work, God is all-powerful. If He so wills a Great Awakening to change the world from this day forward, then it only takes *one*."

And it could be *you*.

So I ask you... Do you feel it?

Do your thoughts drift into visualizations of the gates of Paradise opening for droves and masses who will never feel pain or hurt or sorrow ever again in eternity? Can you close your eyes and see a luminous and dazzling Kingdom with golden streets and brilliant light forever waiting to welcome those who were once lost? Does your heart beat a little faster in your chest when you imagine yourself helping another soul make it into blissful eternity? Do you lay awake at night with your hands laced behind your head wishing you could sleep while your thoughts race with the imagery of new converts stepping into the priesthood of all believers? Have you felt the winds of change blowing you into new shapes and new places for future use in God's Kingdom work? Are you willing to surrender to the Author of the next Great Awakening and be used in any way you can be—regardless of how uncomfortable that position makes you—in order to see the eternal fruits of your labors reflecting in the eyes of those you love and reach out to within this lifetime?

If so, prepare yourself to minister.

Do-It-Afraid-ing

For years, I thought I had my place in the Body of Christ figured out. It wasn't that I believed I was always going to be correct and that God couldn't possibly call me into some other role; I simply believed I knew what I was good at and what was most comfortable. So I prayed repeatedly. "Please, let me be the appendix of the Body." I must have said it a thousand times or more.

First Corinthians 12:12–18 explains that each believer is a part of the unified Body of Christ through the Holy Spirit:

For as the body is one, and hath many members, and all the members of that one body, being many, are one body: so also is Christ. For by one Spirit are we all baptized into one body, whether we be Jews or Gentiles, whether we be bond or free; and have been all made to drink into one Spirit. For the body is not one member, but many.

If the foot shall say, "Because I am not the hand, I am not of the body"; is it therefore not of the body? And if the ear shall say, "Because I am not the eye, I am not of the body"; is it therefore not of the body?

If the whole body were an eye, where were the hearing? If the whole were hearing, where were the smelling?

But now hath God set the members every one of them in the body, as it hath pleased him.

My concept of the appendix, based only upon hearsay layman's understanding, was that it isn't a crucial body part. I had never researched it, but always believed that we don't really know what it does; it's just kind of there—and sometimes it explodes for some reason, which requires surgery to get it taken out. With such a limited perception of this organ's function, I grasped onto that naïve idea and made it a part of my prayer life. I had it all figured out…

I was called—or so I imagined—to sit in the back of a building somewhere and be silent for a living. Nobody needed to know I was ever there except my boss. I would find a career that allowed me to silently pass through a coffee breakroom, grab a cup of fuel, head to a corner chair in a vacant room, and "nerd-out" for eight hours a day. I wanted to use my life in a way that served the Lord, but I also knew there were many parts of the Body, and I had no shame in the notion that I would serve as a quiet one. Paul had made it clear that all parts made up the whole, and I was perfectly secure dreaming about a part that contributed without having to be seen or thought about. Nobody in my circle of friends and family really knew what the appendix did, which made the role even more appealing to me, because it suggested an "out of sight, out of mind" anonymity. Even evolutionists for eons referred to the appendix as a "vestigial organ" (being rendered without function over the course of evolution; literally, an already or soon-to-be useless organ). Plus, if I ever failed in my work, I (or my labors) could be surgically removed so the rest of the Body could move on without me. It was a "win" from every angle.

Mind you, this desire for being unseen or unheard was not by any means a lack of confidence in myself or a disdain for the company of other people. But I was a minister's daughter, and I had seen years of religious abuse during the Satanic Panic era of the 1980s and early '90s. Almost everyone in the Pentecostal denomination in those days linked every problem (national, local, individual, and so on) to a big underground satanic cult conspiracy, so even when there was no merit for it, the Church was gripped in terror, and I was frequently affected by that paranoia.

Let me make it perfectly clear that the religious abuse I witnessed and experienced *never* came from my mom, dad, brother, or sister. On the contrary, we were as close as any family could be, so, when the religious abuse occurred, we fought against it as a unit. However, the memory of all those years of trying to appease the unrealistic expectations of others had taken its toll. Scores of "Christians" throughout my life have found it their religious duty to tell me all the ways I'd let them down. More often than not, it was something ridiculous, and just as frequently it was a blatant contradiction of what the last person said. "You're a lady, so you should wear makeup in church to show God your best," followed by, "That makeup is worldly. If you absolutely must wear it, don't wear it in church." Or: "You're the pastor's daughter, so you of all people should be up at the altar right now praying for these people," followed by, "Would you mind stepping back, please? You can visit the altar any time, but these people need some space with God."

A woman in our church named Nancy once told me I needed to go home and burn all my Mickey Mouse clothes. I was on a kick at the time. I wore a lot of Mickey clothing because my body was shaped maturely for my age and I couldn't find modest girl clothes very often. I was scolded if I dressed "like a boy," so I went through a leggings-and-oversized-Mickey-sweater phase. I was under the impression that Disney's Mickey Mouse would represent innocence and be seen as a good compromise, but no, Nancy said. Disney was evil, because some of their animated features "had subliminal messages hidden in them." If I wore clothing made by the same company, I was "endorsing the wicked and perverse brainwashing of young children" and becoming a "willing participant of their evil." Even Mickey Mouse was a disappointment to the church elders. A "green" believer might have gotten by with it, but *I* was a minister's child, and I had to know better if my soul were to be spared from the enemy's grip.

I never burned my Mickey clothes because my dad (whose hard-earned money paid for them to begin with) thought it was absurd, but there were other instances of this same expectation. Like that one morning with Rick...a "prayer warrior" who had attended our church with a guest speaker.

I had gone to the altar for prayer that day. My reason for being there? I wanted to be closer to the Lord. I wanted to grow in Him. I did not say that I felt there was any kind of sin in my life keeping me from doing so (as I had gone joyfully), but I guess Rick, who met me there for prayer, made that assumption. He asked me why I had come forward, and when I told him, he started walking around me in a circle, eyeing me up and down. Eventually he stopped off to one side and said, "Ah... This here's your problem." I felt a tug on my Tinker Bell earring. "That's a pagan symbol. Did you know that?"

"Uhh... No," I said suddenly wishing that I had stayed quiet in my seat. (Usually at a moment like this I would have scanned the room for my dad, but he wasn't there that day.)

"Yes, yes it most certainly is. You're wearing a mystical, pagan entity in your ears. That's most definitely an open door for Satan."

When he came back to stand in front of me, he started darting his gaze about the air all around me dramatically as if he were watching a fireworks show behind my head. It was as fake an acting job as I've ever seen. Each time Rick's eyes popped to another location, he flickered his eyebrows in mock surprise. I hadn't the slightest clue what was going on, but I knew he was pretending to see something in the supernatural, so I just stood there, waiting for an explanation. When it came, I can't say I was surprised.

"Girl, you have demons all over you!" Rick shouted, and as usual, everyone in the building turned to look at me.

When I didn't immediately recoil in horror and fall to my knees in repentance for wearing those earrings, Rick's expression turned to one of mild embarrassment, as if he knew I wasn't buying it—and now he had an audience. So he then took it up a notch. Before I knew it, he was batting his hands in a slapping motion all around my head, furiously (as if you battle demons with a physical slap...). This went on for what felt like an eternity, and all the while, the onlookers were dazzled by Rick's authoritative stance in raging warfare. Eventually (thank goodness), he finally stopped and came back to a peaceful countenance, as if I had just been delivered. (As a quick aside: If the earrings *had* been "the problem" [that "problem" I never said I had], the fact that I was still wearing them at this point likely means that I would still have the oppression upon me. But I digress...)

He then prayed for me with a grand and thunderous tone, and when he was done, he moved on to the next person at the altar.

Years later, we discovered that Rick was a total fraud after a few major lies were exposed concerning the way he handled administrative reports related to his ministry (although it wasn't rocket science that his religion was also fraudulent, based on his spiritual warfare battling tactics).

Of course, there were other times when my clothing or accessories drew scrutinizing glances, but that was the tip of the iceberg. One guy in one of the churches my dad pastored was all smiles to everyone in the building, but I could do nothing right. (I'll never forget that man. He looked like Abraham Lincoln, and even dressed like him in the pictures [minus the top hat]). His name was Luke, and he constantly turned a blind eye to deeds by other children in the church that he would glare at me for. Like the tricycle incident.

We ran a school out of our church building and kept toys and equipment in the sanctuary store room. One day, the room was left unlocked after a worship service. I was by no means the first kid to run to play with the "off limits" school equipment. In fact, other children had been playing with all of the fun stuff for a good twenty minutes while the adults visited. I finally decided that because all the other moms and dads were allowing it, I was going to play also. I got on a tricycle I spotted, and started zooming around the recess area. Immediately, Luke sauntered over and started shouting at me—like Rick, drawing the attention of the surrounding crowd—that it didn't matter what anyone else did, but that as the minister's daughter, I should set the example and respect the property of the school lest I open a door for the enemy to enter my life.

This was one of those rare occasions when he got onto me within earshot of my mother, who politely explained to him that I wasn't misusing the equipment. He stood there and argued with her for several minutes about all the wrong I was doing and the bad example I was setting, but I became bored and returned to the fun. I found out later that Mom took quite a tongue-lashing that day. When she didn't agree with Luke and refused to scold me, she became the central target for the "bad influence" lecture. But by this time, both my mother and I were used to being "called out for bad behavior" and "usurping authority," so it didn't leave a scar on either one of us. It was merely just another day in the life of the minister's family. It happened all the time. And it certainly was not the last time we had a run-in with Luke, either. However, it didn't take anything specific to earn his expression of dissatisfaction. In fact, I don't remember ever locking eyes with that man—not once in my childhood—when he wasn't at the very least giving me that "I'm watching you" stare.

I grew accustomed to being "the unruly child" who was guilty of "inviting the enemy into my life" whenever I was at church. It was almost constant (and I am *so grateful* for my mom and dad, who always kept me on solid ground theologically). I was either enduring a lecture about life's most menial concerns and how they affected my eternal standing with God, or I was enduring the stare-down. Then there was that third reaction I obtained frequently, which materialized in that "what a pity, she's already a lost cause" head shake or eye roll. Ironically, *outside* the church, I had grown accustomed to hearing people tell my mother how well-behaved I was, how respectfully I spoke to elders, how sweet my nature was, how I followed rules so obediently…and it became apparent that I was only a failure to fellow believers. (As an interesting side note, if our modern Church were to perfectly adhere to the rules of male ministers listed in 1 Timothy 3:2–12 as "absolutes," my "rebellious" behaviors in these situations—and the "harm" that would have caused to my father's reputation—could have resulted in stripping my father's ministerial credentials from him.)

In my teen years, the abuse reached a whole new and debilitating level. This time, it did leave scars. The incidents I witnessed in churches were outright crippling to my early spiritual development, and it is *nothing less than a miracle* that I have overcome that damage. Some of what I saw and experienced are so heretical and offensive (and *all* of which ironically occurred when my father—a man of great discernment—was either not in the building or after he had resigned) that it would take two chapters to scratch the surface, yet the purpose of this book is not to discuss my story. Maybe someday that book will be written, but suffice it to say that, for me, the church was the *last place I would ever look* to find love and acceptance for a solid fifteen years of my adulthood. ("Negative learning" is sometimes as important as "positive learning," and I'm glad for the incidents I observed, because they have made me much more cautious as I go forward in what God has called me to do.) Some Christians (many of whom are leaders) cannot be pleased…and many specifically seek to take advantage of others and/or harm them for selfish gain.

I could list another thousand examples, but the point is, that garbage happened all the time. I was always coming up short somehow, and as long as I was placed at the center of attention because I was the pastor's kid, I was going to have to deal with what that attention delivered.

Life had taught me where the sharks gathered.

By the time I was mature enough to start questioning which "Body part" I was, I simply *did not* want to be in front of people or have any ministry of mine under constant scrutiny.

A back room.

Steaming mug-o-joe.

Silence. Solitude. Independence.

Let me be the appendix, Lord!

So when the winds of change stirred me and I felt the Holy Spirit telling me I was not—as I had hoped—going to get by with existing "out of sight, out of mind," the discomfort that fell upon me was great. I didn't feel right continuing to beg the Lord for another path if I was also telling Him I would be obedient in the path He chose, so I conceded and enlisted myself in one of the country's most highly respected and accredited Bible schools. (It was around this time that the night-imaginings mentioned in the introduction to this book, those moments of "preaching in my head," began.) For years by this time, I had been a professional "appendix," drawing a paycheck for my research and writing in the back of a building where I never had to face anyone outside of a casual hello in passing for a java refill. But if the Lord wanted me to get my minister's license, I knew He would also give me the strength to be used in that arena, so with nervousness and fear, I poured myself into new schooling.

From the start, I was encouraged to see that the courses I enrolled in were addressing some of the same scriptural misinterpretations that I had already spent several years writing about. In fact, I soared through a three-year program in under one year, not because I was in a hurry, but because, ironically, I had already spent two decades writing about these topics. It was refreshing how familiar the materials were to me, and I soaked up information I didn't know as well faster than a dry sponge submerged in water. Over and over, the course materials would refer to a popular misconception from the Bible, and then paint the backdrop from which the Scripture had originally been written (including such details as the author, audience, locality, culture, history, literary genre, etc.) in order to explain the Scripture's true meaning. (Honestly, if all preachers today were required to keep refreshing their study skills in this way, the Christian Church as a whole would not resemble the lackluster social club of handshakes and cookies that it has become. My book, *Radicals*, visits this topic at length. Exegesis—the art of pulling the context out of the text—is simply not being taught or exercised to the degree it should be. If it were, many more Christians would be radical about the true Gospel of Christ.)

Thoroughly encouraged and thriving in these new exegetically rich studies, I found myself saying out loud one day, "I love this stuff. I always have."

Like lightning, a still, small voice responded.

I know you do. I know you have. I know you always will. It's how I created you. After all, you're the appendix.

Wait a minute...

What?

Say *what*?!

That still, small voice we so dearly treasure was telling me I *was* the appendix? That vestigial and nearly useless body part that even science had written off as a hopeless "leftover" of human evolution? I mean, I don't believe in evolution anyway, but the concept that I would be consecrated within the Body of Christ as an organ our human assessment decrees nonvital...

No, I wasn't offended. I was excited! Could it be that God was letting me off the hook after all?

With butterflies in my stomach, I flew to my computer with my typical nerd-research knuckle crack. Nervously, I pulled up a search engine online and typed in "purpose of the appendix to the body." Here I was, having spent years praying about something I didn't even understand—which usually goes against my nature because I'm always self-educating before I pretend to know about a subject—and I hadn't even learned the purpose of the body part I had prayed to become. I felt incredibly silly in that moment, reading hundreds of articles with headlines similar to the following: "Appendix More Important than We Thought, Scientists Say"; "The Appendix: It's Crucial Purpose"; "Your Appendix May Serve an Important Biological Function After All"; "New Research Shows the Human Appendix Essential for Optimum Body Health"; and so on.

At least I wasn't alone in assuming its uselessness, as even scientists were only just learning the purpose of this organ. However, I still couldn't shake the fact that I had been praying so very ignorantly for so very long, and it made me feel sheepish. The appendix may not be so vital that the human body can't live without it, but the body can also survive without fingers, hands, arms, toes, feet, legs, ears, eyes, spleen, and teeth, as well as partial removal of the colon or liver, or living with only one kidney, and so on—and that's not even an exhaustive list. But the "*optimum body health*" requires all these things together to run smoothly, or else the ideal functionality is stunted.

As it turns out:

The function of the appendix appears to be to expose white blood cells to the wide variety of antigens, or foreign substances, present in the gastrointestinal tract. Thus, the appendix probably helps to suppress potentially destructive humoral (blood- and lymph-borne) antibody responses while promoting local immunity. The appendix…takes up antigens from the contents of the intestines and reacts to these contents. This local immune system plays a vital role [note this reference to the "vital role"] in the physiological immune response and in the control of food, drug, microbial or viral antigens.[126]

Put more simply, it's a storage container for good bacteria, exposing white blood cells to foreign substances, so if a person comes down with a digestive illness or infection, good bacteria is repopulated by the appendix to fight off the illness and bring the individual back to superior health. Additionally, if a person has been placed on a steady flow of antibiotics (which will kill both good and bad bacteria), the appendix once again recolonizes the good bacteria, which reboots the digestive system after a hard reset.

The organ is, as the article above stated, "vital" to system immunity!

Without this organ, a person is four times more likely to develop "*Clostridium difficile* colitis—a bacterial infection that causes diarrhoea, fever, nausea, and abdominal pain."[127] Another article by *Global Healing Center Online* describes:

For the past few decades, conventional medicine believed the appendix was an unimportant organ and served very little function. Emerging evidence is painting a strikingly different picture, revealing the startling physiological role the appendix plays in health. It turns out that the appendix may play a vital function [there's that word "vital" again] in the development of the immune system.... Based on current evidence...the appendix serves as a "reservoir" for beneficial gut flora. It's also been shown that individuals without an appendix may be four times more likely to suffer from recurrent *Clostridium difficile* colitis, an irritation of the large intestine by spore-forming bacteria. This condition is often present when the body is running low on gut flora, potentially explaining the connection between the appendix and its role in maintaining probiotic levels. While the research is still a little bare, the conclusion is clear—*the appendix is important for health.*[128]

For as many times as I had heard that the appendix could be removed with a quick surgery, after which the body would function perfectly fine without it, I learned that a rupture of the organ is *commonly* related to major health concerns, including up to three or four hundred deaths per year in America alone.[129]

By the time I had read several recent reports proving the value of the appendix to the human body, there was no need to analyze how that related to my "appendix role" in Christ's Body.

The Body of Christ is fed through the spiritual food of the Word. Without proper digestion of the Word (which requires proper exegetical interpretations of Scripture), illness and infection can occur, which affects the rest of the Body's optimum functionality. The fastest cure for this is exposure to the Bible's "white blood cells" and "gut flora immunity boosters" (correctly interpreted Scripture) to the "foreign substances" (incorrectly interpreted Scripture), alongside the radical repopulation/recolonization of fundamental truths that the Gospel message offers.

And it was this very brand of filtering that I had been writing about for decades: true context of Scripture versus the spread of "misconception bacteria."

I was the appendix after all…and I always had been.

(By no means is this shared to illustrate that my role in the Body of Christ is more important than any other. It's just the part I was assigned, and the part I had prayed for well before I knew what function it carried out. If I had left the fold for any reason, God is all-powerful, and could easily replace me with a new appendix. Our spiritual Body is not limited to complete removal or prosthetic replacements like our corporeal bodies. However, although the Body might continue to live without this organ, the chances of infection or illness [improper digestion of the Word] is greatly increased. If anything, the readers of this book should be encouraged that if the appendix—that seemingly useless and "vestigial" body part disregarded by evolutionists throughout history—has an important purpose within the body, *then so do you* in the Body of Christ!

All parts make up the whole, and yours may be *far* more important than
you know…)

I realized at this point that, just because I was the appendix, I couldn't
expect to stay comfortably silent. I just knew that I knew that I knew:
God was going to ask me to speak up, and when He did, I would have to
make a choice to either obey and assist in our spiritual immunity system
or rupture and cause damage to the Body until God found my replace-
ment. Rupturing and being replaced sounded like a far better plan each
second I listened to my fleshly desires…but I had, in fact, asked for this,
and I had already promised God that I would be obedient when my calling was revealed. God gave me precisely what I asked for. Additionally,
I don't hear many other voices out there begging to be the appendix.
Contrarily, I see many preachers and teachers of the Word perpetuating stereotypical scriptural interpretations that don't have anything to
do with original context, so someone needs to be obedient to this role,
regardless of how uncomfortable it might be.

As such, my own discomfort could not be allowed outweigh what
God had told me to do. I could not hand God my official refusal because
I was afraid.

And that's a serious issue for all of us, isn't it? Fear and discomfort.
God wouldn't call us to fulfill a role that causes us to stretch so far outside our own fleshly desires and comfort bubbles, would He?

Read the Bible from cover to cover. You will find that all those who
were truly in the service of God went where they were supposed to go
and did what they were supposed to do *regardless of how they felt.*

Look at the book of Jonah: God tells Jonah to go to Nineveh and
preach a message of repentance. Jonah doesn't like the Ninevites, and he
doesn't think they deserve redemption, so he doesn't *feel* like doing what
God has told him to do. He gets on a boat headed to Tarshish instead.
God brings a huge storm to the sea where the ship is sailing, and the
waves are crashing all around. When lots are cast, Jonah owns up to the
crew that it is he who has run from his God and angered Him, and their

only chance for survival is to throw him overboard. The crew reluctantly agrees, and as soon as Jonah's off the ship and submerged in the waters below, the storm stops. Jonah is swallowed by a great fish and spends three days in its belly. When he's vomited back up by the fish days later, God does *not* say, "Well, okay, you've paid well enough for your disobedience, and I understand that what I asked you to do was terrifying or uncomfortable. Go home and scrape the digestive acids off your clothes, put your feet up, and drink a restorative cup of fig juice."

Not a chance. God picks right back up where he left off. He says, "Go to Nineveh."

Straight back to square one: God's directive.

When my family and I were studying the book of Jonah together, I used the following example with my son, who was six years old at the time. "Joey, it's like this," I said. "If I tell you to go clean your room, and then you go off in another direction and piddle around because you don't feel like obeying me, I might make you stand your nose in the corner for not doing what I said to do. But then, once you've stood in the corner, I'm not going to say, 'Well, your punishment is over and you paid your price for disobedience, and I can understand that I made you feel uncomfortable by asking you to clean your room, so I guess you can go play.' No, I'm going to say, 'Now that you've stood in the corner and you've been punished, go to your room and clean it up!'" I went on to explain: "After we're done suffering for not doing what God told us to do in the first place, God is going to say, 'Okay Jonah, get up, go where I told you to go and do what I told you to do.'"

The message doesn't change, and it's simple enough that a six-year-old can understand it. The *directive* of God upon one's life doesn't change when that person is afraid. The commands given to followers of the Word don't change when we disobey them because of our feelings.

No matter how many times you begin a sentence with "But God, I *feel…*" it's always going to come back to the same command: "Get up. Go where I've told you to go. Do what I've told you to do."

Following the Lord is a choice we have the free will to make, one way or another. But once we've committed to follow Him, we don't get to choose *how* we will obey. I knew that very well, but I was still struggling internally with the repetitive "but I'm scared" response. It was debilitating to think that I was going to have to face the one thing I feared the most.

So, this time, when I prayed, I changed my tune and asked for the Lord to give me peace about my fear. That same night, I suddenly got the urge to look up that Joyce Meyer woman that I had heard of my whole life but never got around to listening to. I found out immediately that the urge had been sent from the Holy Spirit. Sermon after sermon, she continued to talk about people in my position: people who felt called but were afraid to respond to the calling. Her response was redundant in all the necessary ways. "I know you're afraid," she would say, "but do it afraid. You don't have to make the fear go away completely before you follow God's orders. If you're uncomfortable, do it uncomfortable. If you're afraid, do it afraid. But do what the Lord is telling you to do."

I agreed with her summary.

And I am still in my season of do-it-afraid-ing. Will I ever reach a day when I'm no longer fearful or uncomfortable? Maybe, maybe not. But if the Body needs an appendix, I'm committed to being the best immunity-and-white-blood-cell-booster I can be until I've been given the green light to step down.

You, Yes You, Are Called to Be a Minister; We All Are

If women *do* decide to step into the fullness of their calling, they *will* experience resistance—and it will be uncomfortable. For many, it will produce feelings of fear.

I told you my story, and I can almost guarantee that it's not the same as yours. Many women today may not feel they've been called to be a preacher behind the pulpit, but if she has the Holy Spirit working within her, and if she has dedicated herself to being used by God, then *she is called* to be the best *minister* of God that she can be. She may be called to be a great wife, or mother, or schoolteacher, or business woman, or Starbucks barista, but she *is* called by God to be a minister.

The word "minister" today typically refers to someone in the clergy of a church. A vocabulary study of the word, however, reveals: "When you minister to someone, you take care of them. All…meanings of minister—both as a noun and as a verb—contain a grain of the original Latin [*ministrare*] meaning, 'servant.'"[130] So the idea that a minister is one who preaches or leads a congregation is a Western-religion idea. If you are a Christian, *you are called to be a minister*, whatever servant position in life that means for you.

Second Timothy 1:8–9 says, "Be not thou therefore ashamed of the testimony of our Lord, nor of me [Paul] his prisoner: but be thou partaker of the afflictions of the gospel [be ready to be made uncomfortable and face resistance for the sake of the Gospel] according to the power of God; Who hath saved us, and *called us* with an holy calling, not according to our works, but according to his own purpose and grace, which was given us in Christ Jesus before the world began" (emphasis added). God has called *us*, the collective Body made up of *all believers*, with all parts intact. Romans 8:29–30, again the words of Paul, says, "For whom he [God the Father] did foreknow, he also did predestinate to be conformed to the image of his Son…. Moreover whom he did predestinate, them he also *called*" (emphasis added).

Some confuse Matthew 22:14 ("For many are called, but few are chosen") to mean that some are called into ministry (smaller audience), some are chosen into greatness as God's elect (larger audience), and then there's a third group of people who believe in Christ, but aren't called or chosen into ministry of any kind. (Others interpret the verse to mean a kind of Calvinistic, predestination theology idea, suggesting that only those who are "chosen" by God will make it into Heaven, and the rest of the world is doomed.) However, this verse follows Christ's Parable of the Wedding Feast, which dealt with the heavy Jews-and-Gentiles issue and salvation, and once properly understood (once the pop culture and Western-religion concepts are removed), it's clear that only two groups are being referred to: a) the many who hear the Gospel, and b) those who choose to believe in Christ and live their lives accordingly.

From a hindsight view, these two categories can potentially converge into a people who have both heard the Gospel *and* subsequently decided to live for Christ, assuming both are met positively through such a decision. Some will belong to the first category (those who hear the Gospel message), but not the second (those who choose to believe and live their lives accordingly), because they will reject the message. This interpretation is unanimous amongst the early Church Fathers. The classic *Pulpit Commentary* says as much: "All the Jews had first been called; then all the Gentiles; many were they who obeyed not the call; and of those who did come in, many were not of the inner election, of those, that is, *whose life and character were worthy of the Christian name*, showing the graces of faith, holiness, and love."[131] Even the historian, Origen, said:

> If any one will observe the populous congregations, and inquire how many there are who live a better kind of life, and are being transformed in the renewing of their mind [those who live like Christians]; and how many who are careless in their conversation and conformed to this world [the lost who reject the Gospel openly, or the lost who pretend to be Christians but whose lifestyles oppose true Christianity], he will perceive the use of this voice of our Saviour's, "Many are called, but few chosen;" and in another place it has been said, "Many will seek to enter in, and shall not be able" (Luke 13:24); and, "Strive earnestly to enter in by the narrow gate; for few there be that find it" (Matthew 7:13, 14).[132]

Therefore, we must regard Matthew 22:14 as an isolated warning following the Parable of the Wedding Feast. Its references to the "called" and "chosen" stand apart from 2 Timothy 1:8–9 and Romans 8:29–30, which speak to the believer who has already heard the Gospel message and decided to live for Christ.

There is no unrecorded "third category" of believers who are not called or chosen, but who live ordinary, non-ministerial lives. Any *true* follower of Christ who has the Holy Spirit in his or her heart *has already been called* as a minister (servant) of God, according to these verses in Romans and 2 Timothy. It does *not* mean that every true follower of Christ has to fulfill the role of a preacher. But whatever your calling is, "whatsoever ye do, do it heartily, as to the Lord" (Colossians 3:23).

Embrace your own season of do-it-afraid-ing, so that whatever you've been called to do, you can prepare yourself to minister without allowing your potential to be stunted later on by human emotion.

For women who do believe they've been called to stand behind a pulpit: expect resistance. I cannot tell you that your path will always be easy. But if you're willing to be the kind of radical, on-fire leader like the many women leaders of the Bible, if you're willing to carry out your calling while afraid and uncomfortable, you *can* see many lives changed for all eternity as a result.

Many women feel defined by the darker moments in their lives. They feel that they will never get beyond how "broken" they are. Never forget that your past, your traumas, the abuse you've encountered, and your bouts with emotional extremes (depression, loneliness, anxiety, despair) do not define you. God is the only One who defines you. He will not use you just *despite* of who you are and what you've been through; He will use you *because of* who you are and what you've been through.

Lastly, always remember that resistance, too, has a purpose. Have you ever been to the gym? Have you ever met with a personal trainer?

Do you know even the first fundamental concept of lifting weights. Then you will know already that no muscle within the body is capable of building growth and strength without first pressing against an encumbrance or burden.

Sometimes it is only when ministers press against the resistance around them that they, as a part of the Body, become stronger.

Prepare.

I will close this book with a beautiful piece of poetry by my ministry acquaintance, Randy Conway. This masterful work is called "UP"—which is ironically the same word Judge Deborah authoritatively shouted to Barak just before she led Israel into a victory that resulted in forty years of peace for God's people (Judges 4:14):

> It seems we live in a world dedicated to its own dissension,
>   Ruled by Principalities from a dark dimension.
> Every day the news tells of another who snapped under the
>   tension,
> And even the Christians rise to face the day with apprehension.
>
> But as he slept, a young man was given a dream of serving God
>   in the courts;
> As she drove, a young woman had a vision of feeding the
>   hungry through the sea ports;
> A wealthy entrepreneur is on his knees seeking God as to how
>   he can serve,
> And a housewife is witnessing to her neighbor because she
>   finally got the nerve.
>
> Precept by precept and line upon line, God's people are coming
>   around.
> A fire that has been ignited in the hearts of believers is taking
>   ground.

A generation finding strength to turn the battle at the gate:
Knowing there is a sure foundation not just an accidental fate.

For too long have we clung to our favorite tenants of religion,
But very soon we will see heaven and earth make a dimensional
collision.
Listen for the voice of the Father that says "This is the way,
walk in it."
God is calling out today building up not religion but a
remnant.

Do you see the people waking up and getting up?
They are bracing up and praying up in order to stand up:
Standing up and facing up to the darkness that desires God's
place—
God will lift us up and fill us up but we must seek His face.

God's people are getting fed up, stirred up, and shaken up,
Filled up, geared up, prayed up, and speaking up!
The old man has been put up—
And just when satan thinks he has things sewed up.

Look out and look up because God is going to show up!
It is time to get revved up, stoked up, pumped up, and fired
up,
Worked up, freed up, studied up; time for God's people to
reach up.
We're going to tell the devil to shut up every time he tells us
we're washed up.

People want to know the Truth and we are going to lift the
Truth up,

And when He is lifted up all men are drawn to Him close-up.
More than any time in our history, God's people need to be
    looking up,
For when time for this age is all used up, He is coming back to
    take us up!

Notes

1. This interview is available at the following link: Donna Howell, *The Jim Bakker Show*, aired June 6, 2017, 19:58–26:51, https://www.jimbakkershow.com/video/angels-prophecies-day-2/.

2. "Does the Future of the Church Belong to RADICALS?" a YouTube video, uploaded by SkyWatch TV on June 13, 2017, https://www.youtube.com/watch?v=d_P8JBVqtlk&t.

3. "2 Peter 3:16 Commentary," *Barnes' Notes on the Bible*, as shared by *BibleHub*, last accessed July 7, 2017, http://biblehub.com/commentaries/barnes/2_peter/3.htm.

4. Ibid; emphasis added.

5. Ibid; emphasis added.

6. John Jalsevac, "Queen James Bible: Publisher Releases 'Gay-Friendly' Bible Translation," December 13, 2012, *Life Site News*, last accessed July 17, 2017, https://www.lifesitenews.com/news/queen-james-bible-publisher-releases-gay-friendly-bible-translation.

7. Ibid.

8. "Strong's G4395," *Blue Letter Bible*, last accessed July 16, 2017, https://www.blueletterbible.org/lang/lexicon/lexicon.cfm?Strongs=G4395&t=KJV.

9. "Strong's G846," *Blue Letter Bible*, last accessed July 16, 2017, https://www.blueletterbible.org/lang/lexicon/lexicon.cfm?Strongs=G846&t=KJV.

10. "Strong's G2406," *Blue Letter Bible*, last accessed July 16, 2017, https://www.blueletterbible.org/lang/lexicon/lexicon.cfm?Strongs=G2406&t=KJV.

11. See: "ham·baś·śə·rō·wt," *Bible Hub*, last accessed August 23, 2017, http://biblehub.com/hebrew/hamvasserot_1319.htm; and: "Psalm 28:11," *Bible Hub*, last accessed August 23, 2017, http://biblehub.com/interlinear/psalms/68-11.htm.

12. For more information on this, I highly recommend: David A. deSilva, *Honor Patronage, Kinship, & Purity: Unlocking New Testament Culture* (Downers Grove, IL: InterVarsity Press, 2000).

13. "Romans 16:3," *Bible Hub*, last accessed July 15, 2017, http://biblehub.com/commentaries/romans/16-3.htm.

14. Ibid.

15. Ibid.

16. "Strong's G4904," *Blue Letter Bible*, last accessed July 16, 2017, https://www.blueletterbible.org/lang/lexicon/lexicon.cfm?Strongs=G4904&t=KJV.

17. "Synergy," *Dictionary Online*, last accessed July 16, 2017, http://www.dictionary.com/browse/synergy?s=t.

18. "Strong's G1249," *Blue Letter Bible*, last accessed July 16, 2017, https://www.blueletterbible.org/lang/lexicon/lexicon.cfm?Strongs=G1249&t=KJV; emphasis added.

19. Ibid.

20. Ibid.

21. Eddie Hyatt, "Did Paul Have a Woman as His Pastor?" *Charisma News*, last accessed August 30, 2017, https://www.charismanews.com/opinion/65047-did-paul-have-a-woman-as-his-pastor; emphasis added.

22. Dr. Deborah M. Gill and Dr. Barbara L. Cavaness Parks, *The Biblical Role of Women* (Springfield, MO: Global University, 2008), 120.

23. Eddie Hyatt, *Paul, Women, and Church* (Kindle edition, Grapevine, TX: Hyatt International Ministries, Inc., 2016), Kindle locations 359–361.

24. Dr. Deborah M. Gill and Dr. Barbara L. Cavaness Parks, *The Biblical Role of Women*, 120.

25. "Strong's G4368," *Blue Letter Bible*, last accessed July 17, 2017, https://www.blueletterbible.org/lang/lexicon/lexicon. cfm?Strongs=G4368&t=KJV.

26. "Strong's G4291," *Blue Letter Bible*, last accessed July 17, 2017, https://www.blueletterbible.org/lang/lexicon/lexicon. cfm?Strongs=G4291.

27. "Deaconesses," *The New Advent Catholic Encyclopedia*," last accessed July 16, 2017, http://www.newadvent.org/ cathen/04651a.htm.

28. Eldon Jay Epp, *Junia: The First Woman Apostle* (Kindle edition, Minneapolis: Fortress Press, 2005), location 346.

29. Bernadette Brooten, *Women Priests* (Costa Mesa, CA: Paulist Press, 1977), 142–143.

30. Rena Pederson, *The Lost Apostle: Searching for the Truth About Junia* (Kindle edition, San Francisco, CA: Jossey-Bass, 2006) Kindle locations 2470–2484.

31. "Junia," *The Full Wiki*, last accessed August 3, 2017, http://www. thefullwiki.org/Junia. However, note that this quote can be found in almost every discussion on Junia anywhere. A simple Google search of the words "Junia Chrysostom" reveals hundreds of references.

32. "Strong's G653," *Blue Letter Bible*, last accessed July 17, 2017, https://www.blueletterbible.org/lang/lexicon/lexicon. cfm?Strongs=G652&t=KJV.

33. Ann Graham Brock, *Mary Magdalene, the First Apostle: The Struggle for Authority* (Cambridge: Harvard University Press, 2003), 147; emphasis added.

34. "Strong's G1722," *Blue Letter Bible*, last accessed July 17, 2017, https://www.blueletterbible.org/lang/lexicon/lexicon. cfm?Strongs=G1722&t=KJV.

35. Ibid.

36. Eldon Jay Epp, *Junia*, locations 955–956.

37. Ibid., location 958.

38. Ibid., locations 990–1006.

39. Gilbert Bilezikian, *Beyond Sex Roles: What the Bible Says about a Woman's Place in Church and Family: 3rd Edition* (Kindle edition, Grand Rapids, MI: Baker Publishing Group, 2006), 133.

40. John Ortberg, *Who Is this Man?: The Unpredictable Impact of the Inescapable Jesus* (Kindle edition, Grand Rapids, MI: Zondervan, 2012), 53.

41. John Temple Bristow, *What Paul Really Said about Women: The Apostle's Liberating Views on Equality in Marriage, Leadership, and Love* (Kindle edition, San Francisco, CA: HarperCollins, 2011) 51.

42. D. H. Madvig, "Corinth," *The International Standard Bible Encyclopedia* (revised edition; Grand Rapids: Wm. B. Eerdmans Publishing Co.), 773.

43. William Barclay, *The Letters to the Corinthians* (revised edition; Philadelphia: Westminster Press, 1975), 4.

44. Troy W. Martin, "Paul's Argument from Nature for the Veil in 1 Cor. 11:13–15: A Testicle instead of a Head Covering," *Journal of Biblical Literature*, 123:1 (2004), 78–80.

45. "Strong's G1538," *Blue Letter Bible*, last accessed July 20, 2017, https://www.blueletterbible.org/lang/lexicon/lexicon. cfm?Strongs=G1538&t=KJV.

46. "Strong's G3551," *Blue Letter Bible*, last accessed July 21, 2017, https://www.blueletterbible.org/lang/lexicon/lexicon. cfm?Strongs=G3551&t=KJV.

47. "Strong's G181," *Blue Letter Bible*, last accessed July 20,

2017, https://www.blueletterbible.org/lang/lexicon/lexicon. cfm?Strongs=G181&t=KJV.

48. "Tumult," *Merriam-Webster Online*, last accessed July 20, 2017, https://www.merriam-webster.com/dictionary/tumult.

49. John Temple Bristow, *What Paul Really Said about Women*, 61.

50. Dr. Deborah M. Gill and Dr. Barbara L. Cavaness Parks, *The Biblical Role of Women*, 128; emphasis added.

51. Dr. Deborah M. Gill and Dr. Barbara L. Cavaness Parks, *The Biblical Role of Women*, 140.

52. Ibid., 143.

53. Ibid., 157.

54. Ibid., 125.

55. Richard Clark Kroeger and Catherine Clark Kroeger, *I Suffer Not a Woman: Rethinking 1 Timothy 2:11–15 in Light of Ancient Evidence* (Kindle edition, Grand Rapids, MI: Baker Academic Publishing Group, 1992) 72–73.

56. Gilbert Bilezikian, *Beyond Sex Roles: What the Bible Says about a Woman's Place in Church and Family: 3rd Edition* (Kindle edition, Grand Rapids, MI: Baker Academic Publishing Group, 2006) 132.

57. Strong's G5615," *Blue Letter Bible*, last accessed July 24, 2017, https://www.blueletterbible.org/lang/lexicon/lexicon. cfm?Strongs=G5615&t=KJV; emphasis added.

58. "Strong's G2532," *Blue Letter Bible*, last accessed July 24, 2017, https://www.blueletterbible.org/lang/lexicon/lexicon. cfm?Strongs=G2532&t=KJV.

59. "Strong's G127," *Blue Letter Bible*, last accessed July 22, 2017, https://www.blueletterbible.org/lang/lexicon/lexicon. cfm?Strongs=G127&t=KJV.

60. 1 Timothy 2:9, Interlinear," *Bible Hub*, last accessed July 22, 2017, http://biblehub.com/interlinear/1_timothy/2-9.htm. Notice, however, that this very website even gets it wrong, which

shows how often this error occurs. In the interlinear comparison, the word for "and" (*kai*) is clearly shown between "braided hair" (*plegmasin*) and "gold" (*chrysio*) in the Greek line; later in the same Greek line, we see "or" (*ē*) as distinct. But in the English translation line, it is "or" all three times.

61. Richard and Catherine Kroeger, *I Suffer Not a Woman*, 74.

62. Dr. Deborah M. Gill and Dr. Barbara L. Cavaness Parks, *The Biblical Role of Women*, 138.

63. Mishna Sotah 3:4, as translated by: Herbert Danby, D.D., *The Mishnah: Translated from the Hebrew with Introduction and Brief Explanatory Notes* (New York, NY: Oxford University Press, 1933), 296.

64. "Lechery," *Merriam-Webster Online*, last accessed July 24, 2017, https://www.merriam-webster.com/dictionary/lechery.

65. "Inordinate," *Merriam-Webster Online*, last accessed July 24, 2017, https://www.merriam-webster.com/dictionary/inordinate.

66. "Strong's 2271," *Blue Letter Bible*, last accessed July 24, 2017, https://www.blueletterbible.org/lang/lexicon/lexicon.cfm?Strongs=G2271&t=KJV.

67. "Strong's G5292," *Blue Letter Bible*, last accessed July 24, 2017, https://www.blueletterbible.org/lang/lexicon/lexicon.cfm?Strongs=G5292&t=KJV.

68. John Temple Bristow, *What Paul Really Said about Women*, 71.

69. Richard and Catherine Kroeger, *I Suffer Not a Woman*, 75.

70. Gilbert Bilezikian, *Beyond Sex Roles*, 135.

71. John Toews, *The Bible and the Church: Essays in Honor of Dr. David Ewert* (Shillington, Hillsboro, KS: Kindred Press, 1983), 84.

72. "Strong's G1850," *Blue Letter Bible*, last accessed July 24, 2017, https://www.blueletterbible.org/lang/lexicon/lexicon.cfm?Strongs=G1850&t=KJV.

73. "Strong's G1849," *Blue Letter Bible*, last accessed July 24,

2017, https://www.blueletterbible.org/lang/lexicon/lexicon.
cfm?t=kjv&strongs=g1849; emphasis added.

74. Ibid.

75. Henry George Liddell, Robert Scott, *A Greek-English Lexicon*,
revised and augmented throughout by Sir Henry Stuart Jones,
with the assistance of Roderick McKenzie, Oxford, Clarendon
Press, 1940, last accessed July 25, 2017, http://www.perseus.tufts.
edu/hopper/text?doc=Perseus%3Atext%3A1999.04.0057%3Aen
try%3Dau%29qe%2Fnths.

76. List obtained from: Gail Wallace, "Diffusing the 1 Timothy
2:12 Bomb: More On Authority (Authentein)," *The Junia
Project*, last accessed July 25, 2017, http://juniaproject.com/
defusing-1-timothy-212-authority-authentein/.

77. Scott Bartchy, "Power, Submission, and Sexual Identity among
the Early Christians," *Essays on New Testament Christianity*
(Cincinnati, OH: Standard Publishing, 1978), 71–72.

78. Walter Liefeld, "Women and the Nature of Ministry," *Journal of
the Evangelical Theological Society* (30:51), 1987.

79. "The Meaning of Authenteo," *Bible Discussion Forum*, last
accessed July 25, 2017, http://www.thechristadelphians.org/
forums/index.php?showtopic=14052.

80. Richard and Catherine Kroeger, *I Suffer Not a Woman*; As it
relates to the subject of sexually aggressive women/priestesses in
ancient culture surrounding Ephesus, the entire book makes this
argument. Although I do not agree with some of the conclusions
this couple makes, I strongly suggest this as a staple research book
for every serious student of New Testament culture and history.

81. Ibid., especially page 89.

82. Ibid., especially chapters 6–9 and appendices 1–2.

83. Ibid., 90.

84. Albert Wolters, "A Semantic Study of *Authentein* and Its
Derivatives," *Journal for Biblical Manhood and Womanhood,*

2006, 11.1.54; originally published in *Journal of Greco-Roman Christianity and Judaism*, 2000, 1.145–175; emphasis added.

85. As quoted in: "1 Timothy 2:12 in Context (Part 4)," *Marg Mowczko*, last accessed July 25, 2017, http://margmowczko. com/1-timothy-212-in-context-4/.

86. "Usurp," *Merriam Webster's Dictionary Online*, last accessed August 23, 2017, https://www.merriam-webster.com/dictionary/ usurp.

87. "Strong's G1135," *Blue Letter Bible*, last accessed July 25, 2017, https://www.blueletterbible.org/lang/lexicon/lexicon. cfm?Strongs=G1135&t=KJV.

88. For instance: Dr. Deborah M. Gill and Dr. Barbara L. Cavaness Parks, *The Biblical Role of Women*, 144–146.

89. Gilbert Bilezikian, *Beyond Sex Roles*, 139.

90. Gilbert Bilezikian, *Beyond Sex Roles*, 132.

91. Derek Gilbert, "NEW ONLINE SERIES: The Great Inception Part 1: The Mountain of Eden," January 28, 2017, *SkyWatch Television Online*, last accessed December 5, 2017, http://www.skywatchtv.com/2017/01/28/ new-online-series-great-inception-part-1-mountain-eden/.

92. Dr. Deborah M. Gill and Dr. Barbara L. Cavaness Parks, *The Biblical Role of Women*, 39.

93. "Genesis 3," *Gill's Exposition of the Entire Bible*, last accessed August 1, 2017, http://biblehub.com/commentaries/gill/ genesis/3.htm; emphasis added.

94. "Genesis 3," *Ellicott's Commentary for English Readers*, last accessed August 1, 2017, http://biblehub.com/commentaries/ellicott/ genesis/3.htm; emphasis added.

95. Richard and Catherine Kroeger, *I Suffer Not a Woman*, 20.

96. Loren Cunningham and David J. Hamilton, *Why Not Women?* (Kindle edition, Seattle, WA: YWAM Publishing, 2000), locations 1488–1492.

97. "Strong's H8199," *Blue Letter Bible*, last accessed August 2, 2017, https://www.blueletterbible.org/lang/lexicon/lexicon.cfm?Strongs=H8199&t=KJV.

98. Roberts Liardon, "Deborah," YouTube video uploaded on August 22, 2014, by Roberts Liardon, 5:09–6:16, last accessed August 3, 2017, https://www.youtube.com/watch?v=LD7Bpfk0wGA; emphasis placed where it was vocally delivered from the footage.

99. Ibid., 7:09–7:42.

100. Ibid., 12:56–13:12; emphasis placed where it was vocally delivered from the footage.

101. Ibid., 17:45–17:51.

102. Ibid., 19:35–20:00; emphasis placed where it was vocally delivered from the footage.

103. Bernadette Brooten, *Women Leaders of the Ancient Synagogue* (Chico, CA: Scholars Press, 1982), 11.

104. Ross Kraemer, *Maenads, Martyrs, Matrons, Monastics* (Minneapolis, MN: Fortress Press, 1988), 219.

105. The quotations in this section are taken from: Leonard Swidler, *Biblical Affirmations of Women* (Philadelphia, PA: Westminster Press, 1979), 154–157.

106. Ibid., 155.

107. David deSilva, *Honor, Patronage, Kinship, & Purity: Unlocking New Testament Culture* (InterVarsity Press, Downer's Grove, IL: 2000), 23.

108. Ibid., 24.

109. Dr. Deborah M. Gill and Dr. Barbara L. Cavaness Parks, *The Biblical Role of Women*, 73.

110. Linda Belleville, *Women Leaders and the Church: Three Crucial Questions* (Baker, 1999), 149.

111. Dr. James B. Hurley, *Man and Woman in Biblical Perspective* (Eugene, OR: Wipf and Stock Publishers, 2002), 82–23.

112. Jodi Hooper, "Jesus and the Samaritan Woman," July 19, 2011,

Bible.org, last accessed August 14, 2017, https://bible.org/seriespage/4-jesus-and-samaritan-woman-john-41-42.

113. Mark Raburn, "The First Gospel Preacher: The Samaritan Woman at the Well," October 10, 2013, *Mark Raburn*, last accessed August 14, 2017, https://mikeraburn.com/2013/10/10/red-letter-year-1010/.

114. Judith VanOsdol, "Intimate Encounters…The First Preacher of the Good News of Jesus, the Christ, John 4:1–39," last accessed August 14, 2017, http://www.overcomingviolence.org/fileadmin/dov/files/wcc_resources/dov_bible_studies/The_First_Preacher_of_Jesus.pdf.

115. Note that this is the most frequent explanation behind why the Samaritan woman would be found at the well in the middle of the day, since most often the drawing of water happened at dusk. She was there midday, scholars postulate, because she was avoiding the humiliation of the scornful glances from other women who drew water in the evening.

116. Note that there is a popular variation of the story here. According to some historians, the men were taken out to be crucified, and they hung there four days. When Nero's servants went to see if the believers were still alive, they were blinded upon their arrival. It is said that angels appeared and released the believers, who thereafter took pity on Nero's servants and prayed for their eyesight to be returned. Their prayers were successful, and the servants escorted the men back to prison where they awaited further judgment, but not before they converted to Christianity and were baptized.

117. Pope John Paul II, "Apostolic Letter *Mulieris Dignitatem* of the Supreme Pontiff John Paul II on the Dignity and Vocation of Women…" *La Santa Sede Vatican*, last accessed August 17, 2017, https://w2.vatican.va/content/john-paul-ii/en/apost_letters/1988/documents/hf_jp-ii_apl_15081988_mulieris-dignitatem.html.

118. Heidi Schlumpf, "Who Framed Mary Magdalene?" *US Catholic*, last accessed August 17, 2017, http://www.uscatholic.org/articles/200806/who-framed-mary-magdalene-27585.

119. Professor Barbara Bowe, as quoted by: Ramona V. Tausz, "Mary Magdalene, Feminist Icon?" last accessed August 17, 2017, https://www.firstthings.com/web-exclusives/2017/07/mary-magdalene-feminist-icon.

120. "Gender Composition," *Pew Research Center*, last accessed August 23, 2017, http://www.pewforum.org/religious-landscape-study/gender-composition/.

121. "The Gender Gap in Religion around the World: Women Are Generally More Religious than Men, Particularly among Christians," March 22, 2016, *Pew Research Center*, last accessed August 23, 2017, http://www.pewforum.org/2016/03/22/the-gender-gap-in-religion-around-the-world/.

122. Danielle Paquette, "Men Say They Work More than Women: Here's the Truth," June 29, 2016, *Washington Post*, last accessed August 23, 2017, https://www.washingtonpost.com/news/wonk/wp/2016/06/29/men-say-they-work-more-than-women-heres-the-truth/?utm_term=.311a41783ac4.

123. Ibid.

124. Melinda Gates, "More Time," in the 2016 annual letter, "Two Superpowers We Wish We Had," *GatesNotes*, last accessed August 23, 2017, https://www.gatesnotes.com/2016-Annual-Letter.

125. "Visual Privacy Productivity Study: Commissioned by 3M," October 2012, *Ponemon Institute*, last accessed August 23, 2017, https://www.ponemon.org/local/upload/file/Visual_Privacy_Productivity_Study.pdf.

126. "What Is the Function of the Human Appendix?..." *Scientific American*, last accessed July 10, 2017, https://www.scientificamerican.com/article/what-is-the-function-of-the-human-appendix-did-it-once-have-a-purpose-that-has-since-been-lost/.

127. BEC Crew, "Your Appendix Might Serve an Important Biological Function After All," January 10, 2017, *Science Alert*, last accessed July 10, 2017, https://www.sciencealert.com/your-appendix-might-serve-an-important-biological-function-after-all-2.

128. Dr. Edward Group, "What Does the Appendix Do?" December 26, 2014, *Global Healing Center*, last accessed July 10, 2017, https://www.globalhealingcenter.com/natural-health/what-does-the-appendix-do/; emphasis added.

129. Ibid.

130. "Minister," *Vocabulary Online*, last accessed July 10, 2017, https://www.vocabulary.com/dictionary/minister.

131. "Matthew 22:14," under the heading "Pulpit Commentary," last accessed July 10, 2017, http://biblehub.com/commentaries/matthew/22-14.htm.

132. Ibid.